Nurturing 'Difficult Conversations' in Education

Bloomsbury Critical Education

Series Editor: Peter Mayo

Books in this series explore the relationship between education and power in society and offer insights into ways of confronting inequalities and social exclusions in different learning settings and in society at large. The series will comprise books wherein authors contend forthrightly with the inextricability of power/knowledge relations.

Advisory Board:

Antonia Darder (Loyola Marymount University, USA), Samira Dlimi (École Normale Supérieure, Rabat, Morocco), Luiz Armando Gandin (Federal University of Rio Grande do Sul, Mexico), Jose Ramon Flecha Garcia (University of Barcelona, Spain), Ravi Kumar (South Asian University, India), Antonia Kupfer (University of Dresden, Germany), Peter McLaren (Chapman University, USA), Maria Mendel (University of Gdansk, Poland), Maria NIkolakaki (University of Peloponnese, Greece) and Juha Suoranta (University of Tampere, Finland)

Also available in the series:

Course Syllabi in Faculties of Education: Bodies of Knowledge and Their Discontents, International and Comparative Perspectives, edited by André Elias Mazawi and Michelle Stack

Critical Education in International Perspective, Peter Mayo and Paolo Vittoria

Critical Human Rights, Citizenship, and Democracy Education: Entanglements and Regenerations, edited by Michalinos Zembylas and André Keet

Ecopedagogy: Critical Environmental Teaching for Planetary Justice and Global Sustainable Development, Greg William Misiaszek

Education, Individualization and Neoliberalism: Youth in Southern Europe, Valerie Visanich

Hopeful Pedagogies in Higher Education, edited by Mike Seal

Pedagogy, Politics and Philosophy of Peace: Interrogating Peace and Peacemaking, edited by Carmel Borg and Michael Grech

Feminism, Adult Education and Creative Possibility: Imaginative Responses, edited by Darlene E. Clover, Kathy Sanford and Kerry Harman

Itinerant Curriculum Theory: A Declaration of Epistemological Independence, edited by João M. Paraskeva

Forthcoming in the series:

Decolonizing Indigenous Education in the US, Samuel B. Torres

Nurturing 'Difficult Conversations' in Education

Empowerment, Agency and Social Justice in the UK

Edited by Katarzyna Fleming and Fufy Demissie

BLOOMSBURY ACADEMIC
LONDON • NEW YORK • OXFORD • NEW DELHI • SYDNEY

BLOOMSBURY ACADEMIC
Bloomsbury Publishing Plc, 50 Bedford Square, London, WC1B 3DP, UK
Bloomsbury Publishing Inc, 1359 Broadway, New York, NY 10018, USA
Bloomsbury Publishing Ireland, 29 Earlsfort Terrace, Dublin 2, D02 AY28, Ireland

BLOOMSBURY, BLOOMSBURY ACADEMIC and the Diana logo
are trademarks of Bloomsbury Publishing Plc

First published in Great Britain 2024
This edition published in 2026

Copyright © Katarzyna Fleming and Fufy Demissie, 2024

Katarzyna Fleming and Fufy Demissie have asserted their right under the Copyright,
Designs and Patents Act, 1988, to be identified as Editors of this work.

For legal purposes the Acknowledgements on p. xxiv constitute
an extension of this copyright page.

Series design by Catherine Wood
Cover image © Studiojumpee/Shutterstock

All rights reserved. No part of this publication may be: i) reproduced or transmitted in any form, electronic or mechanical, including photocopying, recording or by means of any information storage or retrieval system without prior permission in writing from the publishers; or ii) used or reproduced in any way for the training, development or operation of artificial intelligence (AI) technologies, including generative AI technologies. The rights holders expressly reserve this publication from the text and data mining exception as per Article 4(3) of the Digital Single Market Directive (EU) 2019/790.

Bloomsbury Publishing Plc does not have any control over, or responsibility for, any third-party websites referred to or in this book. All internet addresses given in this book were correct at the time of going to press. The author and publisher regret any inconvenience caused if addresses have changed or sites have ceased to exist, but can accept no responsibility for any such changes.

A catalogue record for this book is available from the British Library.

Library of Congress Cataloging-in-Publication Data
Names: Fleming, Katarzyna, editor. | Demissie, Fufy, editor.
Title: Nurturing 'difficult conversations' in education : empowerment, agency and social justice in the UK / Edited by Katarzyna Fleming and Fufy Demissie.
Description: New York, NY : Bloomsbury Academic, 2024. | Series: Bloomsbury critical education | Includes bibliographical references and index. | Summary: "This book offers critical discussion on the necessity for 'difficult conversations' to take place in education, drawing on studies from across the UK. The chapters cover a range of topics including: supporting children with SEND, parent and carer engagement, childhood trauma, race, disability, the climate emergency, research methods and draw on the theoretical work of Linda Martin Alcoff, Maurice Blanchot, Paulo Freire, and Maureen Lipman. The contributors argue against the prevailing deficit-based perspectives about marginalized communities and students, and invite deep thinking about the nature of oppression and the complicity of many education professionals in it"– Provided by publisher.
Identifiers: LCCN 2024010991 (print) | LCCN 2024010992 (ebook) | ISBN 9781350332119 (hardback) | ISBN 9781350332157 (paperback) | ISBN 9781350332133 (epub) | ISBN 9781350332126 (ebook)
Subjects: LCSH: Communication in education–Great Britain. | Social justice and education–Great Britain. | Students with social disabilities–Great Britain. | Special education–Great Britain.
Classification: LCC LB1033.5 .N87 2024 (print) | LCC LB1033.5 (ebook) | DDC 370.15/23–dc23/eng/20240321
LC record available at https://lccn.loc.gov/2024010991
LC ebook record available at https://lccn.loc.gov/2024010992

ISBN:	HB:	978-1-3503-3211-9
	PB:	978-1-3503-3215-7
	ePDF:	978-1-3503-3212-6
	eBook:	978-1-3503-3213-3

Series: Bloomsbury Critical Education

Typeset by Integra Software Services Pvt. Ltd.

For product safety related questions contact productsafety@bloomsbury.com.

To find out more about our authors and books visit www.bloomsbury.com
and sign up for our newsletters.

For Erica, and her infectious questioning of the world around us that inspires my own critical thought and openness to the diverse perspectives of others.

For Adday and Yared, whose youthful energy and insightful perspectives inspired this project, and to Ben for his ongoing support throughout.

Contents

List of Figures	ix
List of Table	x
List of Contributors	xi
Series Editor's Foreword	xiv
Foreword *Joshua Forstenzer*	xviii
Preface	xxiii
Acknowledgements	xxiv
Summary of Chapters	1

1 Introduction: Why Difficult Conversations Matter – In Search for Transformation and Personal Growth *Katarzyna Fleming and Fufy Demissie* ... 7

Part One 'Difficult Conversations' in Educational Settings

2 Transforming Autistic Children and Young People's School Experiences through Difficult Conversations between Educators *Jo Billington* ... 23

3 'Conversations' without 'Mouth Words': A Challenge or Learning for Transformative Educational Practice? *Katarzyna Fleming and Julie Calveley* ... 41

4 Should I Be Having This Conversation about Death? *Tracy Edwards* ... 59

5 Co-Production between Parents and Special Educational Needs Coordinators (SENCOs) – A Route to Transform Working Together *Lorna Hughes* ... 73

Part Two 'Difficult Conversations' in Higher Education

6 Using a Community of Philosophical Inquiry Approach to Explore Race and Inequality in Higher Education Contexts *Fufy Demissie* ... 93

7   Challenging Hierarchical Barriers through Co-Creation of Curricula in HE: Students-Lecturers Reflection on Critical Dialogue *Elizabeth Collins and Hannah Wilson*   111
8   Free Speech, Conversation and the 'Difficulty' of Academic Freedom *Seán Henry*   129
9   'Engaging Educators in Conversation on Our Climate and Ecological Emergency' *Elena Lengthorn*   145

Part Three 'Difficult Conversations' in the Research Context

10 (Looking) Behind the Mask: How Difficult Conversations in Research Can Illuminate the Complex Inner Worlds of the Teacher and the Researcher *Sally Hinchliff*   167
11 Enabling Difficult Conversations about Childhood Trauma with Care Experienced Children and Young People in the Home: A Conversation between a Researcher and an Adoptive Mother *Debbie Watson and Alison Crowther*   185
12 Ethical Complexities of Having Difficult Research Conversations: A Reflective Account and a Cautionary Tale on Speaking for 'Others' *Antonios Ktenidis*   203
13 Fairness, Fruitfulness, Fact: An Argument for the Belonging of People with Profound Intellectual and Multiple Disabilities within Research *Joanna Grace*   223

Afterword   239

Index   242

Figures

5.1	Overview of the EHCP timescales and development when a request is made (DfE/DoH, 2015, p. 154)	76
6.1	Becoming anti-racist behaviour, adapted from www.SurgeryRedesign.com	98
11.1	Sarah's sandbox (20-year-old care leaver)	192
11.2	Esme's sandbox	193
11.3	Granulating identity	198
13.1	Jo and Chlöe chat	232
13.2	Jo and Chlöe with the tissue paper	232
13.3	Jo and Chlöe embrace	233

Table

6.1 Stimulus for Enquiry 2   102

Contributors

Jo Billington is a doctoral researcher in the Centre for Autism at the University of Reading, UK. She has a particular interest in mental health, and her work aims to enhance child well-being through increased public understanding and acceptance of difference and diversity. Twitter @MsJoBillington

Julie Calveley, Dr, is a learning disability nurse, psychology graduate, parent and founder director of NAC, a community-interest company dedicated to the emotional well-being of people with severe and profound intellectual disabilities. She carries out research and delivers training and consultancy on mental health, trauma, regulation, co-regulation and intensive interaction with families and for health, social care and education services. Twitter @NACWellbeing

Elizabeth Collins is a postgraduate student at the Carnegie School of Education, Leeds Beckett University, UK. Following on from the Primary Education Hons Degree, she embarked on the journey to become a teacher. Her interests lie within dialogic pedagogy and inclusive education.

Alison Crowther is a facilitator, trainer and coach in the fields of conflict resolution, trauma, positive psychology, and stakeholder and public dialogue. She specializes in environmental, social and science issues and has advised the UK government for sixteen years on how to work with the public to create new policy on complex science. She helps organizations to be trauma-informed around climate change and its many repercussions through her organization MadeToLast Resilience. Twitter @AlisonCrowther

Fufy Demissie, Dr, is a senior lecturer in the Sheffield Institute of Education at Sheffield Hallam University, UK. Her research interests include dialogic pedagogy, teachers' continuous professional development, education for global citizenship and philosophy for children. Twitter @DemissieFufy. https://shup4c.wordpress.com/

Tracy Edwards has an extensive background in teaching, school leadership, education research and consultancy. She has undertaken commissioned work for a number of local authorities, multi-academy trusts and the UK Department of Education. Currently, she is a lecturer at Leeds Beckett University, where she leads the National Award in SEN Coordination. Twitter @TracyEd1

Katarzyna Fleming, Dr, is a senior lecturer and researcher in Sheffield Institute of Education at Sheffield Hallam University, UK. Her research interests encompass parent-practitioner partnerships, co-production, co-creation in higher education, inclusive education, community of philosophical enquiry and critical pedagogies. Katarzyna is also a founder of Co-productive Partnerships Network. Twitter @kfleming100 @co_productive. https://katarzynafleming.com/

Joshua Forstenzer is a senior lecturer in Philosophy and Co-Director of the Centre for Engaged Philosophy at the University of Sheffield, UK. He works mostly on John Dewey, the tradition of American pragmatism, democratic education, and other related topics. His work has been supported by the British Academy, the Yale Centre for Faith and Culture, and Higher Education Innovation Funding.

Joanna Grace is a sensory engagement and inclusion specialist, author, trainer, TEDx speaker and founder of The Sensory Projects. Joanna's doctoral studies focus on identity and belonging for people with profound intellectual and multiple disabilities. In all her work Joanna seeks to contribute to a future where people are understood in spite of their differences. Joanna is autistic. Twitter @jo3grace

Sean Henry, Dr, is a lecturer in education at the Department of Secondary and Further Education, Edge Hill University, UK. His research explores questions of religion, education, sexuality and gender from a philosophical perspective. More recently, he has turned his attention to questions of academic freedom. He is currently completing a monograph for Routledge's Religion and Education series entitled *Queer Thriving in Religious Schools*. Twitter @seandhenry

Sally Hinchliff is a senior lecturer in the Sheffield Institute of Education at Sheffield Hallam University, UK. Her research interests include teachers' navigation of their beliefs and values in their work, the emotional dimensio n of training to teach and Philosophy for Teacher Education (P4TE). She is a part-time doctoral student. Twitter @hinchliffsally

Lorna Hughes is a senior lecturer in special educational needs and inclusion at Canterbury Christ Church University, UK. She teaches the National Award for SEN Coordination and Postgraduate Certificate in Dyslexia. Her PhD studies focus on the role of parents and schools in the co-production of Education Health and Care Plans for children. Twitter @LornaHughes29

Antonios Ktenidis, Dr, is a lecturer in education in the School of Education at the University of Sheffield, UK. His research interests include critical disability studies, sociology of education, heightism, and non-normative bodies in education. He is the lead for the Identity and Marginalised Communities research cluster and member of iHuman. Twitter @AntonisKtenidis

Eleanor Lengthorn, a teacher educator at the University of Worcester, UK, is exploring sustainability education in our time of climate and ecological emergency. Her recent Green Impact research projects include: Climate Assembly Approaches with Secondary Teachers, Embedding the SDGs in Primary Education, Nature Connectedness in ITE and Intergenerational Flood Education. Twitter @ELengthorn

Debbie Watson is a professor of child and family welfare in the School for Policy Studies at the University of Bristol, UK. Her research interests focus on identity and well-being for children and families living in adverse circumstances including those in poverty and care experienced. Her research is interdisciplinary, creative and co-produced. Twitter @debbiew63152670

Hannah Wilson is an aspiring primary teacher currently undertaking postgraduate studies at the Carnegie School of Education, Leeds Beckett University, UK. Her chosen specialism is English as a Second Language. Prior to this, Hannah completed her undergraduate degree studies in primary education, which led her to taking part in a co-creation project and thus developing an interest in co-creation and dialogic pedagogy. Twitter @hannahcurstaidh

Series Editor's Foreword

This new book series was introduced against an international background that comprised and continues to comprise situations that are disturbing and intriguing. The onset of Covid-19 has thrown into sharp relief arguably the major casualty of this pandemic, an unprepared, failed state. We have been left with a state shorn of the facilities and provisions one would expect of a purportedly 'democratic' entity that dances not only to the tune of capital accumulation but also to that reflecting the concerns of all people under its jurisdiction. The latter is certainly not the case as, with regard to the provision of social safeguards, the state has, in many places, almost been rendered threadbare by its accommodation of nefarious neoliberal policies which leaves everything outside the demands of capital to the market and voluntary organisations. While wealth is concentrated, as a result, in the hands of a few, there are those who are left to struggle for survival in a Darwinian contest that rewards the 'winners' and renders others disposable. Questionable wealth is concentrated in the hands of a few, who take advantage of their network of spin doctors and 'fake news' soothsayers, to play the victim with regard to the pandemic. They and the many policymakers who accommodate them deflect their responsibility onto ordinary citizens and further justify curtailing the state's social spending, to the detriment of the many, 'the multitudes', as referred to by Michael Hart and Toni Negri.

The series was launched at a time when the 'social contract', ideally one which transcends the capitalist framework (as Henry Giroux astutely remarks), is continuously being shredded as several people are removed from the index of human concerns. Many are led to live in a precarious state. Contract work has become the norm, a situation that renders one's life less secure. There is also criticism targeted at the very nature of production and consumption with their effects on people and their relationship to other social beings and the rest of the planet, hence 'questionable wealth'.

They are also difficult times because the initial enthusiasm for the popular quest for democracy in various parts of the world has been tempered by eventual realism based on the fact that strategically entrenched forces are not removed simply by overthrowing a dictator. Far from ushering in a 'spring', the uprisings in certain countries have left political vacuums – fertile terrain for religiously motivated terrorism that presents a real global security threat. This threat, though having to be controlled in many ways, not least tackling the relevant social issues at their root, presents many with a carte blanche to trample on hard-earned democratic freedoms and rights. The situation is said to further spread the 'culture of militarisation' that engulfs youth, about which much has been written in critical education. Terrorist attacks or aborted coups allow scope for analyses on these grounds, including analyses that draw out the implications for education.

The security issue, part of the 'global war on terror', is availed of by those who seek curtailment of human beings' right to asylum seeking and who render impoverished migrants as scapegoats for the host country's economic ills. The issue of migration would be an important contemporary theme in the large domain of critical education. This phenomenon and that of Covid-19, as with any other pretext, are availed of by powers acting exclusively in the interest of capital. This leads to a further siege mentality marked by increasing otherising, scapegoating, surveillance and incarceration. Security extends beyond the culture of fear generated through terrorism to include health issues such as the pandemic, the latter said to be spread by those who, in reality, are the least equipped to work and live safely in their homes, including rejected asylum seekers and other migrants denied citizenship, those who live in restricted and overcrowded spaces or who do not have a home – period. They face a stark choice: exposure or starvation. Barbarism, in Rosa Luxemburg's sense of the term, is a key feature of this choice and the society in which many live.

The series was introduced at a time when an attempt was made for politics to be rescued from the exclusive clutches of politicians and bankers. A more grassroots kind of politics has been constantly played out in globalized public arenas such as the squares and streets of Athens, Madrid, Istanbul (Gezi Park), Cairo, Tunis and New York City. A groundswell of dissent, indignation and tenacity was manifest and projected throughout all corners of the globe, albeit, as just indicated, not always leading to developments hoped for by those involved. Yet hope springs eternal. Some of these manifestations have provided pockets for alternative social action to the mainstream, including educational action. Authors writing on critical education have found, in these pockets, seeds for a truly and genuinely democratic pedagogy that will hopefully be explored and developed, theoretically and empirically, in this series.

It is in these contexts, and partly as a response to the challenges they pose, that this new series on Critical Education was conceived and brought into being. Education, though not to be attributed powers it does not have (it cannot change things on its own), surely has a role to play in this scenario – from exposing and redressing class politics to confronting the cultures of militarization, consumerism, individualism and ethnic supremacy. The call among critical educators is for a pedagogy of social solidarity that emphasises the collective and communal in addition to the ecologically sustainable.

Critical educators have for years been exploring, advocating and organizing ways of seeing, learning and living that constitute alternatives to the mainstream. They have been striving to make their contribution to changing the situation for the better, governed by a vision or visions of systems that are socially more just. The ranks of the oppressed are swelling. Hopefully, it is the concerns of these people that are foremost in the minds and hearts of those committed to a social-justice-oriented critical education. I would be the first to admit that even a professed commitment to a critical education can degenerate into another form of radical chic or academic sterility. We need to be ever so vigilant toward not only others but also ourselves, coming to terms with our own contradictions, therefore seeking, in Paulo Freire's words, to become less incoherent.

This series offers a platform for genuinely socially committed critical educators to express their ideas in a systematic manner. It seeks to offer signposts for an alternative approach to education and cultural work, constantly bearing in mind the United Nations Sustainable Development Goals that, albeit difficult to realize, serve as important points of reference when critiquing current policies in different sectors, including education. The series' focus on critical education, comprising the movement known as critical pedagogy, is intended to contribute to maintaining the steady flow of ideas that can inspire and allow for an education that eschews the 'taken for granted.'

In this particular volume, the editors, Katarzyna Fleming and Fufy Demissie, assemble a team of writers who foreground difficult conversations in education and social enquiry, connected with the ever-so-urgent theme of social difference within the larger context of biodiversity. This is what critical education is all about. It is about the carving out of safe spaces where thorny issues are not kept under the carpet or at best skirted around but are confronted head-on by people who, in Paulo Freire's words, are different but not antagonistic. Difference is the hallmark of critical education. This means facing difficult issues, loves, enabling situations in the interest of bolstering a substantive as opposed to a sham 'formal' democracy. It would for instance be ridiculous to organise a conference about democratic education and make next to no reference, save for a token gesture, to the human carnage and genocide raging in Gaza in a form of collective punishment as reprisal for a reprehensive callous terrorist attack targeting civilians. Otherwise the whole activity or effort would be phoney and smacking of cloud cuckoo land. Conflict and difference, with the various suffering through different aggressions, macro or micro, these entail. Disablement and racism feature prominently in the difficult discussions in this volume. They feature together with many other issues.

Critical enquiry and education is all about difficult, unsettling questions and coming to terms with often deep-seated antagonistic dispositions. This is what this book series is intended to focus on, and this specific volume suits this series admirably, paving the way for other and more difficult conversations in future.

Peter Mayo
Series Editor,
UNESCO Chair in Global Adult Education,
University of Malta,
Msida, Malta

Foreword

Joshua Forstenzer

Difficult conversations are the stuff of life. They are, for many of us, the most personally meaningful interactions we can ever hope to engage in. They allow us to interact and share in our authentic vulnerability. But they also are the most emotionally demanding of interactions. They stretch, challenge, transform and even – as the chapters in this volume demonstrate – educate us, because they invite us to confront the other in their full otherness, replete with unexpected particularities and idiosyncrasies. This, in turn, forces us to recognise that we too are always inevitably an other to our conversational partners. Each of us is capable of being surprising, somewhat mysterious and sometimes even downright inscrutable to others, as others can be – and often are – to us. It is only through the process of conversation that this otherness that seems to separate conversational partners can be apprehended and overcome. But this otherness is not overcome in the sense of being destroyed or left behind once and for all. Rather conversation permits the interplay of commonality and difference to move to the foreground of our awareness, pushing our unavoidable existential separateness (the uniqueness of our journey from 'womb to tomb', as Cornel West often puts it) to the margins of our awareness, at least for a while.

Conversations, even the seemingly gentle ones, involve risk: the risk of being misunderstood, of being shunned or shamed, of failing to understand or be understood – in short, of exposure. But in every conversation there is also a chance that the opposite will occur: we may be deeply understood, affirmed and supported; we may more genuinely understand our self and others; we may learn and share, be heard, respected and honoured for our individual thoughts, feelings and expressions.

We can be transformed by conversations. Perhaps the most transformative feature of conversation is that it allows one to learn about oneself. How often have I caught myself mid-conversation saying to my interlocutor something which I had not previously known that I believed or felt? Rather often. In fact, the more emotionally or intellectually demanding the conversation, the more I expect a new part of myself to reveal itself to me and – whether I like it or not – to my conversational partner. Perhaps it was a version of this experience that inspired Socrates in a famous passage of the *Theaetetus* to characterize philosophy as a kind of conversational 'midwifery': a space in which ideas are born. Of course, Socrates maintained that his philosophical method of maieutics aimed at truth and involved confronting the pain of perplexity and doubt. I, for one, rather suspect that Socrates oversold the pain involved in philosophical discussion (he thought it greater than the pain of giving birth to a child!) and undersold its joys.

However, even in the most challenging of conversations we find a kind of existential respite. A sense of being tethered to one another, to one's sense of self in a deeper way than our internal monologues allow for, and perhaps even to the human conversation itself. Conversation is therefore a kind of bridge. It can be a bridge between different parts of the self, between people, between places, between cultures, between times and between subject positions. As conversations always occur in a wider sociopolitical context, one in which some forms of expression are praised or taken as 'natural' because they are those employed by the dominants, while other ways of communicating are trivialized or treated as 'deficient' because they are those employed by the marginalized or the oppressed, conversations must be understood as shaped by power and yet also as offering the possibility of breaking through lines of enduring difference. As the feminist cultural critic Aimee Carrillo Rowe (2010, p. 218) explains: 'To engage an/other is to reach across the power lines that would separate us; it is to place ourselves vulnerably in the hands of an/other and strive to acknowledge the position of an/other.'

Difficult conversations are those conversations where the bridge is shakier, the cliffs deeper and the stakes higher. They are conversations where our mere habitual modes of interaction won't cut it, where words might fail us, where existing structures and hierarchies most threaten mutual understanding, where we must most actively produce and reproduce, invent and reinvent the interpersonal bridge connecting self with others.

The chapters in this volume eloquently and intelligently speak to the pedagogical promise and challenges involved in centring difficult conversations at the heart of the educational task. They invite us as educators to go beyond what Freire famously called 'the banking model' of education, to consider our role in shaping the nature of our interactions with our students, and to overcome many of our preconceived ideas about the nature and purpose of conversation in schooling and beyond. In short, they make a compelling case for the pedagogical value (and, perhaps ultimately, the necessity) of fostering difficult conversations in education. This superbly edited set of chapters provides a series of academically informed and well-grounded reflections about the educational value of difficult conversations across a wide range of contexts and subject matters. Each chapter provides a fascinating insight into a unique context fraught with challenges and rich hermeneutic possibilities. In addition, the editors and the contributors to this volume successfully engage us – their readers – in a conversation about our own pedagogical practices and experiences. They do this by interspersing the text with questions directed at us to wrestle with, to sit with, to discuss with others. In other words, this volume is in and of itself an invitation to take part in difficult conversations about the nature and aims of education, about the place of vulnerability in education and ultimately about what we believe to be the authentic roles of the educator and the learner in pedagogic interactions. It is in the spirit of that conversation that I will now share a brief biographical reflection of my own on what I have learnt about the value of difficult conversations in education.

In the first chapter of *The Courage to Teach*, Parker Palmer (2010, p. 23) lets us in on his private feelings as an educator, when he writes: 'Long into my career I harbored a secret sense that thinking and reading and writing, as much as I loved them, did not qualify as "real work". Growing up in France in the 1990s, attending school as a foreigner, I came to believe something quite similar about 'conversation': I 'learnt' that conversation – and especially difficult conversation – was purportedly the antithesis of 'real learning'. I did not so much 'learn' this from my own secondary school, which was rather liberal compared to neighbouring schools and had a handful of truly excellent teachers who were supportive of questioning, conversation and of the use of the often forbidden word 'je' ('I'). Rather I learnt it from my wider community of friends who went to more traditional schools. I learnt from them that one could get thrown out of class for asking too many questions to the teacher about the content of the lesson, for asking a friend for a pen or a pencil, for telling a teacher that one did not understand something, for asking a teacher what evidence they had to back up their assertions, for asking a teacher for help, for asking a teacher for their first name, for asking to go to the toilet too often or even for asking a question with a tone which the teacher found to be 'insolent'. Students rarely spoke directly to one another in an open forum about the content of the learning, because in French traditional schools (whether state-run or Catholic), my friends informed me, speaking for students was typically reserved for answering the teacher's questions, usually by repeating the teacher's own words back to them, and even then, only when explicitly called upon. The parents of one of my French friends once explained the social significance of being educated in this manner as learning how to inhabit 'one's proper place' in the social order: 'It prepares the young for the real world', they told me, 'a world in which speaking one's mind out of turn is not a mark of intelligence, or of social prestige, or an asset for obtaining employment, but rather a potential stain on one's reputation, a mark of a lower social rank and of a failure to fit in'. Lest the reader get the wrong idea, allow me to fill in the edges: though parcellary, the image of France as a country filled with rebellious radicals, where passionate debates are carried out over coffee or wine (and cigarettes) long into the night on the terraces of Parisian cafes is not wholly inaccurate. But this somewhat widespread political mood of self-actualizing personal and collective sovereignty may well be a direct reaction to the type of overbearing schooling I have just described: when meaningful self-expression is impossible in the classroom, it will eventually emerge somewhere else.

I personally only became fully aware of the depth of the aversion to fostering challenging conversation in education when I was in my penultimate year of *lycée* (high school) and the *directrice* (Headmistress) of my own relatively liberal school saw fit to remind us that the *liberté de parole* (freedom of speech) and open inquisitiveness she thought we had practised there would almost certainly not be tolerated once we graduated. She added that we had to anticipate heavy repercussions should we dare to speak our minds too freely at university or in the classes *préparatoires aux grandes écoles* (preparatory classes for the most prestigious French tertiary institutions).

I took that warning to heart, and I left for Britain to undertake my undergraduate education. It was there that I first experienced the seminar, namely, a space of learning where discussion is the sole and entire point, where educators are disappointed by silence and facile agreement, and where joy is found in the struggle to think together and against one another. But this remained for a long while a mere space for minds to debate, rather than a space for whole people to meet and converse. It was only when I began to take part in facilitating philosophy with children that I discovered a pedagogical outlook (rooted in Matthew Lipman's P4C) that included feelings and challenging experiences alongside thoughts in the list of valued educational contributions. The effect this had on me cannot be overstated: it hit me like a lightning rod, like discovering something that I had somehow always known. True education is of the whole person – psyche and soma in equal measure – and is produced as much out of the experiences, thoughts and feelings of the learners as out of those of the educators. Today, I firmly believe that learning how to engage in difficult conversations is the highest educational good, for it is the one experience that can unleash most meaningfully all other forms of learning. It teaches us to withstand and ultimately treasure the tremendous discomfort that comes from admitting to ourselves all that we do not yet know and all that we most deeply yearn to learn.

May the voices in this volume be a bridge to support your own journey into conversational risk and may they light your way to ever-new conversational horizons – they already have for me.

References

Carillo Rowe, A. (2010) Entering the inter power lines in intercultural communication. In T. K. Nakayama, & R. T. Halualani (Eds.). *The Handbook of Critical Intercultural Communication*. Blackwell.

Palmer, P. J. (2017). *The courage to teach: Exploring the inner landscape of a teacher's life*, 20th Anniversary edition. Jossey-Bass.

Preface

This edited collection of critical discussions about 'difficult conversations' arose out of personal and collaborative reflections we undertook as colleagues working in Teacher Education in the UK. As educators, we strongly feel that the more stories about difficult conversations and their transformative nature are told, the better chances that education can create a socially just world. This collection unravels some of the intricacies of how to conduct a difficult or challenging conversation and why they are needed (Stone, Patton & Heen, 2011; Osborn & Canfor-Dumas, 2018; Ferner & Chetty, 2019). It also aims to inspire, transform and enrich our ways of being and becoming, and to ignite change that leads to a more inclusive society. We hope, therefore, to provoke in-depth reflections about 'difficult conversations' as a window for richer and ethical discussions, where everyone's stories can be told and listened to with compassion and empathy, where assumptions can be challenged constructively and where ideas for a change can be ignited by a diverse collective.

We truly hope that our intention to create an accessible work that can appeal to a broad range of audiences enables our readers to use this collection in their varied contexts. While we take you through the landscape of educational endeavours presented in each chapter, we also hope that the golden thread of human connection can inspire you to create a space where your thinking or practice can be transformed.

We would like to take this opportunity to thank our readership for engaging with this collection and convey our excitement and enthusiasm for your own transformative journeys through 'difficult conversations'. We would be humbled to hear your story should you wish to share it with us.

Acknowledgements

First and foremost, we would like to thank our chapter contributors for bringing their expertise and passions to interrogate the topic of 'difficult conversations' for transformative practice and understanding, and all the participants in their research without whom these contributions to knowledge would not be possible. Our thanks go to all the colleagues whom we have been privileged to work with and who shared our enthusiasm for this volume, asked insightful questions and always encouraged us to persist with the task at hand. We would also like to recognize the indirect impact that our doctoral and professional journeys have had on our ability to engage in the editorial endeavour with diligence, compassion and criticality – special thanks here are due to Dr Lisa McGrath, Prof. Nick Hodge and Roger Sutcliffe. We are grateful that Sheffield Hallam University supported some of the editorial costs of this publication. We would also like to extend our gratitude to our colleague Sharon Smith, who contributed with insight to the initial ideas for this collection. Finally, but not least, we would like to acknowledge the support and kindness of our colleagues, friends and our families for their unwavering faith in our abilities, courage and ideas for the conceptualisation of this book.

Summary of Chapters

Introduction

This volume exemplifies a range of empirical and theoretical research from professional, doctoral, early career and established researchers, on topics such as inclusive practice, disability, communication, sustainability, race, trauma, ethics and higher education pedagogies. Each chapter illustrates how 'difficult conversations' in a myriad of contexts can become a vehicle for discussions that many consider challenging and demanding of criticality about the world around them as well as about the assumptions they carry within themselves. While these conversations are imbued with a level of risk in experiencing the uncomfortableness of the unknown and unfamiliar, we argue that engaging in difficult conversations opens the vistas for the transformation of many traditional or entrenched behaviours, systems and beliefs existent in our society that have recently been questioned for their ethical value.

This book would be of interest to a range of audiences who wish to engage in critical reflection on how 'difficult conversations' can provide an affective space where transformation in thinking and practice can take place. These would include professionals in public and private services, students, academics and researchers alike.

Although exemplified 'difficult conversations' utilise different theoretical frameworks and philosophies, they serve more as an opening to further explorations, discussions and reflections, rather than encompass an exhaustive array of lenses through which the reader can engage in their own 'difficult conversations'.

The structure of the book

Whether you are a student, practitioner, academic or a member of the public, you are encouraged to explore this book by first attending to the introductory

Chapter 1, where the main concepts of what we consider 'difficult conversations' entail are critically discussed; these include the theoretical underpinning of dialogue, liminal spaces, transformation and ethics of care. Here, the editors also position their educational journeys in relation to the value and transformative potential of these conversations for socially just education and therefore society.

The book is divided into three parts: (1) transforming dialogues in schools, (2) transforming dialogues in higher education settings and (3) transforming dialogues in research. To different degrees, each part focuses on theorizing difficult conversations, the value of difficult conversations to bridge differences, and the kind of individual and societal transformations that might arise from participation in 'difficult conversations'.

Part One

The authors in Part One focus on 'the difficult conversations' around inclusion in school contexts.

In Chapter 2 autistic children's experiences of schooling are discussed. This discussion leads to a position where the author challenges the popular view that locates the problem of autistic children in the deficit model with the solution of 'fixing' their traits rather than respecting and working with their neurodiversity. Alternative rhetoric positions this issue within the teachers' and policymakers' attitudes and deep-seated beliefs and invites their engagement in 'difficult conversations' where perceptions and assumptions are examined to recognise the value of autistic pupils in our learning communities.

Chapter 3 presents the complexities of non-verbal cues and 'conversations' without 'mouth words' within the diverse communication modalities. The authors discuss with insight how the ability to engage in communication with others whose modes of interactions might differ from one's own can serve as a moment of transformation for socially just action and education. However, this transformation requires the interlocutors to enter a liminal space where their entrenched ways of being might need to be temporarily abandoned in place of a sense of uncertainty or discomfort. The authors propose a range of techniques and considerations that can enable these liminal spaces to be embraced with self/compassion.

Chapter 4 offers a poignant reflection about difficult internal conversations a teacher engages in as she realises that her attempts to include a student with multiple learning needs in a class discussion about death poses complex ethical dilemmas. Thus, the difficult conversation not only lies within the internalized dialogue of the teacher but also poses an opportunity for professional dialogue about the inclusive practice where emotive and somewhat abstract topics are introduced to learners. In this chapter, the author articulates the transformative impact of reflecting on the dissonance between teacher's values surrounding the inclusive practice and their enactment in the classroom.

Chapter 5 explores the potential that the practice of co-production can have on establishing and enriching partnerships between Special Education Needs Coordinators (SENCos) and parents and carers of children categorized as having Special Needs and/or Disabilities (SEND). The author highlights the socio-emotional aspects of these relationships, the role of open, honest and transparent communication, and how this communication is imbued with 'difficult conversations'. Furthermore, she proposes that by underpinning partnerships with shared values of respect, reciprocity, trust and agency, all stakeholders can participate in the transformation of their interactions with each other, and the ethos of the communities they form for socially just inclusive practice.

Part Two

Part Two focuses on transforming dialogues in the higher education context. All four chapters in this part focus on the power of dialogue for transforming both students and their educators' perspectives on a range of issues.

Chapter 6 offers a critique of English universities' response to the Black Lives Matters movement. While acknowledging the renewed focus on institutional enablers for racism, the author argues that meaningful change also requires transformation at the individual level. Reflections from staff development workshops are used to illustrate the power of dialogue to question and challenge assumptions, using a community of philosophical inquiry approach (CoPI). Through these reflections, the essence of the collaborative, caring, creative and critical nature of the CoPI methodology is brought to the fore to illustrate how this approach can be used to enable academics and students to enter 'difficult conversations' about race and surrounding injustices with self/compassion.

Chapter 7 presents a co-reflection between two students who participated in the co-creation of a curriculum within a primary education course through a community of philosophical inquiry (CoPI) approach. The authors critically discuss the hierarchies existent between the lecturers and students in higher education (HE), and how these orders influence students' perception of their agency within their studies. A discernment into the conflict between the 'banking model of education' and critical pedagogy illustrates how students can enact their values and engage actively in their learning. An evaluation of CoPI is used to demonstrate how 'difficult conversations' about students' agency can be facilitated to enable more inclusive collaborative practices in HE.

Chapter 8 offers a valuable analysis of the concept of academic freedom and its politicizations in higher education institutions worldwide. The chapter challenges the view that freedom of speech is necessary to enshrine academic freedom. Instead, the author argues that conversations offer a more humane and meaningful route to academic freedom, interpersonal relations and understandings. The argument is supported by reflection from a classroom debate about an individual's right to express ideas that is rejected by the majority. This chapter is an attempt to guide educators to reflect on the limits and possibilities of free speech, and the possibilities of dialogue and conversation to strengthen academic freedom.

Chapter 9 offers a timely contribution to the climate and ecological emergency. Following a discussion of the policy developments in the UK and worldwide, the author draws on a range of statistical findings to emphasize the criticality of 'difficult conversations' about the climate crisis. The challenges of those conversations are further examined in the context of education. The author calls for urgent action within education that would address eco-anxiety in students, as well as teachers' preparedness to engage in dialogue about the climate emergencies that contribute to this phenomenon. Furthermore, the author offers insight into how the 'difficult conversations' about climate emergency can be scaled up in different contexts.

Part Three

Part Three offers examples of the transformation through 'difficult conversations' within a range of research projects, bringing to the fore personal and societal values, individual and interpersonal fears of 'uncomfortable conversations', and exploring ways in which these can be embraced.

Chapter 10 is centred in the teacher education context and explores the power of difficult conversations in the research encounter. Using data from doctoral research on teachers' values and beliefs, the author reflects on how difficult conversations can be navigated through a life history methodology. These conversations enabled the author to listen deeply to hidden stories of teachers' struggles, to negotiate their beliefs in the face of challenging policy contexts, and how this in turn unravelled the author's own hidden beliefs and values. These kinds of conversations were joyful, painful and cathartic, but also transformed the researcher's and participants' awareness about how purpose and agency are connected in their work and life histories.

Chapter 11, through a conversation between authors, provides an insightful discussion on how 'difficult conversations' are pivotal to healthy and supportive relationships with children and young people who are care experienced. The authors draw on the findings from an ESRC-funded impact project which involved a co-created training resource with child and adult stakeholders. The 'difficult conversations' in this context are presented as transformational and a means to improving relationships, placement stability, and better identity outcomes for children and families. Lastly, the authors offer some considerations for how adults can, through liminal spaces, develop their openness to engage in these dialogues.

Chapter 12 explores the ethical issues that arise in the relationship between the researcher and the researched in a study on young people with dwarfism. The author's reflexive account highlights how conversations between the researcher (as privileged) and the participants (margnilalised) could have problematic ethical implications. The author adopts Alcoff's (1991) framework for interrogative practices to draw researchers' attention to ethical practices in qualitative research. This chapter is a cautionary tale for qualitative researchers to consider, reflect and act on the challenges of balancing the researcher's aims with the needs and interests of the researched.

Chapter 13 reports on the conceptualisations of conversations with people with profound intellectual and multiple disabilities (PMLD), who do not use mouth words and do not have access to standardized forms of communication. Through some preliminary findings from doctoral research which is funded through the South Coast Doctoral Training Partnership UKRI, the author considers why these conversations might be worth having, how they impact the sense of belonging for people with PMLD, and how the barriers faced by people seeking to have these conversations can be addressed. An example of such a conversation culminates the chapter to exemplify its nature.

Conclusion

All chapters in this collection highlight the contested, ambiguous and problematic nature of life in a fast-changing world. Old assumptions and beliefs about how the world works and how it should work are increasingly being challenged. Activists' work over the past decade on structural inequalities is providing marginalised groups with the confidence to question their place and role in society and to challenge the hidden and overt inequalities that result from this. If these inequalities are going to be tackled in a mature and grown-up way, then 'difficult conversations' are needed about the nature of and impact of assumptions that have privileged the few and disadvantaged the many. This edited book aims to start the conversation about the nature of difficult conversations and their potential value in transforming individuals and societies. We, therefore, invite you to explore the many contexts in which 'difficult conversations' are and could make meaningful change at societal and individual level.

Introduction: Why Difficult Conversations Matter – In Search for Transformation and Personal Growth

Katarzyna Fleming and Fufy Demissie

Introduction

We consider a difficult conversation to be the kind of conversation where participants hold different views or perspectives about a contentious issue. Whether it is in a personal or professional context, we often encounter life events that necessitate 'difficult conversations' in potentially challenging circumstances. For example, negotiating separation, disclosing our sexuality, advocating for others who might be classified as less able to do so, approaching a neighbour about the ongoing issue of noise or a broken fence or asking for a pay rise. We see these 'difficult conversations', as a way of resolving dilemmas, enacting critical pedagogies, and realizing a more socially just future – a 'future that does not repeat the present' (Giroux, 2022, p. 177).

'Difficult conversations' are also crucial for life in democratic and progressively diverse and inclusive societies. For example, there is an increasing awareness of the impact of structural racism and social inequalities on individuals' lives, as evidenced by the disproportionate impact of the pandemic on marginalised groups such as people with disabilities or in disadvantaged communities. Furthermore, it is widely known that people of colour have less access to elite universities or get a good degree, whilst the gender pay gap continues to persist (House of Parliament, 2022). It seems inevitable, therefore, that challenging or difficult conversations are vital to begin the process of transformation towards a more equal and just society (Dawson, 2015). Importantly, Giroux (2022) points out how the current educational climate is deprived of 'the soul' that education should foreground – the democratic, critical and humanising role it should play in the growth and progression of our society. Instead, he argues, the critical pedagogues are prevented from criticality, civic courage and agency that contribute to the resistance of oppression – the crisis of critical pedagogy. It is, therefore, more imperative than ever that, at this historical juncture where liberalism and authoritarianism are at headlocks, we must create hope by evoking different stories and, therefore, different futures. These stories can only be unravelled when spaces for them to be told are created, even if these spaces might be imbued with 'difficult conversations'.

Through a range of contexts in the chapters, we show how conversations about contested issues (such as inequality or discrimination) are often 'difficult' and challenging as they often confront world views, threaten power differentials or expose vulnerabilities. We also argue that difficult conversations are inevitable and necessary because when there are power differentials, those with vested interests (e.g. teachers, social workers or policymakers) often resist any challenge to the status quo, perpetuating social inequalities.

To situate the topic of 'difficult conversations' within the pertinent theoretical landscape, we now turn to discuss the five main themes which are interwoven into the fabric of this book: dialogue, the difficulty in 'difficult conversations', liminal spaces, transformation and ethics of care.

'Difficult conversations' – a theoretical perspective

The ability to communicate is one of the defining aspects of our humanity. Through conversations (whether verbal or non-verbal), we interact with each other, gain new knowledge and develop our sense of self and its meaning within society (Kizel, 2016). At a basic level, conversation can be considered a mere exchange of feelings, of thoughts, of information or understanding (Lipman, 2003). But conversation is also a deeply human phenomenon, signifying 'an encounter … mediated by the world … (that) cannot be reduced to one person "depositing" ideas in another' (Freire, 1970, p. 45).

Conversation as a mutual exploration and inquiry (Lipman, 2003) is closely aligned with dialogue. Many philosophers have extolled the importance of dialogue in our social life. Dewey perceived dialogue as an essential requirement for democratic societies because, for him, society only exists 'by communication, and, *in* communication … and communication is the way in which they [individuals] come to possess things in common' (1966, p. 4), whilst Buber (2002) considered dialogue as a process that enables humans to know themselves and the world they live in and as a means for transforming culture

(Bohm, 2000). Similarly, Freire (1970) asserted the importance of dialogue as a tool for consciousness raising about how we come to know about the world, whereas for Habermas (2018), rational dialogue was important to transforming the world into a more just society. As the book's aim is to explore the potential of difficult conversations for individual and societal transformation, we draw on Buber and Freire's perspective of dialogue as a process of self-realization (1970, 2002), rather than as a means of achieving consensus (Bohm, 2000; Habermas, 2018).

The authors also interweave a range of theoretical lenses to depict the intricacies of 'difficult conversations' within their respective contexts to frame their conceptualizations of the transformative potential of these conversations (e.g. Bojesen, Alcoff, Spivak and hooks).

Many will attest to the value of 'difficult conversations', but the essence of embedding fruitful dialogue around controversial topics can be problematic. According to Lipman (2003), transformative dialogue is more likely when relationships are nurtured, and participants have the skills to question and reason, in a caring and collaborative atmosphere. Lipman's community of philosophical inquiry pedagogy (CoPI) or the creative approach of *trove* explored in one of the chapters might be helpful tools to foster difficult conversations in education, and beyond. We believe that self-reflection can be a starting point to enable critical questioning and therefore inquisitive nature of our interactions with others. To prompt self-reflection and awareness of what constitutes 'difficult' in our individual circumstances, we offer a short discussion on the 'difficult' in the 'difficult conversations' that follow.

The 'difficult' in 'difficult conversations'

In a world that is ridden by a rapid change, organisations and therefore individuals need to be able to conduct difficult conversations effectively to survive and adapt to these changes (Stone, et al., 2021). Despite the necessity for two-way communication to address differing viewpoints, we continue to avoid difficult conversations as they are, far too often, entangled in feelings of anger, fear, hurt or guilt (Stone, et al., 2021). However, these difficult conversations are unavoidable in our daily lives, with our children, family members, neighbours, colleagues, customers or business partners (Ahmed, 2018; Stone, et al., 2021). Instead of avoiding the somewhat problematic nature of the difficult conversation, Stone, et al. (2021) encourage us to engage in developing our skills of expression in a world where we will always encounter a gulf in experiences, beliefs and feelings, in various contexts, including personal, institutional and even international relations. This chasm of difference can become a space for growth through 'difficult conversations' which can become a vehicle to address the criticality within human interactions, where the power of telling one's story and speaking to the heart of the matter is transformative (Ahmed, 2018; Cherry, 2021; Freire, 1970; Giroux, 2022).

One of the compelling arguments put forward by Stone, et al. (2021) is the realisation that although we always fear engaging in 'difficult conversations', whether we do or not will always have consequences as the subject of the matter that needs to be discussed remains unaddressed. Learning how to handle 'difficult conversations' in a constructive manner takes time, and effort, and often requires us to 'sit in the uncomfortable' (Ahmed, 2018; Stone, et al., 2021) with 'no quick fixes for long-term progress' (Ahmed, 2018, p. XXX); however, difficult conversations help resolve tough topics and awkward situations which in turn strengthen relationships (Lipman, 2003). We argue that overcoming the fears and apprehension about entering 'difficult conversations' can begin by reflecting on why difficult conversations threaten our sense of self and established distinguish steps to engage in these reflection as follows:

1. 'What happened' – differing perspectives cause the divergence between what each person perceives took place. Most often the assumptions about the 'truth', the intentions and who is to be blamed for what had happened create the tension in the conversations. Ensuring these assumptions are explored, compared and understood is essential to effectively handle the difficult conversations.
2. 'The feelings' – difficult conversations evoke strong feelings, and without recognizing them, naming them and sharing them with the other person, we can't expect them to understand the impact of this conversation on us. However, expressing feelings, particularly in a professional context, might make us feel vulnerable and uncomfortable. This is one of the main reasons people would often avoid discussing 'the feelings'. However, feelings are the core of difficult conversations and therefore, when not addressed, can exasperate the anxiety about having difficult conversations.
3. 'The identity' – even only the awareness of the impact of difficult conversations on your identity is a step forward. This aspect of difficult conversations focuses on what the conversation tells you about yourself, for example, your self-image, self-esteem, prosperity in the future, or self-doubt.

Once we realise and appreciate the complexity of the aspects involved in difficult conversations, we might shift your own intention from delivering a message based on your own perception to sharing information, asking questions and engaging with the viewpoint of the other person.

Considering the impact 'difficult conversations' may have on many spheres of our lives, it is natural that engagement in them can feel risky. However, what we present in this collection is the sheer vastness of circumstances where avoiding difficult conversations can have catastrophic consequences for individuals, communities and humanity itself. Moreover, the chapters demonstrate the strength of agency in various contexts that can be transferred across a variety of difficult conversations we all might need to engage in across our life spans.

Whilst considering the narratives presented in the book, we would like to draw your attention to the reflective space that is often formed during 'difficult conversations', a space that we refer to as a 'liminal space' or a 'space in-between'.

Liminal space and 'sitting in the uncomfortable'

Originally coined by Arnold Van Gennep (1909), liminality was identified as a period existing between a set of structures that resides within a rite of passage and follows three stages: separation, liminal period and re-assimilation. For example, when a child is born, a person (previously not a parent) enters a new phase in their life, and following the liminal period where they learn how to function in their new role, they re-assimilate into their social structure with a changed identity (of a new parent). However, Turner's (1995) further research on liminality resulted in the development of the term 'liminoid experience', which described a transitional moment in time that didn't always culminate in a change of identity. Liminality, therefore, can be described as a state of ambiguity concerning the individual's or group's identity and the space occupied during the transition which is characterised by a 'disturbance' of the established or polarized societal structures (Bhabha, 2004). Moreover, Bhabha (2004, as cited in Kalua, 2009, p. 25) describes it as 'an act of unleashing that post-dialectical moment when people reject structures and hegemonies and occupy any one of the heterogeneous spaces where they negotiate narratives of their existences as well as of particular spaces of meanings and different identities'.

This understanding of liminality is particularly important in this collection as the chapters invite the reader to consider the perspectives of others whose lived experiences might differ from the reader's values and their enactment, and therefore the reader's identity and everything they had known, cherished or believed in. More importantly, while the 'twisting' of the traditional, conventional conceptions of identities takes place, it doesn't require an immediate alteration of the self; instead, by embracing the liminal spaces, one is invited to ruminate over the foundations of their identity, while 'resisting the drive to immediately perform, redirect, or proclaim new directions' (Tesar & Arendt, 2020, p. 1104). Therefore, the liminal spaces allow time to process and consider our positionalities and understandings for as long as required in particular contexts.

In the context of collaborative work, liminality can also refer to the progress and the connections that a group can achieve in the liminoid period, also known as 'communitas' (Turner, 1969). The shared experiences of the liminal spaces can result in a shared sense of marginality, and therefore intensify the group's solidarity and togetherness (Buechner, Dirkx, Konvisser, Myers & Peleg-Baker, 2020). The group's interconnectedness can, therefore, develop an 'immediate and genuine sense of the other' (Turner, 2012, p. 6). This sense of the other is essential to emphasise with those whose lived experiences differ from our own. While this book might serve as an ignition for self-reflection, we recognise that it might also be a stimulus for group conversations or an attempt to ignite a change in a given social structure, such as, a classroom, an institution or a community group. Therefore, as Freire (1970, p. 20) argued, 'even when one must speak to the people, one must convert the "to" to the "with" people. And this implies respect for the 'knowledge of living experience'. Undertaking the role of a learner despite often having had rich life experiences already can enable us to act with humility while engaging with others, and to appreciate the multi-dimensional aspect of all experiences. Likewise, liminality encompasses the state of temporality and becoming while privileging process over structure (Neumann, 2012); therefore, recognising difficult conversations as liminal spaces, one should consider the value of the process of being in those spaces rather than focusing on how to be in them.

Being open to the possibility of entering and engaging in liminal spaces often leads to a discomfort. This discomfort might be related to the realisation of one's own biases; however, to become an agent of change one must recognise and challenge them (Ahmed, 2018). Pondering over our sense of self, years of lived experiences, choices we have made and the consequences of those choices comes at a price of a realisation that what once constituted a safe harbour of the known and predictable becomes destabilised and comes under question. Perhaps admitting flaws and shortcomings in our own behaviour, assumptions or sets of beliefs is the harshest outcome of the endeavour of critical reflection. However, the learning that occurs through critical reflection always leads to change and growth, while it also often sparks transformation of practice, thinking and being that humanises our interactions.

Transformation through 'difficult conversations'

Transformation 'always requires engagement with what or who is other', in a dialogical process that is frequently difficult and frustrating, and without guaranteed outcomes (Biesta, 2013, p. 3). The global pandemic, the Black Lives Matter, the LGBTQ+ the Disability Rights movements and the Ukrainian and Gaza Wars have all fuelled debates around traditions, identity and social justice, with voices that were once marginalized and disregarded becoming central to the sociological debate (Macionis & Plummer, 2005). Unsurprisingly, the recognition of previously silenced experiences stimulates 'difficult conversations' in a range of contexts, e.g. educational institutions, workplaces, in the community or simply around the dinner table. Such conversations can result in discomfort; however, as Ball (2017) describes, this might not only be unavoidable but it is also necessary for social transformation to occur. This necessity has also been corroborated by Stephen Hawking who warned that 'mankind's greatest achievements have come about by talking, and its greatest failures by not talking'.

'Difficult conversations' are uncomfortable because they can threaten established hierarchies, privileges and traditional identities (Freire, 1970), while they might also pose challenges from a practical perspective, e.g. communicating with loved ones through the internet rather than being able to spend time with them to develop meaningful conversations and connections (Osborn & Canfor-Dumas, 2018). However, the ability to adopt open-minded non-judgemental attitudes, curiosity and empathy is not innate and, therefore, it must be cultivated (Lipman, 2003). To better understand the experiences of others, we should practise being learners who engage in conversations with humility and ask questions when we don't understand (Ahmed, 2018).

One of the ways to engage in being a learner is to learn from people's stories. Goodson (2013) emphasises the egalitarian and inclusive power of stories from diverse communities as a most familiar form of everyday existence. And it is through learning from these stories that we become more attuned with our fellow humans, some of whose lived experiences might differ from polarised ways of thinking (Ahmed, 2018; Cherry, 2021); it is through the decentring of what we perceive as a 'norm' that we are inspired to ponder, question and reflect (Cherry, 2021), and therefore begin to change – to enter the 'state of becoming'.

If, as Hawking argues, 'talking' is central to human achievement and progress, it is important to consider the role of the educator. Humans have the capacity to engage in meaningful dialogue, but for many, the ability to participate in meaningful and transformative 'talk' is problematic (Osborn & Canfor-Dumas, 2018). We often struggle to express our thoughts, listen to others and fail to operate within what Buber calls the 'I-thou' space – a space characterised by mutuality, directness, intensity and ineffability (Buber, 1970). At the same time, policy discourses continue to prioritise the acquisition of knowledge and skills through didactic curricula and pedagogy, even though the societal challenges we face require educational experiences that value talk and dialogue. The issues addressed in this book are urgent. This means that educators, in whatever context they operate, need to seek out opportunities to engage their communities in 'difficult conversations' and develop their own skills to create and facilitate these dialogic spaces. Adopting the principles of relational pedagogy, such as open and trusting relationships with students and modelling an open-minded and critical attitude to knowledge claims, are key to the educators/facilitators' professional repertoire (Gravett, 2023). While, as a reader, you engage in self-reflection on how and why to conduct 'difficult conversations' in your circumstances, we would like you to consider how you might nurture these conversations by contemplating ways in which you look after your own well-being and create physical and mental space to learn and grow.

Ethics of care: how to nurture 'difficult conversations'

Conversations become difficult when they threaten one's identity, power and ways of understanding the world. A commitment to engage in/facilitate 'difficult conversations', therefore, has an ethical dimension. Nodding's theory of the ethics of care can be a valuable way of conceptualising the ethical elements of 'difficult conversations'. As a feminist philosophical perspective, the ethics of care draw on 'traditional' feminine values and dispositions such as empathy and compassion. Nodding's notion of the 'ethical ideal' involves reciprocity, in which the 'carer' and 'cared for' take part in a relationship (Caine et al., 2020). Likewise, the relational human arrangements underpinned by ethics of care have the potential to re-affect the objectified world around us and to redefine boundaries of new possibilities in our thinking and being (Puig de la Bellacase, 2017). It is through dialogue, without which, argued Noddings (2018), the caring cannot not be modelled. 'When we care, we receive the other in an open and genuine way' (Noddigns, 2018, p. 231), which foregrounds establishing a mutual frame of reference for each other's lived experiences. The focus on understanding the lived experience of the other person in 'difficult conversations' has been at the forefront of the discussion above; however, nurturing one's well-being when engaging in those discussions is equally crucial.

While we present a diverse discussion on the importance and the transformative nature of 'difficult conversations' in education and beyond, we recognise the necessity to consider what nurturing these conversations entails. Likewise, we encourage our readers to engage in nurturing their own liminal spaces while working through this book. As explored by Bhabha (2004), and Turner (1969), liminality is often associated with the space 'in-between' where tensions of unknown and often uncomfortable can decentre our thinking, feelings or even our identity. Therefore, we would like to draw our readers' attention to how engagement in 'difficult conversations' affects their embodied experience of entering these liminal spaces. Part of being able to immerse oneself in the liminality is to be aware of what fears, doubts, assumptions and deep-seated beliefs we hold about the topic or community of people engaged in the 'difficult conversation' (Stone, et al., 2021). When this awareness is achieved, one may start exploring the reasons for 'the uncomfortable' to enrich their own understanding of their identity and world view (Bhabha, 2004). This process of transformation can be complex and therefore we outline a number of considerations to encourage you to facilitate this process:

- Nurturing yourself as a reader and as a conversationalist through difficult conversations
- Developing expressive skills gradually
- Allowing yourself to 'not know'
- Treating others and oneself with compassion for a learner
- Developing self-confidence and self-efficacy to express one's own viewpoints in a constructive way
- Remembering that the difficult conversations are often situated in liminal spaces, on the journey, and are rarely a destination or a final negotiation – they are a part of the transformative process.
- Knowing that the learning and transformation processes are often uncomfortable and may be met with a great level of resistance from others – it is a choice that not everyone can take at a particular junction of their life.
- Ensuring that any emotional labour of engaging in change or being in 'the uncomfortable' is supported by a form of supervision or a time for reflection and restoration of balance if it has been decentralized.

While the premise of this collection is to solicit your reflection and to provide encouragement for you to engage in 'difficult conversations', it would be unethical of us not to point out that there will be times and places where self-care and self-preservation may be more necessary than seeking opportunities for transformation through 'difficult conversations'. As Ferner and Chetty (2019, p. 137) argue, 'sometimes walking away is the most sensible course of action', for if your interlocutor is unable to engage in a productive dialogue, listen, be open to challenge their own assumptions or ignorance, you might find that your energy would be better spent on not engaging with that dialogue.

'Why should one engage in conversations that carry such a level of risk?' we hear you ask. As educators, we see it as our role, if not a duty, to continually develop our horizons, what we think, how we perceive the world, and to uphold the ethical responsibility to enable spaces where our students or pupils can also grow, critically question what's in front of them, and take lessons from what has gone before us to ensure the future doesn't replicate the injustices of the past (Giroux, 2022). The price for this discomfort is, therefore, worth incurring in our eyes. Above all, enduring this discomfort positions educators as able to intervene and express their agency in what and how they 'believe things ought to be' (Greene, 1995, p. 9), rather than merely serving as compliant enactors of the governments' missions to meet national economic and technical needs.

Conclusion

As the 'cogs' in the educational system, we, the educators, face the challenge of channelling our efforts and commitments to inspire growth, curiosity and critical thought in our students and ourselves. However, it is our 'responsibility to persist in the struggle to build a more compassionate, equitable, and sustainable world (Leopando, 2022, p. 19). While we endeavour to enable these transformations and create safe spaces for our students to discuss and question their own and others' assumptions, views, and beliefs' (Mezirow, 1997), we face the constant pressure of meeting the expectations of the performative tasks of assessments, standardizations and instrumentalization of contemporary schooling (Leopando, 2022). And, as these pressures mount around us, we might begin to ask ourselves and others around us about the purpose and the direction of our profession. It is these questions that led us to compose this book; to create the possibilities to re-imagine an educational future that points towards more relationally centred pedagogies which we foster in our work.

In our quest to answer some of the questions, we were humbled to collaborate with the authors of the chapters whose own philosophies led them to embrace collective resistance, disturbance, empathy or radical imagination of what might be (Giroux, 2022). The courageous conversations that are presented in each of the chapters resemble our commitment to education as an act of social justice, always striving to 'think against the grain'. These difficult conversations matter to us as they have the potential to awaken consciousness, challenge common sense, and recognise and provoke action when rights are denied and injustices are enacted. This collection is our call for collective resistance to what might be present in educational practice – our burning torch for social justice.

While we journeyed with you in this introductory chapter, our intention was to inspire your reflection on the position and relevance of some of the powerful concepts connected to 'difficult conversations'. We hope that the key themes will encourage you to immerse in the liminal spaces in your contexts despite the discomfort or vulnerabilities that they may bring to the fore. Whether you are seeking to affect individual or societal transformation, we hope that ethics of care and self-compassion will accompany the 'difficult conversations' you might experience in your endeavours. While we encourage you to 'dare greatly' (Brown, 2015), we are truly hopeful that you find inspiration, challenge and hope in these chapters.

References

Ahmed, S. K. (2018). *Being the change. Lessons and strategies to teach social comprehension*. Heinemann.
Ball, S. J. (2017). School politics, teachers' careers and educational change: a case study of becoming a comprehensive school. In *Education and Social Change* (pp. 29–61). Routledge.
Bhabha, H. K. (2004). *The location of culture*. Routledge.
Biesta, G. J. (2013). *Beautiful risk of education*. Routledge.
Bohm, J. (2000). *Public deliberation: Pluralism, complexity, and democracy*. MIT Press.
Brown, B. (2015). *Daring greatly: How the courage to be vulnerable transforms the way we live, love, parent, and lead*. Penguin.
Buber, M. (1970). *I and Thou (Vol. 243)*. Simon and Schuster.
Buber, M. (2002). *The Martin Buber Reader: Essential Writings*.
Buechner, B., Dirkx, J., Konvisser, Z. D., Myers, D., & Peleg-Baker, T. (2020). From liminality to communitas: The collective dimensions of transformative learning. *Journal of Transformative Education, 18*(2), pp. 87–113.

Caine, V., Chung, S., Steeves, P., & Clandinin, D. J. (2020). The necessity of a relational ethics alongside Noddings' ethics of care in narrative inquiry. *Qualitative Research, 20*(3), pp. 265–76.

Cherry, L. (2021). *Conversations that make a difference for children and young people: Relationship-focused practice from the frontline*. Routledge.

Dawson, M. (2015). Sociology as conversation: Zygmunt Bauman's applied sociological hermeneutics. *Sociology, 49*(3), pp. 582–87.

de La Bellacasa, M. P. (2017). *Matters of care: Speculative ethics in more than human worlds*. University of Minnesota Press.

Dewey, J. (1966). Democracy and education (1916). In J. A. Boydston (Ed.). *The Middle Works of John Dewey, 9* (pp. 1899–924). Southern Illinois University Press.

Dewey, J. (1998). *The essential Dewey: Pragmatism, education, democracy* (Vol. 1). Indiana University Press.

Ferner, A., & Chetty, D. (2019). *How to disagree: Negotiate difference in a divided world.: 20 thought-provoking lessons*. White Lion Publishing.

Freire, P. (1970). *Pedagogy of the oppressed*. Routledge.

Freire, P. (1973). *Pedagogy of hope*. Routledge.

Giroux, H. A. (2022). *Pedagogy of resistance: Against manufactured ignorance*. Bloomsbury.

Gravett, K. (2023). *Relational pedagogies: Connections and mattering in higher education*. Bloomsbury Publishing.

Green, M. (1995). *Realising the imagination: Essays on Education, Arts, and Social Change*. Jossey-Bass Publishers.

Habermas, J. (2018). Interview with Jürgen Habermas. In A. Bächtiger, J. Dryzek, & J. Mansbridge (Eds.). *The Oxford handbook of deliberative democracy*. Oxford University Press.

House of Parliament (2002). *The gender pay gap*. Available at: https://commonslibrary.parliament.uk/research-briefings/sn07068/.

Kalua, F. (2009). Homi Bhabha's third space and African identity. *Journal of African cultural studies, 21*(1), pp. 23–32.

Kizel, A. (2016). Philosophy with children as an educational platform for self-determined learning. *Cogent Education, 3*(1), p. 1244026.

Leopando, I. (2022). Toward a critical pedagogy of spirituality and healing. In T. M. Kress, C. Emdin, & R. Lake (Eds.). *Critical Pedagogy for Healing. Paths Beyond 'Wellness', Toward a Soul Revival of Teaching and Learning* (pp. 19–26). Bloomsbury.

Lipman, M. (2003). *Thinking in education*. Cambridge university press.

Macionis, J. J., & Plummer, K. (2005). *Sociology: A global introduction*. Pearson Education.

Mezirow, J. (1997). Transformative learning: Theory to practice. *New Directions for Adult & Continuing Education, 74*(74), pp. 5–12.

Neumann, I. B. (2012). Introduction to the forum on liminality. *Review of International Studies*, *38*(2), pp. 473–9.

Noddings, N. (2018) *Philosophy of Education*. Routledge.

Osborn, P., & Canfor-Dumas, E. (2018). *The talking revolution. How creative conversation can change the world*. Port Meadow Press.

Stone, D., Patton, B., & Heen, S. (2021). *Difficult conversations: How to discuss what matters most*. Penguin.

Tesar, M., & Arndt, S. (2020). Writing the human 'I': Liminal spaces of mundane abjection. *Qualitative inquiry*, *26*(8–9), pp. 1102–9.

Turner, V. (1969). Liminality and communitas. *The ritual process: Structure and anti-structure*, *94*(113), pp. 125–30.

Turner, V. (1995). *The ritual process: Structure and anti-structure*. Transaction Publishers.

Turner, E. (2012). *Communitas: The anthropology of collective joy*. Springer.

Van Gennep, A. (1960 [1909]). *The rites of passage*. University of Chicago Press.

Part One

'Difficult Conversations' in Educational Settings

2

Transforming Autistic Children and Young People's School Experiences through Difficult Conversations between Educators

Jo Billington

Introduction

In accordance with national and international legislation intended to promote the social and educational inclusion of children with disabilities (Children and Families Act, 2014; United Nations, 2006), 72 per cent of identified autistic children in the English state school system are educated in mainstream settings (Department for Education, 2022b). However, despite the inclusive ideology that forms the basis of special educational needs provision in England, many autistic children and young people have difficult school experiences and impoverished educational outcomes.

Of the autistic children in mainstream schools, around three-quarters do not meet the criteria for an Education Health and Care Plan (Department for Education, 2022b) and have been determined by their local authorities[1] as capable of accessing a mainstream education without the specialist multidisciplinary support provided by such plans. Therefore, one might expect the attainment data for this particular group of children would be more or less in line with national averages. However, the attainment gap between autistic and non-autistic pupils is long-standing and well documented (Keen et al., 2016). At the time of writing, the 2022 key stage 2 (year 6 SATs) and 4 (year 11 GCSEs) attainment data has not yet been published and figures during the height of the Covid-19 pandemic are not necessarily reliable due to the disruption caused by lockdowns and exam adjustments. However, the last set of reliable pre-pandemic figures showed that 32.5 per cent of autistic children achieved the equivalent of five A*–C grades at GCSE in 2018/19 compared with 63.9 per cent of the general school population in the same period (Department for Education, 2020). An even wider attainment gap existed at the end of Key Stage 2 (year 6), with 25 per cent of autistic children reaching expected levels in reading, writing and maths compared with 70 per cent of the general school population in the same academic year (Department for Education, 2019).

The causes of this disparity have not been clearly identified, and while previous research evidence has highlighted several potential factors including an uneven academic profile in autistic learners (Griswold et al., 2002; Jones et al., 2009), time spent away from the classroom undoubtedly plays a part. Recent research has shown that in primary school, children regarded as having the highest level of need spend the equivalent of more than a day a week separated from their teacher, their peers and the curriculum engaged in various out-of-class activities and interventions (Webster, 2022). Autistic children are also more likely to display behaviour described as 'disruptive' resulting in significantly higher formal exclusion rates than children with no special educational needs (Brede et al., 2017), and are an over-represented group in Pupil Referral Units[2] (Department for Education, 2022a). Moreover, charities such as the National Autistic Society have been concerned for some years about the rise in unofficial exclusions. Such unlawful exclusions include being sent home to 'cool off' when showing signs of distress or overwhelm and being excluded from school trips and extracurricular activities. The extent of these exclusions is difficult to pinpoint because they are not recorded in official statistics, but in a recent survey of 3,470 parents and carers of autistic children, more than one in five respondents reported that their child had been informally excluded at least twice in the last year (National Autistic Society, 2021).

Furthermore, there is an increased awareness of the growing number of autistic children who find school so stressful that they are unable to attend regularly or at all, resulting in burnout or protective self-exclusion (Dalrymple, 2022; Totsika et al., 2020). Research suggests that central to the issue of attendance difficulties is the fact that autistic children and young people are considerably more likely to experience bullying, peer vicitimisation and social isolation than their non-autistic peers (Humphrey & Hebron, 2015; Maïano et al., 2016), all of which undoubtedly play a significant role in the disproportionate rates of mental distress in the autistic child population (Strang et al., 2012; White et al., 2009).

Arguably key to addressing this crisis is the level of understanding and acceptance there is of autistic pupils in mainstream schools. The level of support that is available to autistic children in English mainstream schools is highly variable and largely teacher-dependent, leading some families to describe the process of securing the right support for their child as a lottery. Given the central role of the individual teacher in the success or otherwise of an autistic child's school experience, it is troubling to know that some teachers have ambivalent views towards including children with disabilities in mainstream classrooms (see De Boer et al., 2011 for a review), and others do not necessarily feel confident about their ability to provide the right support to autistic pupils, citing insufficient funding, resources and autism-specific training (Humphrey & Symes, 2013; Ravet, 2018; Roberts & Simpson, 2016). I argue that this development of understanding and acceptance can be reached through engagement in what might be considered difficult conversations, which I discuss in the next section.

Why difficult conversations are needed

There has been considerable debate among researchers, teachers, parents, policymakers and others about how best to improve the experiences and outcomes for autistic children and young people in mainstream settings (e.g. Dillon *et al.*, 2014; McKinlay *et al.*, 2022; Walsh & Hall, 2012; Warnock & Norwich, 2010). However, this conversation has not fully included autistic people and has often failed to honour and value autistic ways of being (Milton & Bracher, 2013). Instead, the conversation has largely been confined to non-autistic people (adults, mainly) and has tended to focus on the changes autistic children need to make in order to fit into the education system rather than identifying how changes in the structures, practices and cultures in our schools might actively disadvantage neurodivergent pupils (Milton, 2014). This one-sided perspective poses a difficulty for all involved as it emphasises that the current ways of working are not inclusive and require a shift not only in practical terms but also in relation to traditional attitudes and principles that underpin current practice. Attitudinal shifts of this kind are always challenging as they destabilise the status quo and prompt everyone to examine their own assumptions (Ahmed, 2018; Bhabha, 2004). However, not engaging in these difficult conversations carries ethical risks that our schools will remain ill-equipped to support autistic pupils – a risk that, in my view, must be addressed and mitigated.

While we unquestionably still have a long way to go, our education system has progressed in recent decades in terms of recognising and celebrating ethnic, cultural, sexual, religious and gender diversity. However, it is arguable that neurodiversity is still a largely under-recognised and poorly understood concept in English schools. Rather than an identity worthy of respect and appreciation, autism (and other neurodivergent conditions such as ADHD and dyslexia) is still viewed by many as an economic burden or a problem to be solved (e.g. Buescher et al., 2014; Rogge & Janssen, 2019), and this can have a catastrophic impact on the health and well-being of autistic children and their families. It is my belief that these social and attitudinal factors are at the heart of the challenges faced by autistic children and young people in mainstream schools, and indeed for autistic people of all ages across society. One way to address the stigma around neurodiversity could be to engage in critical conversations, some of which may be difficult and uncomfortable due to the fact that they require us to examine our values and beliefs in novel ways. For example, it is possible that we may have never considered the privilege and power that comes with being of a dominant neurotype. Furthermore, we may have never examined our attitudes towards neurodivergent pupils and how these attitudes might shape our interactions with them, our assessment of their strengths and difficulties and, in turn, the support we offer to them.

I am frequently asked by school staff and families how conversations about autism can be had in the classroom but prior to any conversation with pupils, arguably the most important place for these conversations is the staffroom. Conversations that explore the idea that our education system may be inadvertently causing harm to autistic children are challenging but necessary. As I aim to explain in this chapter, this is a subject that needs to be discussed, however difficult it may be for us as educators to critically engage with the unintended consequences of educational and societal neuronormativity. It is necessary that we 'sit in the uncomfortable' (Ahmed, 2018; Stone et al., 2011) if we are to identify and break down potentially oppressive practices within our education system. It is my intention in this chapter to set out why I believe this to be the case and offer some ideas for reflection. I will do this by outlining two aspects of research evidence: (1) a short review of relevant theory and (2) my own empirical research with autistic young people. To become agents of urgently needed social change we must harness the transformative power of difficult conversations and lean into the discomfort of this liminal space because, as I will discuss later, the lives of autistic people may, quite literally, depend on it.

> **Pause for reflection**
>
> - What are your attitudes towards the inclusion of autistic children and young people in mainstream schools?
> - What experiences contributed to the formation of your attitudes?
> - What are the barriers to the successful inclusion of autistic learners in your particular educational setting, if any?

Moving from the medical model to the neurodiversity model of autism

Historically, autism has been understood predominantly through a medical lens, one that makes a binary distinction between 'normal' and 'abnormal' development. In the clinical literature, autism is classed as a 'neurodevelopmental disorder' (American Psychiatric Association, 2013, p. 31) and autistic ways of being which differ significantly from non-autistic norms are pathologised as deficits and impairments with the implication that autistic behaviours are defective and in need of treatment or correction. This has fed into what Stone and Priestley (1996) refer to as the 'personal tragedy model' (p. 701), where a diagnosis of autism for a child may be seen as a blight on the person and their family. This view has also undoubtedly contributed to the interventionist culture of autism support in English education. Indeed, the statutory guidance set out in the SEND Code of Practice maintains that the process of identifying if a child has special educational needs is determined by their need for support which is 'additional to or different from that made generally for other children or young people of the same age' (Department for Education and Department of Health, 2015, p. 16) – an assessment which is largely determined by how far a child may have deviated from a perceived 'normal' developmental trajectory determined by their chronological age.

In the case of autistic children, the deviation from the norm, be it determined behaviourally or otherwise, carries with it the supposition that the autistic child is in some way broken and needs to be fixed – the end goal being not that the child is encouraged to be their authentic autistic selves and supported to lead a full and flourishing life on their own terms, but that they behave and function as closely as possible to a norm set by their non-autistic peers of roughly similar age. Given the paucity of critical autism education in teacher training and the interventionist nature of governmental guidance (Department of Health and Social Care and Department for Education, 2021), it is easy to see how these views are shared by many who work in mainstream schools to the extent where they are rarely questioned. I propose that these views are examined critically in order to expand the understanding of educators' own attitudes towards teaching autistic pupils and the impact those attitudes have on this group of pupils. This is because, despite being unintended, the consequences of this approach can and do cause harm and they need to be considered carefully – a theme I will expand on as this chapter continues.

Due to how entrenched the medical model of autism is in our society, an autistic-led resistance to its principles has been steadily growing since the early 1990s. A member of the autistic rights movement, Australian sociologist Judy Singer, proposed the term 'neurodiversity' in 1998 to describe the 'emerging social movements for civil rights for people with various devalued, medically labelled neurological conditions' (Milton et al., 2020, p. 3). The term has been interpreted in different ways over the intervening years and, being still very much in its infancy as a concept, is the subject of some debate (den Houting, 2019; Walker, 2021). However, it is essentially rooted in the idea that a 'normal' brain is a social construction and neurological difference is as natural a form of human diversity as, say, differences in ethnicity and sexuality (Singer, 2017).

In this way, the concept of neurodiversity is at the heart of a social justice movement which challenges the deficit model of autism by resisting the pathologisation of autistic ways of being and recognizing the strengths of autistic people while not seeking to dismiss or trivialise their experiences of disablement (den Houting, 2019). The concept of neurodiversity also provides a framework for considering the social and political considerations central to this chapter. It provides an alternative to deficit-based medical-model thinking by exposing the stigma and hostility autistic people face as a minority group in a society largely designed by and for people who are not autistic. Thus, the emphasis on criticality, social change and collective resistance central to the neurodiversity movement is closely aligned with the theoretical foundations of difficult conversations as set out in the introduction of this book by scholars such as Giroux (2022), who underlines the importance of critical thinking and challenging the status quo in the quest to build a more equitable society.

> **Pause for reflection**
>
> - Do you identify as 'neurotypical' (i.e. majority neurotype) or 'neurodivergent' (i.e. minority neurotype), or is it something you've not thought about before?
> - How might your neurotype affect your expectations of others?
> - How might the values and attitudes of those with the majority neurotype adversely affect those of minority neurotypes?
> - How might the power relations between adults and children of different neurotypes play out in a school setting?

The double-empathy problem: how people of different neurotypes can misunderstand one another

In accordance with the medical model of autism, the social and communication challenges autistic children experience in school are usually attributed to their neurology. Indeed, the deficit model of autism which underpins clinical assessment dictates that 'persistent deficits in social communication and social interaction' (American Psychiatric Association, 2013, p. 31) are diagnostic criteria. As mentioned previously, this has led to a model of autism support, particularly in childhood, in which the child is subjected to a range of formal and informal interventions with the aim of reducing the 'autistic behaviours' in favour of 'non-autistic behaviours'. However, the idea that autistic interaction is defective and in need of modification has been challenged by autistic people for many years (e.g. Baggs, 2007; Sinclair, 1993/2012).

This challenge has been theorised by autistic sociologist Dr Damian Milton as the 'double empathy problem' (Milton, 2012). His theory posits that instead of autistic interaction being 'wrong' and non-autistic interaction being 'right', they are both simply different. Each has its own integrity but the distinct differences between them can lead to mutual misunderstanding. Milton goes on to explain this as 'a "double problem" because both people experience it, and so it is not a singular problem located in any one person' (Milton, 2012, p. 884). However, due to the power imbalances between autistic (minority group) and non-autistic people (majority group), any difficulties or misunderstandings are generally attributed to the autistic person. This leads to the widely accepted belief that it is autistic people who need to adjust their behaviour to more closely match the conventions and expectations of non-autistic people who, in turn, are not usually required to make adjustments because how they behave is not subject to the same scrutiny.

There are serious and sometimes catastrophic consequences to the widely held belief that autistic people need to adapt to the linguistic and behavioural conventions of non-autistic people. The pressure to behave less autistically and adapt to neurotypical norms can lead autistic people to try to camouflage their natural ways of being. Not only is this effortful to the point of exhaustion but it can also lead to feelings of worthlessness and a lack of belonging, both of which have been strongly associated with suicidal behaviours (Cassidy et al., 2020). When we also take into account the fact that suicide is a leading cause of early death in autistic adults (Hirvikoski et al., 2016), the urgency of the need to have conversations about this subject is clear.

Thus, the double empathy problem offers an alternative way of thinking since it proposes the solution to the misunderstandings between autistic and non-autistic people is not one that rests entirely with autistic people but is one that is shared. It implies that instead of autistic people needing intervention in order to behave more typically, non-autistic people need to learn how to interpret, understand and appreciate autistic ways of being. However, given the stigma associated with autism, this learning process arguably needs to begin with non-autistic people examining how their internalised beliefs and assumptions might impact on their engagement with autistic people. This is where difficult conversations aimed at sensitively exploring one's own preconceptions can play a crucial role in overcoming the double empathy problem. In engaging in conversations of this nature, we lay the foundations for a deeper understanding of ways of being which may be very different to (but no less valuable than) one's own (Buber, 2002; Freire, 1970).

Autistic young adults' reflections on the double empathy problem in mainstream primary schools: A qualitative study

But, how does the double empathy problem play out in schools, and what is its impact on autistic children and young people? To answer this question, I will now refer to a focus group study (The University of Reading Research Ethics Committee, approval code 2017-196-FK) I conducted with six autistic young adults (4 female, 2 male) aged between 19 and 25 years in which they were asked to reflect on their experiences of mainstream primary school (Billington, et al., forthcoming). The group discussion was recorded, transcribed verbatim and then analysed in order to identify themes across the participants' contributions. Three themes were constructed from the data which I will briefly describe below and illustrate with participant quotes. Pseudonyms are used throughout.

Theme 1: The undesirability of difference

Although most of the participants did not know they were autistic until well into their adolescence, they all knew they were different from a very early age. They described their experience of being different in negative terms which they attributed to interactions with peers, teachers and occasionally parents. They also reported that their earliest memories of primary school were of a place where they did not belong and were not necessarily welcome:

> I was just so different from everyone else that not even the teachers really knew how to address me, and I just felt really ... like I wasn't meant to be there at all. (Sophie)

In addition to feeling on the outside of the everyday business of school, the participants reported that when they interacted with teachers and peers, their natural approaches to communicating, learning and socialising were often misunderstood. They spoke of unwittingly making social mistakes which in some cases were perceived as wilfully defiant. In these instances, it could lead to criticism or sanctions from teachers:

> [I was] always being told off for things which I didn't understand were wrong. (Georgia)

Recent research suggests that having a formal diagnosis of autism earlier in life may be helpful in developing a more positive self-concept (Gould & Ashton-Smith, 2011), but for some participants this wasn't the case and the sense of being 'other' that came with their diagnosis was distressing:

> I really didn't like [having an autism diagnosis] because I always thought that was what made me different and I was trying ... I remember sitting there thinking trying to work out ways to get un-diagnosed and not liking it, basically. Basically trying to work out how to be normal and get rid of it. (Daniel)

As demonstrated by the participants' expressions, feeling different or continually being treated differently by crucial community members can have a profoundly lasting impact on one's sense of belonging. Turner (2012) posits that spaces where these differences can be explored can help the group to develop a greater sense 'of the other'. These spaces are not aimed at merely creating a consensus about a set of behaviours (Bohm, 2000) but at empowering the engaged to learn through the liminality of these spaces where one is allowed to 'not know' and to arrive at realisations about own assumptions or prejudices (Cherry, 2021).

> ### Pause for reflection
> - How did you feel when reading the quotes from the autistic young people above?
> - Can you recall any instances from your life that made you feel different or 'othered'? How would you have liked to enable people to better understand your experience?
> - How might you begin to have conversations with colleagues about the themes raised in this section?

Theme 2: The various guises of bullying

Daniel's description of not feeling 'normal' cited above was one that was expressed by others in the group who described examples of how being different made them targets for bullying. Most of the participants could recall numerous instances of obvious bullying by peers such as name-calling or physical assaults, but much of the bullying reported was less overt. These more subtle forms of bullying typically involved some form of social exclusion:

> *… being picked later for sports teams or just not having people to sit with at lunch … or kind of having difficulties like finding the right things to talk about that people would be interested in … or not being invited to birthday parties. (Holly)*

The participants also reported bullying not just from their peers but also from their teachers. However, they perceived the teachers' bullying to be different from their peers. While peers engaged in physical and verbal assaults, their teachers' bullying tended to centre on the implication that if they were 'less autistic', life would be easier for them:

> *[I] remember a teacher … basically saying … the way that you'll get bullied less if you act like a normal person … and the reason he said that was that I liked to just sit read a book erm, and not go play football. (Daniel)*

When I asked the group what might have motivated this behaviour from their teachers, they responded that it was possible that their teachers were acting in their best interests, as exemplified by Georgia:

> [She] told me that she was doing it for my own good. I was very clear I didn't want friends and she thought that made me, like, selfish, like 'one day you're going to regret you didn't make friends when you were younger'. (Georgia)

However, even though the participants acknowledged there was a possibility that this treatment from their teachers came from a place of concern, this did nothing to minimise the invalidation and shame they experienced. In some cases, it led to fear and anxiety so overwhelming that they would regularly struggle to attend school:

> The main person that put me off [attending school] in primary school was my year 5 teacher who used to bully me quite a lot ... I don't know why she had such a problem with me but ... she just seemed to have this real dislike for me and I don't know why. (Jack)

While the participants' accounts above illustrate the extent to which the bullying related to their difference was prevalent in their school experiences, I would like to draw your attention to the issue of teachers' assumptions about normalcy. If, as educators of neurodivergent children, we only accept the non-autistic definitions of normalcy, how can we be open to the needs and realities of those who are different? Engaging in conversations about what we consider 'normal' and what we consider 'different' can be challenging since these concepts are often based on deeply entrenched ideas. As such, we might be required to 'sit in the uncomfortable' of what these conversations might unravel (Ferner & Chetty, 2019). With this risk of the discomfort in mind, please consider the following points for reflection:

Pause for reflection

- Is it ethical to avoid potentially difficult conversations about normalcy in educational settings?
- How can educators provide support to autistic children that is identity-supporting rather than identity-invalidating?

Theme 3: The emotional labour of 'being good'

Given the level of hostility towards their differences, it is unsurprising that the participants reported being under significant pressure to behave in more neurotypical ways and engage in more neurotypical activities, despite the discomfort and distress that caused:

> *I was always very nervous about trying to fit in potentially so like, making sure I didn't go do anything that would be not normal. (Daniel)*

All participants reported feeling overwhelmed by the emotional labour involved in either blending in or coping with the fallout of non-conformity. Invariably, the effort expended in attempting to cope with others' attitudes towards their differences led some participants to suppress their emotional response while in school and release some of the tension in the safety of their homes:

> *In school, I would bottle it up. And try and be good to kids and good to teachers. And that's probably why me and my mum never got on because I probably just exploded on her really. Like, just let rip because then I knew that I wasn't going to get bullied from people that way. I could just be angry at her. (Sophie)*

This idea of 'trying to be good' was central to the participants' experience of primary school. They worked hard to have a good school experience, but, as expressed by Katie below, many felt that their efforts to fit in were not reciprocated by school staff and peers:

> *I liked school, but school didn't like me. (Katie)*

The data also suggest that the costs of the challenges experienced during primary school were borne by the participants, and these costs were not just felt at the time. The impact has been long-lasting and is still something many of the participants feel they are paying for in adulthood:

> *Now I'm angry, I'm unforgiving, I'm cold, and I never used to be like that ... y'know? (Sophie)*

These themes clearly show the double-empathy problem in practice. The participants all felt undesirably different from an early age because of the way in which they were perceived by the people around them. Whenever misunderstandings occurred, they were seen as solely responsible and were either sanctioned or shunned. They were subject to bullying by peers and invalidation by their teachers. In response, they felt the pressure to conform in ways that were effortful and distressing. The results of this study suggest that the participants' primary school experience was characterised by routine invalidations and hostilities which had long-lasting implications for their self-esteem and self-concept. It is important to note that all the participants in this study completed their compulsory schooling and went on to enrol in post-16 education, with most studying for a university degree. As such, they represent the minority of autistic young people who continued their education to tertiary level. A key question to contemplate though is, at what cost?

Freire (1970) argues that education should offer opportunities to challenge hierarchies, privileges and traditional identities, and it is important to recognise the position of power and authority educators occupy within the circumstances illustrated in this chapter. This position of power, albeit traditionally embedded in accountability and performativity measures (Ball, 2017), carries the danger of lifelong negative impacts on pupil identity when it is not reviewed critically. I propose that difficult conversations are considered as a way of opening an inclusive dialogue where the double empathy problem can be addressed, where children and young people's experiences are brought to the forefront to inform educational practice, and where the learning community can engage in the 'liminal space' to learn with and from each other's difference (Turner, 2012).

Pause for reflection

- How can we develop a learning environment in which autistic learners do not feel under pressure to conform to neuronormative expectations?
- How can we as educators critically reflect on the unintended consequences of the authority we might exert over children of different neurotypes to our own?

Conclusion

Consequently, in the words of disability rights activist Elly Chapple, we need to 'flip the narrative' (Chapple, 2019) around how autistic children are supported in our schools. The idea that autistic children are a group in need of highly specialist (and costly) approaches has steadily gained ground in recent years, but in an education system with ever-decreasing access to resources, and a group of children with ever-deteriorating outcomes, the focus on funding and training is potentially misleading and distracts from what I see as the bigger issues of equity and social justice. Instead of locating the challenges experienced by autistic pupils solely within the children themselves, as educators we need to carefully consider our own roles in those challenges. Instead of the conversation continuing to centre on concerns about resources and interventions designed to increase greater conformity, we need to pause to consider what are undoubtedly more pressing questions.

In the work that I have done with teachers and families over the last ten years, I have become increasingly aware that mainstream school can be completely intolerable for many autistic children. For those who are not traumatised to the point of crisis or permanently excluded, school is all too often a place where autistic children need to dig deep, don their masks and try their best to cope. As previously highlighted, not only can this pattern of behaviour lead to catastrophic consequences including self-harm and suicide, coping is a long way from flourishing and living a rewarding and enjoyable life. Simply trying to just get through each day cannot be our aspiration for this group of young people. But the idea that school and the attitudes of the people in it could be at the heart of the challenges an autistic child is experiencing is not one that is readily or openly discussed. We need to acknowledge that harm may still be caused despite the very best of intentions, and this is where our difficult conversations need to begin. For those of us who identify as part of the majority neurotype, this may challenge the way we see the world and how we define our role as educators. Engaging in these difficult conversations with ourselves and our colleagues may involve threats to our identities with the acceptance that the dominantly neurotypical culture of our education system might be part of the problem. Care needs to be taken so that we can navigate this complex process of transformation, but before we can look at specific support for individual pupils, we first need to acknowledge that maintaining the status quo in our education system is no longer an ethical option.

Notes

1 Local Authorities (LAs) are organisations responsible for governmental administration of public services at a geographically localised level. They have a legal duty to ensure that children and young people identified as having Special Educational Needs and Disabilities (SEND) have access to suitable education provision.
2 Pupil Referral Units are alternative educational institutions designed for children and young people who are unable to attend mainstream or specialist schools due to illness, exclusion, or having needs that cannot be otherwise met.

References

Ahmed, S. K. (2018). *Being the change: Lessons and strategies to teach social comprehension*. Heinemann USA Imprint.

American Psychiatric Association, A. (2013). *Diagnostic and statistical manual of mental disorders (DSM-5®)*. American Psychiatric Pub.

Baggs, M. (2007). *In my language* [video]. https://www.youtube.com/watch?v=JnylM1hI2jc.

Ball, S. J. (2017). School politics, teachers' careers and educational change: A case study of becoming a comprehensive school. In *Education and Social Change* (pp. 29–61). Routledge.

Bhabha, H. K. (2004). *The location of culture*. Routledge.

Billington, J., Knott, F. K., & Loucas, T. (Forthcoming). 'I liked school, but school didn't like me': Reflections on the autistic mainstream primary school experience.

Brede, J., Remington, A., Kenny, L., Warren, K., & Pellicano, E. (2017). Excluded from school: Autistic students' experiences of school exclusion and subsequent re-integration into school. *Autism & Developmental Language Impairments*, 2, 2396941517737511.

Bohm, J. (2000). *Public deliberation: Pluralism, complexity, and democracy*. MIT Press.

Buber, M. (2002). *The Martin Buber Reader: Essential Writings*. AIAA.

Buescher, A. V. S., Cidav, Z., Knapp, M., & Mandell, D. S. (2014). Costs of autism spectrum disorders in the United Kingdom and the United States. *JAMA Pediatrics*, *168*(8), pp. 721–8. https://doi.org/10.1001/jamapediatrics.2014.210.

Cassidy, S. A., Gould, K., Townsend, E., Pelton, M., Robertson, A. E., & Rodgers, J. (2020). Is camouflaging autistic traits associated with suicidal thoughts and behaviours? Expanding the interpersonal psychological theory of suicide in an undergraduate student sample. *Journal of Autism and Developmental Disorders*, *50*(10), pp. 3638–48. https://doi.org/10.1007/s10803-019-04323-3.

Chapple, E. (2019). Diversity is the key to our survival: The Shoeness of a Shoe. TEDx Norwich [video]. https://www.ted.com/talks/elly_chapple_diversity_is_the_key_to_our_survival_the_shoeness_of_a_shoe.

Cherry, L. (2021). *Conversations that make a difference for children and young people: Relationship-focused practice from the frontline*. Routledge.

Children and Families Act (2014). https://www.legislation.gov.uk/ukpga/2014/6/contents/enacted.

Dalrymple, E. (2022). School attendance and anxiety: A parental perspective. In D. A. Moore, K. Finning, & T. Ford (Eds.). *Mental Health and Attendance at School* (pp. 162–80). Cambridge University Press. https://doi.org/DOI:10.1017/9781911623151.010.

De Boer, A., Pijl, S. J., & Minnaert, A. (2011). Regular primary schoolteachers' attitudes towards inclusive education: A review of the literature. *International Journal of Inclusive Education*, *15*(3), pp. 331–53.

den Houting, J. (2019). Neurodiversity: An insider's perspective. *Autism*, *23*(2), pp. 271–3. https://doi.org/10.1177/1362361318820762.

Department for Education (2019). *National curriculum assessments: key stage 2, 2019 (revised)*. Retrieved from https://www.gov.uk/government/statistics/national-curriculum-assessments-key-stage-2-2019-revised.

Department for Education (2020). Key stage 4 performance 2019 (revised). https://www.gov.uk/government/statistics/key-stage-4-performance-2019-revised.

Department for Education (2022a). Schools, pupils and their characteristics. https://explore-education-statistics.service.gov.uk/find-statistics/school-pupils-and-their-characteristics.

Department for Education (2022b). Special Educational Needs in England. https://explore-education-statistics.service.gov.uk/find-statistics/special-educational-needs-in-england.

Department for Education and Department of Health (2015). Special Educational Needs and Disability Code of Practice.

Department of Health and Social Care and Department for Education (2021). National strategy for autistic children, young people and adults: 2021 to 2026. https://www.gov.uk/government/publications/national-strategy-for-autistic-children-young-people-and-adults-2021-to-2026.

Dillon, G. V., Underwood, J. D. M., & Freemantle, L. J. (2014). Autism and the U.K. Secondary school experience. *Focus on Autism and Other Developmental Disabilities*. doi:10.1177/1088357614539833.

Ferner, A., & Chetty, D. (2019). *How to disagree: Negotiate difference in a divided world: 20 thought-provoking lessons.* White Lion Publishing.

Freire, P. (1970). *Pedagogy of the oppressed.* Routledge.

Giroux, H. A. (2022). *Pedagogy of resistance: Against manufactured ignorance.* Bloomsbury Publishing.

Griswold, D. E., Barnhill, G. P., Myles, B. S., Hagiwara, T., & Simpson, R. L. (2002). Asperger syndrome and academic achievement. *Focus on Autism and Other Developmental Disabilities*, *17*(2), pp. 94–102.

Gould, J., & Ashton-Smith, J. (2011). Missed diagnosis or misdiagnosis? Girls and women on the autism spectrum. *Good Autism Practice (GAP)*, *12*(1), pp. 34–41.

Hirvikoski, T., Mittendorfer-Rutz, E., Boman, M., Larsson, H., Lichtenstein, P., & Bölte, S. (2016). Premature mortality in autism spectrum disorder. *The British Journal of Psychiatry*, *208*(3), pp. 232–8.

Humphrey, N., & Hebron, J. (2015). Bullying of children and adolescents with autism spectrum conditions: a 'state of the field' review. *International Journal of Inclusive Education*, *19*(8), pp. 845–62. https://doi.org/10.1080/13603116.2014.981602.

Humphrey, N., & Symes, W. (2013). Inclusive education for pupils with autistic spectrum disorders in secondary mainstream schools: teacher attitudes, experience and knowledge. *International Journal of Inclusive Education*, *17*(1), pp. 32–46. https://doi.org/10.1080/13603116.2011.580462.

Jones, C., Happé, F., Golden, H., Marsden, A. J., Tregay, J., Simonoff, E., & Charman, T. (2009). Reading and arithmetic in adolescents with autism spectrum disorders: Peaks and dips in attainment. *Neuropsychology*, *23*(6), p. 718.

Keen, D., Webster, A., & Ridley, G. (2016). How well are children with autism spectrum disorder doing academically at school? An overview of the literature. *Autism*, *20*(3), pp. 276–94. https://doi.org/10.1177/1362361315580962.

Maïano, C., Normand, C. L., Salvas, M.-C., Moullec, G., & Aimé, A. (2016). Prevalence of school bullying among youth with autism spectrum disorders: A systematic review and meta-analysis. *Autism Research*, *9*(6), pp. 601–15. https://doi.org/https://doi.org/10.1002/aur.1568.

McKinlay, J., Wilson, C., Hendry, G., & Ballantyne, C. (2022). 'It feels like sending your children into the lions' den' – A qualitative investigation into parental attitudes towards ASD inclusion, and the impact of mainstream education on their child. *Research in Developmental Disabilities*, *120*, p. 104128. doi:https://doi.org/10.1016/j.ridd.2021.104128.

Milton, D. (2012). On the ontological status of autism: The 'double empathy problem'. *Disability & Society*, *27*(6), pp. 883–7. https://doi.org/10.1080/09687599.2012.710008.

Milton, D. (2014). So what exactly are autism interventions intervening with? *Good Autism Practice (GAP)*, *15*(2), pp. 6–14.

Milton, D., & Bracher, M. (2013). Autistics speak but they are heard. *Journal of the BSA MedSoc Group*, *7*, pp. 61–9.

Milton, D., Ridout, S., Murray, D., Martin, N., & Mills, R. (2020). *The Neurodiversity Reader: Exploring concepts, lived experiences and implications for practice*. Pavilion.

Nations, U. (2006). Convention on the rights of persons with disabilities. Retrieved from https://www.ohchr.org/en/hrbodies/crpd/pages/conventionrightspersonswithdisabilities.aspx.

Ravet, J. (2018). 'But how do I teach them?': Autism & Initial Teacher Education (ITE). *International Journal of Inclusive Education*, *22*(7), pp. 714–33. https://doi.org/10.1080/13603116.2017.1412505.

Roberts, J., & Simpson, K. (2016). A review of research into stakeholder perspectives on inclusion of students with autism in mainstream schools. *International Journal of Inclusive Education*, *20*(10), pp. 1084–96.

Rogge, N., & Janssen, J. (2019). The economic costs of autism spectrum disorder: A literature review. *Journal of Autism and Developmental Disorders*, *49*(7), pp. 2873–900. https://doi.org/10.1007/s10803-019-04014-z.

Sinclair, J. (2012). Autism network international: The development of a community and its culture. In J. Bascom (Ed.), *Loud Hands: Autistic People, Speaking* (pp. 17–48). Washington, DC: The Autistic Press. Retrieved from http://www.autreat.com/History_of_ANI.html.

Singer, J. (2017). *Neurodiversity: The birth of an idea*. Self-published.

Society, N. A. (2021). School report 2021. https://s2.chorus-mk.thirdlight.com/file/24/0HTGORW0HHJnx_c0HLZm0HWvpWc/NAS-Education-report-2021-A4%20%281%29.pdf.

Stone, D., Patton, B., & Heen, S. (2011). *Difficult Conversations: How to discuss what matters most*. Portfolio Penguin.

Stone, E., & Priestley, M. (1996). Parasites, pawns and partners: Disability research and the role of non-disabled researchers. *The British Journal of Sociology*, *47*(4), pp. 699–716. https://doi.org/10.2307/591081.

Strang, J. F., Kenworthy, L., Daniolos, P., Case, L., Wills, M. C., Martin, A., & Wallace, G. L. (2012). Depression and anxiety symptoms in children and adolescents with autism spectrum disorders without intellectual disability. *Research in Autism Spectrum Disorders*, 6(1), pp. 406–12. https://doi.org/https://doi.org/10.1016/j.rasd.2011.06.015.

Totsika, V., Hastings, R. P., Dutton, Y., Worsley, A., Melvin, G., Gray, K., & Heyne, D. (2020). Types and correlates of school non-attendance in students with autism spectrum disorders. *Autism*, 24(7), pp. 1639–49. https://doi.org/10.1177/1362361320916967.

Turner, E. (2012). *Communitas: The anthropology of collective joy*. Springer.

Walker, N. (2021). *Neuroqueer heresies: Notes on the neurodiversity paradigm, autistic empowerment, and postnormal possibilities*. Autonomous Press.

Walsh, N., & Hall, I. (2012). The autism strategy: Implications for people with autism and for service development. *Advances in Mental Health and Intellectual Disabilities*, 6(3), pp. 113–20. doi:10.1108/20441281211227166.

Warnock, M., & Norwich, B. (2010). *Special educational needs: A new look*. Bloomsbury Publishing.

Webster, R. (2022). *The Inclusion Illusion: How children with special educational needs experience mainstream schools*. UCL Press.

White, S. W., Oswald, D., Ollendick, T., & Scahill, L. (2009). Anxiety in children and adolescents with autism spectrum disorders. *Clinical Psychology Review*, 29(3), pp. 216–29.

3

'Conversations' without 'Mouth Words': A Challenge or Learning for Transformative Educational Practice?

Katarzyna Fleming and Julie Calveley

Introduction

In this chapter of the collection, we would like to invite a critical reflection on the pertinence of non-verbal cues in education as well as in communication with pupils who are considered as those who do not use 'mouth words' or, what you might have experienced in practice, often being classified as 'non-verbal'. Although this chapter is situated in the sphere of education, we'll also make some connections to lifelong learning and learning with people who are in care or beyond the remit of what traditional meanings of education may imply, for we consider learning, and therefore education, a lifelong endeavour.

We explore two different dimensions of communicative processes here. First, we examine the importance of the ability to read and generate non-verbal cues within educational settings to enrich attunement with the other. Secondly, we discuss how multimodal interactions can contribute to more inclusive and just education. While we recognise that the phrase 'non-verbal' pupils are commonly used in practice and some research, we accentuate the concept of using 'mouth words' to invite reflection on whether a person considered as 'non-verbal' communicates through other modalities of words. 'For example, a situationally mute person may not use mouth words but still use other words to communicate such as writing/typing or using sign/gestures' (Aucademy, n.d.). This phrase is a preferable term used within the community groups conducting research about lived experiences of autism, which emphasises the value in divergent modes of communication without the exclusionary or perhaps inferior role of those modalities in relation to spoken language. While drawing your attention to this term, our intention is to encourage your reflection on how you use language in your context, and whether the term 'mouth words' can be more appropriate to employ to recognise that those of us who don't communicate through 'mouth words' should not be classified as non-verbal but as communicators who use diverse communicative modalities.

Often, the communicative exchanges are planned by the speaker who uses 'mouth words', and who takes the lead in designing and the trajectory of those 'conversations'. Although this set-up may enable the interlocutor who doesn't use 'mouth words' to become a participant in some of the everyday structures and activities in a setting, we argue that it is crucial to consider the agency, the sense of belonging of that speaker and the potential the speaker may gain in their autonomy to lead some of those interactions. Therefore, the aims of this chapter are:

1. To encourage the reader to consider the non-verbal cues and their role in communication in their context.
2. To emphasise the potential of multimodal interactions in enabling attunement with the other.
3. To discuss how the perceived difficulty in communication with pupils who don't use 'mouth words' can be transformed into a learning opportunity for more socially just exchanges.

While focussing on the value and place of 'conversations' without 'mouth words' in the context of education, we will be drawing on Bhabha's (2004) argument for 'sitting in the uncomfortable and unfamiliar' to spark courage in educational practitioners, students and communities to critically examine their ways of communicating. Furthermore, we will be inviting a consideration of how Freire's (1970) notion of 'learning with' rather than teaching to, or 'doing to', can enrich the inclusion of those of us who communicate through exchanges that may not contain 'mouth words' in our educational settings, as well as in our communities.

The value of non-verbal communication in conversations

Communicating through non-verbal language

You might have come across Albert Mehrabian's commonly referenced notion that there is a set ratio of 7 per cent verbal, 38 per cent vocal and 55 per cent facial elements of communication that occurs when a message is conveyed through spoken words (Lapakko, 1997). Although this position has been challenged and undermined due to the complexity of factors that impact the individuals' ability to communicate (Lapakko, 1997), the debate on the implications of non-verbal cues within education continues. Likewise, despite that educational settings continue to focus on spoken language for social interactions (Chen, Ninh, Yu, & Abramson, 2020), the non-verbal cues are considered essential in the knowledge of and practice of communication in different fields as they are considered to be the 'tools' for a more attuned understanding of diverse interlocutors in the sphere of education and beyond (Chen et al., 2020).

Research into the effects of non-verbal communication within education illustrates how important and powerful non-verbal cues are in everyday practice. For example, they are used to establish an emotional connection between the teacher and a student (Comadena, Hung, & Simonds, 2007), to maintain classroom culture and rules without necessarily relying on verbal reiterations (Sime, 2006) or to provide a reassurance for pupils' behaviour and achievement while fostering their confidence and self-awareness (Houser & Frymier, 2009). However, all of these effects relate to the educators' ability to express non-verbal cues and to enable pupils to understand them and apply their interpretations to the context of the setting. Although this element of non-verbal communication is pivotal in education, it places the focus on educators as the ones who instigate the non-verbal cues, rather than the ones who need to become attuned to noticing the non-verbal communication. While it can be asserted that educators 'scan' the classroom at all the time, looking out for expected behaviours, the tension we perceive in this act is that of 'looking for what we want to find' often in accordance with the performative measures, rather than tuning-in to what the behaviour or non-verbal cues are alerting us to. This affective attunement to the other can also be hindered by the sheer number of tasks that educators engage with during their day-to-day activities, which might leave them with a limited space to pause for reflection and put aside time to investigate 'the beyond'. Nonetheless, we can agree that the more we 'look behind' the obvious in our pupils' behaviour, the more we discover the functions of their actions, and what they might be communicating to us through their behaviours. Therefore, perhaps for different reasons, we draw connections here between mainstream and non-mainstream educational settings to illustrate the role of non-verbal cues and communication without 'mouth words' from both perspectives.

From the mainstream perspective, we argue, educators benefit not only from generating non-verbal cues, and communicating their expectations to pupils, but also from developing the 'sense of the other' (Turner, 1969) when they explore the unspoken messages from their pupils. This assumption that there is always a reason for all behaviour can result in a transformative opportunity for developing safe spaces between educators and pupils where issues, dilemmas and reasons can be explored, and where meaningful relations can flourish – a space where the traditional teacher-pupil relationship aimed at acquisition of knowledge is surpassed into a more reciprocal partnership. Lipman (2003) argued that these spaces are essential for education to serve its role as a vehicle to a democratic and just society where children can learn from the very onset of their educational journey to question inquisitively and to think critically. Moreover, the ability to infer meaning from sources beyond the spoken language can enable educators in all settings to become more attuned to a range of needs of children, needs that often aren't conveyed through spoken words. For example, consideration should be afforded to children who have alexithymia (difficulty in understanding and expressing emotions) and those who have experienced trauma and might not be in a place where they can articulate their emotions or needs. Conversations about trauma might not only present difficult but may also not be possible at a time; reading non-verbal cues and responding to them through the affective attunement can foster an environment where the trauma-experienced child might feel safe to commence the process of understanding and healing from their experiences (Cherry, 2021). We will return to these implications in the section that explores tuning-in and creativity in the diverse classroom later.

On the other hand, within the context of specialist provisions, where a larger proportion of pupils might be using augmentative and alternative communication (AAC), practitioners might be more experienced and knowledgeable in understanding the role of non-verbal cues and in using diverse modalities of communication. And although mainstream settings are becoming increasingly more diverse, and therefore, ACC approaches aren't only to be considered in the realm of specialist settings, it can be said that specialist settings would experience a higher level of students using these means of communication as part of everyday routine. Therefore, educators who use AAC approaches to communicate with their pupils frequently might perceive attunement with non-verbal cues displayed by pupils as an unequivocal part of their role. Nonetheless, this attunement requires awareness and preparation before it can be developed and before it becomes a part of the educator's pedagogy. Furthermore, it is important to us to emphasise here that the educators are most often people who predominantly use spoken language for social interaction; therefore, communicating through AAC will, most likely, require them to step onto the periphery of their predominant modes of communication which may create a level of discomfort (Bhabha, 2004) that needs to be explored to be addressed. We will discuss these implications in more detail when we present the approach of Intensive Interaction (II) to illustrate the intricacies of the tuning-in practice in the next section.

> ### Pause for reflection
>
> - How do you develop attunement with pupils/students in your context?
> - Do you rely on non-verbal cues when building relationships or creating a community of practice in your setting?
> - What does the phrase 'non-verbal' mean to you and how do you use it?

However, before we turn to discuss the approach of II, we will examine the tensions within the space where affect attunement can be developed and fostered while the interlocutor who uses 'mouth words' explores means of responding in ways that are different from their own.

Disrupting the position of the 'more knowledgeable'

It is encouraging to witness a shift in the diversity of the educators in our settings, with increasingly inclusive practices in teacher education that enable neurodivergent students to pursue the teaching profession (Stevenson & Dalacio, 2017). Not only do neurodivergent educators pave the paths of representation for pupils who are considered neurodivergent, they also enrich the realm of education by contributing their knowledge of lived experiences to the expanding understanding of difference which can better inform our practice and policies. However, it is still common that the majority of educators have limited lived experience of neurodivergence, and therefore it is imperative that whatever our difference or a perceived lack of (and we note that everyone is unique and has a unique lived experience that none else is more knowledgeable of or can completely speak to), we relinquish the position of a facilitator or a constantly 'more knowledgeable other' (Vygotsky, 1978) in place of a position as a learner.

This position of a learner can have a dual impact on our practice. First, it can destabilise our sense of purpose within our professional identity which is often linked to the presumed expectations that educators provide answers and transmit their knowledge to others who are considered less knowledgeable. Secondly, it can unravel aspects of our identity and deep-seated assumptions that aren't always at the fore of our reflections, and that can contribute to a 'disturbance' of the norms and structures we have created or have become part of throughout our personal and professional lives (Freire, 1970). Therefore, becoming a learner who is open to reassess their world view, and in the context of the 'conversations' without 'mouth words', to explore the unfamiliar and potentially uncomfortable new knowledge and practice, can be a challenging undertaking. The difficulty in this transition between the educator and the learner can be accompanied by the fear of exposing any vulnerability that a learner might experience when acquiring new knowledge or developing a new skill. The quality of espousing vulnerability in education isn't considered a virtue, (Brown, 2015) or indeed, perhaps it is often perceived as the opposite to the notion of the 'knowledgeable'. However, through this vulnerability that can transpire in the transition from the 'unknown' to the 'known', we can create spaces where meaning-making can be shared between all stakeholders, and where the recognition for 'learning with' rather than 'teaching to' can empower a more equal and participatory relationships in education (Freire, 1970).

Furthermore, we consider this transition as a liminal space (Bhabha, 2004) where the learner can examine the 'new territory' while embracing the opportunity to consider how and why they might be experiencing 'the uncomfortable' of this space. We posit that it is through this liminality that the internal tensions can be addressed – the questions about the difference can be explored, and by attending to one's own beliefs and assumptions, affective attunement to others can be developed (de la Ballacasa, 2017; Ahmed, 2018). Importantly, the ramifications on the time span of this liminal spaces cannot be determined as it's closely related to every individual. However, regardless of the period that would be dedicated to this transitional space and practice, it is our role as educators to ensure education is meaningful so it can become transformative for all pupils (Giroux, 2022). Without this engagement in transforming ourselves and our practice, the necessary social change in education won't occur (Ball, 2017) – a change without which the inequalities and injustices will remain unchallenged and the pernicious hierarchical distributions of power will be perpetuated. Are you comfortable being the 'cog' in that system?

While you ponder over this question, we will now present the approach of II to enlist its potential in enabling verbal interlocutors to consider the value and application of this approach in their practice. We hope that by considering the place of imitation, you will be encouraged to explore ways of interacting meaningfully with those in your context who don't use 'mouth words', but also tuning-in into 'the beyonds' in interactions with all pupils.

> ### Pause for reflection
>
> Consider how do you, in your context, enact the role of the 'more knowledgeable other'?
> - Are you willing to learn and explore the tasks/approaches that may be difficult or unfamiliar for you?
> - What sits at the core of your feelings about the new learnings?
> - Could you name these emotions? May it be fear of failing, apprehension about your own abilities to learn or indeed something else?

Intensive Interaction approach: Overcoming the difficulty of how to have 'conversations' with communicators who don't use 'mouth words'

Introduction to Intensive Interaction

To create a classroom where diverse interaction modalities enable social interactions for pupils who don't communicate through 'mouth words' is to adopt inclusive educational practice where all individuals can participate, belong and aren't compromised or marginalised by their difference (Chen et al., 2020). The approach of II facilitates this inclusion as it is a responsive process in which the 'learner' leads an interaction with a tuned-in, responsive partner, to enable communication and social interactivity (Firth & McKim, 2018). The approach was originally developed in the 1980s in the UK, informed by research on parent-infant interaction (Hewett, 2012), and subsequently found to be beneficial when there are communication difficulties associated with autistic spectrum disorders, severe or profound learning or intellectual disabilities, profound and multiple learning disabilities (PMLD), brain injury and dementia.

With the caution against 'formulaic' application of II (Firth & Barber, 2010 p. 113), it is important that communication is treated as fluid and intuitive process. Therefore, the techniques that are offered to depict the dimensions of II are not intended to be followed in a set-piece configuration but can include the following actions:

- Tune-in.
- Convey 'I want to be with you', through all your verbal and non-verbal signals.
- Hold back, avoid prompting, don't do too much and avoid being overcomplicated or too unpredictable.

- Pause and wait.
- Be responsive – convey – 'I hear you and understand you'.
- Use imitation – only when appropriate.
- Have a positive, relaxed approach with no agenda, no task to achieve or target to work towards.
- Position sensitively (and safely).
- Use appropriate tone of voice, facial expression, body language or touch.

The term 'tuning-in' is at the top of this list as it is regarded central and underpinning to II practice and is used to mean 'reading a person's emotional, psychological, cognitive and physiological signals and sensitively responding in a way that is meaningful and conveys understanding. It is the ability to hear, see, sense, interpret, and respond to verbal and nonverbal cues and communicate to the person that they have been genuinely seen, felt, and understood' (Calveley, 2018, p. 39). Critical to 'tuning-in' is 'affect attunement', which Stern (1985) describes as the immediate recasting of the emotional-behavioural state of one person by another person, using emphasised behaviours (Stern, 1985). So, affect attunement is not just an imitation of the behaviour but more an attempt to reflect back the emotion and feelings projected, thereby creating a connection between two people.

The technique of tuning-in in II practice includes emotional or affect attunement, but also attunement to signals from other channels that may reveal something about the person's internal state, including, for example, physical and sensory needs, wakefulness, fatigue, cognitive energy and alertness. The affect attunement needs to be considered as the starting point for the use of imitation and the tunning-in must inform all decisions made about its use. This is key for ensuring that the use of imitation, and Intensive Interaction is practised effectively and respectfully.

II prepares practitioners, through training and reflection to adopt techniques with more conscious thought, awareness and reflection (Nind, 2008). Therefore, it is necessary to sensitise practitioners' observation to possible cues, signals and initiations. One way to achieve this is through the use of video analysis and reflection to observe and also to develop an ability to, and an appreciation of, tuning-in as a valid source from which to inform practice, including making decisions on what, when and how to imitate. With II, the most genuine and sincere participation and attuned responsiveness on the part of the practitioner are key to achieving the authentic social connection.

Adequately conveying the essence of imitation as involving much more than simple behavioural matching of actions is an ongoing challenge. Without correct understanding and appreciation of the complexity and holism inherent in the approach, there is risk of misrepresentation as is also seen with Matthews's (2013, p. 104) suggestion that the use of II implies 'acting' or losing oneself:

> Simply looking at intensive interaction from a practical viewpoint does however neglect some more serious problems. The therapy encourages one of the partners precisely not to be herself. By asking the partner therapist to copy the actions of the other in order to break into the other's world the partner therapist's acts no longer reflect who she is. Moreover, it risks being intrusive instead of a way of 'being with' another in companionship.

This is not the intention with II; but rather to use imitation in a sensitive way that respects the other person's communication and to develop the confidence and comfort in joining in with their way of being, much like we may at first feel uneasy speaking a new language but over time and with practice gain confidence and a sense of ease.

This request to detach from one's communicative identity in order to enter the world of the interlocutor, particularly without causing an intrusion, can prove challenging and indeed create the difficulty in 'conversations' or interactions it is meant to enable. While the interlocutor who uses 'mouth words' engages with this new way of communicating, they could rely on the affordances of the liminal spaces they find themselves in to allow them to work through the experienced difficulty. Here, the ability to reflect on and adapt the position of a curious learner can also be helpful in embracing this liminal space (Bhabha, 2004).

The use of imitation in Intensive Interaction

Although imitation is one of the ways to engage in II, effective use of imitation relies on sensitive responsiveness and making decisions about what behaviours to imitate, how and when, and crucially, when not to imitate. Imitation fosters dialogue-like interactions, allowing for non-verbal conversational turn-taking (Romeo et al, 2018). Such back-and-forth exchanges are thought to be developmentally critical and the quality and number of conversational turns has recently been shown to affect the neural development of processing of language and literacy skills and cognitive development (Romeo et al, 2018). Imitation also provides a basis for connecting other people's experiences to one's own and contributes to developing feelings of empathy and a sense of self (Murray, 2014).

Imitation can also foreground the awareness of the interlocutor's agency in the interaction. With 'agency' here describing the sense of personal power that is realised through having experience and opportunity to decide, act and assume dynamic involvement, inherent in it is a developing understanding of cause and effect, or a knowingness that one can influence the world around them (Murray, 2014). Although the choices of behaviours to be imitated are thought to be unconscious (van Baaren et al., 2009), this behaviour plays an important role in social communication, bonding and rapport, contributing to social, emotional and psychological connection between people (Genschow et al., 2018). Imitation has widely been shown to promote more successful and smoother interactions, feelings of closeness, liking and affiliation, and to create more harmonious relationships (Lieberman, 2000). It is, however, essential to recognise that there might be a danger in perceiving imitation as a form of 'mimicry' which can be deemed as derogatory and disrespectful when working with people with learning disabilities (Caldwell, 2006). To avoid this association, Firth et al. (2010, p. 28) advise ensuring that the imitated behaviours should not be 'a mechanistic reproduction of what the person does. Rather, it is an attempt to reflect back something of what the person is doing and also feeling'.

Considering the emotive elements of imitation, we hope that we unravelled the complexities and the power of this approach in enabling inclusive practice where diverse modalities of communication are cherished and encouraged. While these complexities require practitioners to reflect deeply on the intention, purpose and invest in the development of affect attunement, we argue that by employing imitation and II, educators can demystify the commonly assumed 'inaccessibility' of communication with people who don't use 'mouth words'. Furthermore, by enabling agency of all stakeholders, a more humanised culture can be established where everyone is a valuable part of society despite their differences.

Application in education and beyond

The emphasis on the educational potential of II doesn't preclude the wider application of this approach that we would like to mention here. We assign it importance to stress that we consider difference which is often associated with disability as 'different points on a continuum, rather than opposites because we are all impaired to some extent: "It is the inherent nature of humanity"' (Shakespeare & Watson, 2002, p. 27). While we advocate for this position to be adopted, the II approach has already bridged the gap in education as it enables practitioners to tailor their responses to the mode the individual learner expresses themselves, instead of predetermining the expected mode of communication, therefore allowing for more positive, successful and interactive social involvement to be fostered (Barber, 2008). Likewise, research evidence around paid carers and people in residential care settings suggests that II extends the opportunity for more sustained and meaningful social interactions where the clients appear to be more responsive and these behaviours would transfer into other interactions (Firth et al., 2008). Moreover, somewhere else carers for people with learning disabilities reported a significant improvement in forming relationships which II training afforded for them, alongside the development of their and their clients' confidence in purposeful and meaningful interactions that aim at more attuned exchanges (Nagra, White, Appiah, & Rayner, 2017). Lastly, we would like to accentuate the interrelation between our abilities to 'be with' people who don't use 'mouth words' and the impact our reactions or interactions might have on their family members, particularly siblings who might be our pupils or students. While it is known that the siblings of children with learning disabilities often gain a deeper understanding of advocacy and equal rights through their lived experiences, their knowledge of those disabilities expands as does the empathy and acceptance of diversity toward others (Dyson, 2010,). Stalker and Connors (2004) report on the significance that siblings of disabled people place on the reactions of others to their siblings' difference. By realising our place within those reactions, and by engaging in opportunities to connect with others through the II, we can further enact the acceptance of difference being a continuum of humanity amongst our educational communities and broader society.

Pause for reflection

Consider the potential that affect attunement can have in various sphere of your life:
- Are you aware of how to develop a good understanding of people who use diverse modalities to communicate?
- How do you engage in listening or tuning-in to 'the beyonds' when interacting with others?

Transformation of educational practice for social justice

Celebrating communicative diversity in the classroom

As educators, we have the responsibilities to teach all students. With our classrooms continually evolving into increasingly diverse learning communities, as educators, we are required to adopt practices that will enable inclusion of linguistically, culturally, socially, emotionally and cognitively divergent pupils. To celebrate this diversity, all pupils need to be able to participate, achieve and feel that they belong in the learning community. While adaptive communication is often considered within specialist settings, the ability to communicate and read non-verbal clues can enable educational practitioners in all contexts to more effectively attune to the messages that are communicated by a range of pupils through multimodal communication channels. These instances can include pupils who have English as a second language and have only arrived at the thresholds of our settings from culturally and linguistically different parts of the world, pupils who have experienced trauma, neurodivergent pupils and pupils with auditory or visual impairments. Although not an exhaustive list, it clearly illustrates the significant proportion of these pupils in our learning communities.

To enable these diverse learning communities to thrive, educators have at their disposal a range of techniques and resources that enable supportive and inclusive strategies to be embedded in their classrooms. These may include the Picture Exchange Communication System (PECS) (Preston & Carter, 2009), a range of visual representations of words for EAL pupils (Sharples, 2021), or the use of Makaton – a form of simple sign language (Sheehy & Duffy, 2009). However, we would like to place emphasis on the more abstract aspects of celebrating diversity which are the underlying assumptions and our own beliefs about differences that often shape our practice. These abstract counterparts of our practice are often communicated by non-verbal cues, which can often be 'culturally biased and unconscious' (Helmer & Eddy, 2003, cited in Okon, 2011, p. 38). Although cultural biases can be considered to refer to cultural heritage, we argue, they can also have roots in the cultural or societal influences that inform our perception of differences. Therefore, a pivot in enabling the celebratory ethos of difference is educators' awareness and continuous reflection on their own and their pupils' attitudes towards and understanding of difference. It is important, therefore, to examine how your own beliefs and assumptions impact on your openness to challenge some of the stereotypes and how they influence your ability to consider alternative ways of working (Ahmed, 2018). By modelling acceptance, and openness to the exploration of diverse modalities of communication, you will undoubtedly spark interest and courage for your pupils to follow suit and welcome the diversity in your learning community more readily.

Transforming communication in the classroom for social justice

Whether it is II or any other approach aimed at diverse communication, they require creativity in the design and delivery. Likewise, practitioners involved in these exchanges are required to adapt their practice, expectations and learned responses to enable learners' autonomy in communication. These goals can be very challenging in the system driven by time-bounded targets and accountability measures that often leave limited opportunities for liminal spaces where the teacher can learn from the pupil to enable inclusive communication, and, in turn, foster a more just and inclusive culture in the setting.

This inclusive culture is underpinned by the principles of social justice which 'embodies the vision of a society that is equitable and in which all members are physically and psychologically safe' (Levy & Sidel, 2005, p. 552, cited in Van Gundy & Kapeller, 2013). To enact these principles, people are required to share a common humanity, support equitable treatment and human rights, and fairly allocate community resources. Moreover, social justice stands in direct opposition to discrimination, prejudice or constraints of one's welfare based on gender, sexuality, religion, political affiliations, age, race, belief, disability, location, social class, socioeconomic circumstances or other characteristics of background or group membership (Van Gundy & Kapeller, 2013).

Considering these principles, the subject of non-verbal cues and communication without 'mouth words' could be related to issues of shared common humanity, fair allocation of resources, equitable treatment and potential discrimination based on individual's disability. Therefore, we argue, the act of affect attunement and promotion of diverse modalities of communication has a role in transforming our classroom into spaces that fulfil the premise of social justice. For example, through the use of imitation and by entering liminal spaces where the positionality of a learner can accompany some level of admission to vulnerabilities, educators create spaces where the values of humanity can be mutually shared and appreciated. Expressing vulnerabilities and allowing for them to be explored with humility can be classed as 'daring' in the current educational climate (Brown, 2015); however, it is our imperative, here and now, to ensure that how we educate reflects our attunement with trauma, adversity, difference and above all our reflection on own positionality and privilege (Cherry, 2021). This amalgamation of contexts and concepts to consider further exemplifies the importance of the pluralistic social justice theory (Miller, 1999), which asserts that the learning environment must take into account the complexities of the social context whereby all stakeholders' individual contexts, characteristics and ways of being are considered respectfully and equitably. We refer to this plurality throughout this chapter, whether that constitutes the question of when and how to imitate within the II approach, how to 'read' the non-verbal clues of culturally diverse pupils or how to use these clues to form meaningful relationships within our learning communities where differences are celebrated, and action for change established as an inevitable part of our growth.

If we may, we would like to encourage you to situate the learning opportunities explored in this chapter within the realm of actions for transformation rather than perceiving it as a challenge to overcome – who knows, this change of perspective might be the very prompt that will enable you to take the first step into the 'daring' classroom.

Lastly, we would like to acknowledge that, despite many shortcomings and injustices, the system we are part of is full of 'incredible people, doing incredible things, making an incredible difference' (Cherry, 2021, p. 218), whether that is translated into 'pug memes in appointment letters', that might be an attempt at relational connections or 'being prepared to meet the children in whatever way works', including on the stairs, on the floor or pretty much under the household pet (Ryan, 2021, p. 157). So, look around, notice these 'pockets of brilliance' (Ryan, 2021) and be the change – a change that emanates what some might consider extraordinary, while some may simply name basic humanity.

Pause for reflection

- What is your role in fulfilling the values of social justice while you engage in communication in your context?
- How could you become an agent for change to enable inclusive and diverse communication in your setting?

Considerations for self-understanding

We have established that non-verbal cues and 'conversations' without 'mouth words' are paramount in the diverse education of today, but they can also pose an array of challenges in application. While you consider the liminality of the spaces where you can explore and process the diverse modalities of communication, we would like to emphasise the need for you to contemplate how this learning journey is affecting your own growth, and perhaps causing more questions that you might be finding the answers for. In line with Nodding's (1998) feminist theory of ethics of care, we encourage you to step into a realm where you can allow yourself to be a learner, to critically examine what you feel and why about your actions, and how you respond to the changes created by those actions – to develop self-understanding as it might possibly be the most important, if not most neglected goal of education (Noddings, 2006). While you deepen the understanding of yourself, we hope, you will also allow space to develop self-compassion in order to be able to embrace the uncertainty of this new learning experience. This self-compassion often trickles into other areas of life, as well as enables us to perceive others through a more thoughtful and compassionate lens (Herring, 2017). Therefore, we hope that in your own educational and transformative endeavours, you will dedicate space and time to understand and be with others as well as to understand and exercise self-compassion.

References

Ahmed, S. K. (2018). *Being the change. Lessons and strategies to teach social comprehension.* Heinemann.

Aucademy (n.d.) *Resources, books, articles.* Available at: https://aucademy.co.uk/books/.

Ball, S. J. (2017). School politics, teachers' careers and educational change: a case study of becoming a comprehensive school. In *Education and Social Change* (pp. 29–61). Routledge.

Barber, M. (2008). Using Intensive Interaction to add to the palette of interactive possibilities in teacher–pupil communication, *European Journal of Special Needs Education*, 23(4), pp. 393–402.

Bhabha, H. K. (2004). *The location of culture.* Routledge.

Brown, B. (2015). *Daring greatly: How the courage to be vulnerable transforms the way we live, love, parent, and lead.* Penguin.

Caldwell, P. (2006). Speaking the other's language: Imitation as a gateway to relationship. *Infant and Child Development*, *15*, pp. 275–82.

Calveley, J. (2018). Intensive interaction and complex health needs: Tuning-in, the cornerstone of effective practice. *PMLD Link*, *30*(2) Issue 90, Summer Edition.

Chen, R., Ninh, A., Yu, B., & Abrahamson, D. (2020). *Being in touch with the core of social interaction: Embodied design for the nonverbal.* ISLS.

Cherry, L. (2021). *Conversations that make a difference for children and young people: Relationship-focused practice from the frontline.* Routledge.

Comadena, M.E., Hunt, S.K., & Simonds, C.J. (2007). The effects of teacher clarity, nonverbal immediacy and caring on student motivation, affective and cognitive learning. *Communication Research Reports*, *24*(3), pp. 241–8.

de La Bellacasa, M. P. (2017). *Matters of care: Speculative ethics in more than human worlds.* University of Minnesota Press.

Dyson, L. (2010). Unanticipated effects of children with learning disabilities on their families. *Learning Disability Quarterly*, *33*(1), pp. 43–55.

Firth, G., & Barber, M. (2010). *How to use 'Intensive Interaction' with a Person with a social or communicative impairment.* Jessica Kingsley.

Firth, G., & McKim, J. (2018). Background to intensive interaction. In D. Hewett (Ed.). *The intensive interaction handbook.* Sage.

Firth, G., Berry, R., & Irvine, C. (2010). *Understanding Intensive Interaction: Context and concepts for professionals and families.* Jessica Kingsley.

Firth, G., Elford, H., Leeming, C., & Crabbe, M. (2008). Intensive interaction as a novel approach in social care: Care staff's views on the practice change process. *Journal of Applied Research in Intellectual Disabilities*, *21*(1), pp. 58–69.

Freire, P. (1970). *Pedagogy of the oppressed.* Routledge.

Genschow, O., Klomfar, S., D'Haene, I., & Brass, M. (2018). Mimicking and anticipating others' actions is linked to social information processing. *PLoS ONE*, *13*, pp. 3.

Giroux, H. A. (2022). *Pedagogy of resistance: Against manufactured ignorance.* Bloomsbury.

Herring, J. (2017). Compassion, ethics of care and legal rights. *International Journal of Law in Context*, *13*(2), pp. 158–71.

Hewett, D. (2012). What is intensive interaction? Curriculum, process and approach. In Hewett, D. (Ed.) *Intensive Interaction: Theoretical perspectives.* Sage.

Houser, M.L., & Frymier, A.B. (2009). The role of student characteristics and teachers' behaviours in students' learner empowerment. *Communication in Education*, *58*(1), pp. 35–53.

Lapakko, D. (1997). Three cheers for language: A closer examination of a widely cited study of nonverbal communication. *Communication Education*, *46*(1), pp. 63–7.

Levy, B. S., & Sidel, V. (2005). *Social injustice and public health.* Oxford University Press.

Lieberman, D. (2000). *Get anyone to do anything and never feel powerless again: Psychological secrets to predict, control and influence every situation.* Saint Martin's Press.

Lipman, M. (2003). *Thinking in education*. Cambridge University Press.

Matthews, P. (2013). Communication strategies and intensive interaction therapy. Meet the theology of the body: Bioethics in dialogue with people with profound disabilities. *The New Bioethics, 19*(2), pp. 97–110.

Miller, D. (1999). *Principles of social justice*. Harvard University Press.

Murray, L. (2014). *The Psychology of Babies*. Constable.

Nagra, M. K., White, R., Appiah, A., & Rayner, K. (2017). Intensive interaction training for paid carers: 'Looking, looking and find out when they want to relate to you'. *Journal of Applied Research in Intellectual Disabilities, 30*(4), pp. 648–60.

Nind, M. (2008). Promoting the emotional well-being of people with profound and multiple intellectual disabilities: A holistic approach through Intensive Interaction. In J. Palwyn, & S. Carnaby (Eds.). *Profound Intellectual and Multiple Disabilities: Nursing Complex Needs*. Wiley-Blackwell.

Noddings, N. (1998) *Philosophy of education*. Routledge.

Noddings, N. (2006). *Critical lessons. What our schools should teach*. Cambridge University Press.

Okon, J. J. (2011). Role of non-verbal communication in education. *Mediterranean Journal of Social Sciences, 2*(5), 35–40.

Preston, D., & Carter, M. (2009). A review of the efficacy of the picture exchange communication system intervention. *Journal of Autism and Developmental Disorders, 39*, pp. 1471–86.

Romeo, R.R., Leonard, J.A., Robinson, S.T., West, M.R., Mackey, A.P., Rowe, M.L., & Gabrieli, J.D.E. (2018). Beyond the 30-Million-Word Gap: Children's conversational exposure is associated with language-related brain function. *Psychological Science, 29*(5), pp. 700–10.

Ryan, S. (2021). *Love, learning disabilities and pockets of brilliance: How practitioners can make a difference to the lives of children, families and adults*. Jessica Kingsley Publishers.

Shakespeare, T, & Watson, N. (2002). The social model of disability: An outdated ideology? *Research in Social Science and Disability, 2*, pp. 9–28.

Sharples, R. (2021). *Teaching EAL: Evidence-based strategies for the classroom and school*. Multilingual Matters.

Sheehy, K., & Duffy, H. (2009). Attitudes to Makaton in the ages on integration and inclusion. *International Journal of Special Education, 24*(2), pp. 91–102.

Sime, D. (2006). What do learners make of teachers' gestures in the language classroom? *International Review of Applied Linguistics in Language, 44*(2), pp. 211–30.

Stalker, K., & Connors, C. (2004). Children's perceptions of their disabled siblings: 'she's different but it's normal for us'. *Children & Society, 18*(3), pp. 218–30.

Stern, D.N. (1985) *The interpersonal world of the infant: A view from psychoanalysis and developmental psychology*. Basic Books.

Stevenson, J. L., & Dalasio, N. L. (2017). From awareness to acceptance: Transformative approaches to teaching neurodiversity. In R. Obeid, A. Schwartz, C. Shane-Simpson,

& P. J. Brooks (Eds.). *How We Teach Now: The GSTA Guide to Student-Centered Teaching. Society for the Teaching of Psychology*, pp. 178–92.

Turner, V. (1969). Liminality and communitas. The ritual process. *Structure and Anti-structure, 94*(113), pp. 125–30.

Van Barrenn, B., Jansenn, L., CHartrand, T. L., & Dijksterhuis, A. (2009). Where is the Love? The social aspects of mimicry. *Philosophical Transactions of the Royal Society B, 364*, pp. 1528, 2381–9.

Van Gundy, A., & Kappeler, V. (2013). *Feminist theory, crime, and social justice*. Routledge.

Vygotsky, L. (1978). *Mind in society*. Harvard University Press.

4

Should I Be Having This Conversation about Death?

Tracy Edwards

Introduction

This chapter is based on a story shared by 'Polly' (a pseudonym) with the author of this chapter, as part of a wider ongoing separate research project, which has been analysing dilemmas related to inclusive classroom practice. Such stories serve as 'allegorical exemplars' (Crowther et al., 2017, p. 828) of internal dialogues related to meeting individual needs within diverse classrooms. In this chapter, Polly's dilemma will be explored in relation to key theoretical concepts that can support our thinking around difficult conversations with pupils with complex Special Educational Needs and Disabilities (SEND). In doing this, Schon's notion of having a 'conversation with the situation' (2016, pp. 76–104) will be utilised. This is the idea that we engage in a hermeneutic process of reflection, to learn from our experiences of professional practice.

The young person in the above story, 'Hafsa' is a 14-year-old girl who has multiple diagnoses including Downs Syndrome, autism and Severe Learning Difficulties (SLD). In the story, she attends the mainstream comprehensive secondary school where Polly is the lead teacher for religious education (RE). Polly is also Hafsa's form tutor. Hafsa has difficulties around the 'twin pillars' of 'communication' and 'cognition', which Lacey (2011) associated with complex SEND. These difficulties have implications for having conversations with Hafsa who relies on the images within her 'communication book', which she points at to indicate her wants and needs. In RE lessons, Polly struggles to include Hafsa in dialogues around certain topics on the curriculum and her participation is disrupted daily by her continence issues, epileptic fits, and difficulties with working memory. Despite these barriers, Hafsa's presence within her tutor group has been highly beneficial, from Polly's perspective. Many pupils, she has found, seemed to have developed maturity, empathy, and an appreciation of difference as a result.

One difficulty for Polly however, as an RE teacher, is that it often also does not feel appropriate to her, to talk with Hafsa about issues such as capital punishment, euthanasia, or terrorism. This is because Hafsa does not seem to be developmentally 'ready' to engage in such issues at a meaningful level. This is highlighted in the below quote from Polly:

Should I be even including some of this stuff in their learning?

Or should I miss it out entirely? Is it too difficult? Is it too difficult to talk to a student with complex special educational needs about death? Is it too difficult to talk about some of those emotional realities?

Despite these doubts, Polly ultimately found, at the end of the above story, that her initial reservations were unfounded. In fact, Hafsa very much wanted to talk and had lots of questions. For Polly to have taken an alternative approach with Hafsa, i.e., deciding that it was not appropriate to discuss the issue of death with her, would have in fact been unintentionally negligent, because it would have deprived Hafsa an opportunity to process a recent bereavement. Through taking the bold step to have the conversation, Polly was also able to learn something about Hafsa. Before the lesson, Hafsa had no awareness of what death was and that life inevitably comes to an end. The conversation therefore required what Polly described as *'working through discomfort'*, as well as taking the risk of provoking misconceptions about dying that may not have been possible to address within a short series of lessons. Without making the effort to engage in the difficult conversation, however, Hafsa would have missed out on some important learning:

'Oh, my Grandad's died.' Hafsa asked Polly 'Does that mean he's not coming back?'

'Yes, that is what it means. Your Grandad won't be coming back ... he won't come back to live with us. He won't come back to live with you. He's been in hospital. He was sick and he didn't get better and that can happen sometimes.

The subsequent sections of this chapter will analyse Polly's dilemma around having the difficult conversation about death, ultimately highlighting the importance of 'asking' and 'listening' to young people, rather than deciding for ourselves, as teachers, whether a discussion topic is 'appropriate' or an individual 'ready'.

Beyond the dilemma of difference

The term 'dilemma of difference' refers to a tension between a desire to address individual pupil needs and a desire not to stigmatise individuals by visibly treating them in a different way to others. It is a dilemma which Norwich (2019) traces to the Warnock Report (1978) and highlights as key to the development of policy and practice relating to pupils with SEND. In the experience of the author of this chapter, however, this 'dilemma of difference' is more evident in the concerns of early career teachers, who may be grappling over whether to have separate worksheets for different learners within their class for example, or have a core activity for all learners, even though it may not be accessible to everyone. After a few years in the classroom, however, teachers may feel sufficiently comfortable to create a culture within their classroom, which promotes difference as an inevitable part of the human condition, meaning that it is no longer a 'dilemma'.

Graham and Slee (2008) assert that, rather than assume binary distinctions between 'typical' and 'different' learners, it is possible to view everybody as 'different' in their own way. Polly's tutor group, of which Hafsa was a member, included pupils from deprived backgrounds, and those with English as an additional language, LGBTQI+ identities, and/or from minority ethnic and/or faith groups. This meant that 'difference' was not an exclusive characteristic of a small group of 'different' pupils, but was universal, to everyone. The 'dilemma of difference' therefore, arguably had a minimal role to play in Polly's internal self-dialogue, about approaching the topic of death with Hafsa. Polly's dilemma is less concerned about the labelling effect of Hafsa having a different focus for learning from other pupils, and instead concerned with the appropriateness of the conversation about death. Rather than a 'dilemma of difference', this chapter proposes that Polly's dilemma can alternatively be viewed as a 'dilemma of possibility'. It also proposes that a recognition of the 'dilemma of possibility' should underpin considerations more generally, around difficult conversations in education.

The 'dilemma of possibility'

The term 'dilemma of possibility', established through the analysis of the Polly's story, refers to a dilemma around what is appropriate and/or feasible practice. In grappling with her particular 'dilemma of possibility', Polly is, for example, asking herself whether talking with a bereaved teenager with SLD, about her recently deceased grandad, is permissible within the boundaries of her job role. She is also asking whether her aspiration to include Hafsa in the dialogues on death is realistic. The following questions, underpinning Polly's internal 'conversation with the situation', exemplify this notion of a 'dilemma of possibility':

Do I lack the skills to do this?

Do I first need to do some training, so that I don't do things the wrong way and cause damage?

Am I encroaching on the remit of the SEND department within my school?

Am I being naïve or over-idealistic by wanting to attempt a conversation about sensitive issues with Hafsa?

Would it not be more feasible to teach Hafsa a more sensory curriculum, around topics typically taught in early years or primary, to open up conversations she can more fully immerse herself in?

According to Rouse (2008) inclusive practice involves teachers not only 'knowing' and 'doing' but also 'believing' that they are capable of teaching all children. Polly's story suggests that teachers need to first navigate the 'dilemma of possibility', in order to do this. Is it more appropriate to avoid the difficult conversation with Hafsa due to a perceived lack of specialist skills, or do we have a professional and/or moral duty to channel our capacity to connect with others (in whatever way we find ourselves doing so) as a human being? At what point do we accept that taking a conversation down a particular path with a pupil with SLD is not appropriate or feasible? Such questions are explored in the below sections of this chapter, which each outline principles that may underpin Polly's internal dialogues about the difficult conversations she has with pupils with complex needs within her classroom.

Beyond 'monologue-disguised-as-dialogue'

Should the generic label of Severe Learning Difficulties be the basis upon which decisions should be made about the topics of conversation an individual accesses within their classrooms? If we are deciding in advance which topics are most appropriate (or otherwise), we are not having a conversation, but a 'monologue-disguised-as-dialogue' (Buber, 1958). According to Buber (1958), there are three types of dialogue:

- genuine reciprocal dialogue with another person
- technical dialogue which focusses on explanations of things
- 'monologue-disguised-as-dialogue' which gives the appearance of reciprocity but, in reality, involves talking at 'the other'.

In the experience of the author of this chapter, awareness of Buber's notion of 'monologue-disguised-as-dialogue' can support classroom practitioners' reflections on the quality of their conversations with pupils with SLD. It can serve as a reminder, for example, to wait patiently for a response, rather than assume that an initial vocalisation indicates agreement or the expressing of a preference. An awareness of Buber's notion of 'monologue-disguised-as-dialogue' can also lead to the avoidance of highly stage-managed pupil 'consultation' activities in which a young person with SLD may merely be repeating the last word in a question (e.g. **Teacher:** *Do you like PE or Music?* **Pupil:** *Music*).

With Hafsa, avoiding 'monologue-disguised-as-dialogue' is likely to involve Nodding's 'ethics of care' (Noddings, 2013), which emphasise our moral responsibility to others. For Noddings, ethical conduct is relational and the notion of 'caring' should guide our decision making. With this, Noddings makes a distinction between the 'inferred' needs and 'expressed' needs of children in classrooms (2012). Whereas inferred needs can be a necessary basis for developing school curricula, Noddings argues teachers must also respond to the needs that pupils are expressing. To do this, they need to engage in 'receptive listening' and focus efforts on strengthening relationships. For Polly, as Hafsa's RE teacher, this might, at times, mean adapting the curriculum around the inferred needs of pupils with SLD, in ways that are promoted by Imray and Hinchcliffe (2012), who advocate for different bespoke curricula for different categories of SEND. Beyond this, however, it means entering into conversations with Hafsa and paying attention to the needs she is expressing within them. It also means Polly building a connection with Hafsa and creating a 'climate of caring' (Noddings, 2012) within her classroom.

Avoiding Buber's 'monologue-disguised-as-dialogue' with Hafsa is also likely to involve a related pedagogical investment in understanding Hafsa's lived experience. This might involve supplementing questions relating to the 'dilemma of possibility' within Polly's internal 'conversation-with-the-situation', with questions that support interactive assessment and a posteroi reasoning. Examples of such questions are as follows:

How does Hafsa tend to process language?

How might we know that Hafsa has understood?

How might Hafsa start to comprehend 'difficult' and sensitive topics?

What tools may be effective in supporting Hafsa to formulate her own questions?

Beyond age-appropriateness

Another principle that may steer our thinking in relation to Polly's 'dilemma of possibility' with Hafsa is that of 'age-appropriateness'. An age-appropriate approach to working with teenagers and adults with SLD is one that is cautious against infantalising them. In order to be 'age-appropriate', for example, a teacher of 15-year-olds in a special needs school might avoid singing nursery rhymes or labelling items with characters associated with children's television such as Peppa Pig. The concept of 'age-appropriateness' has informed considerations around appropriate literacy materials for pupils in secondary schools, with a reading age which is significantly below their chronological one (McCray et al., 2001; Shurr & Kromer, 2018). In the experience of the author of this chapter, it has also guided policy dialogues around sex education for pupils with SEND, underpinning powerful arguments for investing in bespoke resources which recognise the intellectual level of pupils, alongside the fact that they have adolescent bodies.

In relation to Polly's dilemma, however, the principle of 'age-appropriateness' arguably starts to fall down. The argument that Hafsa has an entitlement to 'age appropriate' conversations, around age-appropriate topics on the curriculum, is difficult to maintain in situations where she cannot engage in authentic reciprocal dialogue about those topics, such as seems to be the case in the example presented in this chapter. This adds a layer of further complexity to Polly's internal 'conversation with the situation'. The principle of 'age-appropriateness', due to it established nature (Forster, 2010), may have become central to Polly's professional self-concept as an 'inclusive teacher'. Finding herself in circumstances where she starts to rethink the notion of 'age-appropriateness', therefore, prompts her to consider slight shifts in her own overall educator identity. Polly's dilemma, and conversations with Hafsa, places her in a liminal space (Bhabha, 2004) in between alternative ways of defining her role as a classroom practitioner.

According to Wolfenberger (1994), the notion of 'age-appropriateness', in relation to teenagers and adults with special educational needs has roots in the

Social Role Valorisation Theory (SRVT) (Forster, 2010). This theory is based on the argument that, in order to overcome marginalisation, individuals with learning difficulties need to be visible in roles which are valued by society and deemed to be respectable. Rather than allow a 15-year-old with SLD to play with dolls for example, SRVT would, instead, lead us to encourage them to wear make-up and/or talk about anime cartoons or gaming. Therefore, it can be argued that, in line with SRVT, topics of conversation deemed 'childish' should be avoided with 'Hafsa', and that she should instead be encouraged to talk about 'age-appropriate' issues and adopt an 'age-appropriate' teenage identity.

Forster (2010), however, argues that an emphasis on 'age-appropriateness', based on SRVT, can be damaging, representing an attempt to 'normalise' individuals in relation to outdated stereotypes. As well as age, SRVT can be applied to the promotion of gender-based identities with teenagers and adults with SEND, as well as identities relating to hobbies or occupations. The place of SRVT within the twenty-first-century world, in which hybrid and diverse identities are celebrated, is therefore questionable. If people of all ages enjoy anime cartoons, why can't a 14-year-old in a special school be allowed to enjoy watching 'Peppa Pig' on television? If a 20-year-old university student carries a 'Hello Kitty' backpack, why too can't the young person with Down's syndrome, who attends her local college? Deciding whether it is appropriate to talk with Hafsa about terrorism or death involves interaction with complexity, rather than inferred needs, based on generalisations around her diagnosis of SLD, or her age.

Lacey (2006, as cited in Forster, 2010, p. 130) argues that an insistence of 'age-appropriateness' with teenagers and adults with complex SEND can ultimately represent a denial of their human rights. This insistence can serve as a rationale, she argues, for denying access for individuals, to important stimuli (such as nursery rhymes and songs) which can sometimes be the only basis upon which they are responsive and/or can start to engage in reciprocal interaction with others. An insistence on 'age-appropriateness', therefore, quite possibly closes down what could be referred to as a 'person-appropriate' conversation. Whereas we may think 'age-appropriateness' is a principle for inviting young people such as Hafsa to enter into a dialogue, there is a possibility that it is in fact doing the opposite.

However, although a dogmatic approach to 'age-appropriateness' would very likely also be harmful to Hafsa, the reality remains that she is a teenager and not a small child. While having reservations around the principle of 'age-appropriateness', we should also recognise the inevitably that she will be encountering many of the issues being discussed within Polly's RE lessons in her day-to-day life. This makes the challenges around having related 'difficult conversations' with Hafsa a safeguarding issue, as well as an issue related to well-being. Nonetheless, it is important to remember the difference between 'expressed' and 'inferred' needs, alongside the difference between authentically 'having' the conversation and merely emulating one. In the experience of the author of this chapter, SRVT can lead to conversations with young people which are 'performed' using the scripted text within curriculum documents.

At Polly and Hafsa's school, conversations with children and young people with SLD are often supported through signing, symbols and/or augmentative and alternative communication (AAC) devices. However, arguably, without practitioner tools for 'listening' or 'noticing' what is being communicated, the capacity for genuine conversations with learners is undermined and it is 'monologue-disguised-as-dialogue' (Buber, 1958) that prevails. Such tools for 'listening' and 'noticing' may include the use of careful observation and record keeping, to establish any non-verbal ways in which preferences tend to be expressed by an individual. For example, the Engagement Model (Standards and Testing Agency, 2020) and the Engagement Profile and Scale (Carpenter et al., 2011) provide a framework for teachers of pupils with complex SEND, to identify when and how 'engagement indicators' such as 'persistence' are expressed, and shape pedagogical responses accordingly.

Beyond narrow conceptualisation of inclusion

According to Florian (2012, p. 277), 'what appear to be similar events may be inclusive or exclusive'. In explaining this, Florian provides the example of a lone pupil within an observed lesson, being sat at a computer terminal. This could be because they are benefitting from an inclusive learning environment, which encourages independence, yet it could also reflect how they have been neglected by their teacher, who is interested only in keeping this lone pupil 'busy' so she can get on with educating the rest of the class. Similarly, printing a peace dove for Hafsa to colour in, as Polly does in the vignettes below, can arguably simultaneously represent inclusion and exclusion. *"Polly scans her classroom to see Hafsa starring out of the window. She is teaching a lesson on 'Terrorism' which forms part of the Religious Education curriculum at her school. Polly feels awkward and guilty. She doubts that Hafsa can understand the comments from other pupils about the sanctity of life, or about how the notion of 'jihad' can refer to internal battles involving the conscience, rather than physical fights. As the class* set about answering questions, from a book chapter, on different religious extremist groups in history, Polly goes over to Hafsa, wondering how she could adapt things for her. She gives her a printed copy of the book chapter and asks her to highlight the key words. Hafsa sits there, highlighting absolutely everything without actually reading it. By the end of the lesson, Hafsa is colouring in a picture of a peace dove which Polly quickly printed from her computer in desperation. 'What is the point of this?' thinks Polly to herself 'Really, what IS the point?" Is it merely a means to preoccupy Hafsa, so that Polly can get on with the 'main job' of teaching the other pupils in her group? Or is it instead a means to make the complex themes being taught accessible to Hafsa, and enable her participation? Or is it something else?

Although Hafsa may physically be in the RE lesson on terrorism, it could be claimed that she is in fact being excluded within it. She does not have the means to engage or participate in the lesson and is seemingly disconnected from the learning that is happening. Whereas learning in a small group away from the rest of her class may appear to be exclusive, therefore, it may pragmatically be preferable to her merely being 'kept busy' within a mainstream classroom. However, such an approach would have also meant that Hafsa would not have been present in the lesson on death and dying. She would have missed the important opportunity to ask questions because she had been dismissed as not 'ready' to have related conversations.

The elusive and ambiguous nature of inclusion in education, discussed across the related research literature (e.g. Black-Hawkins & Florian, 2012; Florian, 2012, 2014), therefore adds further difficulty to Polly's 'conversation with the situation' around teaching Hafsa. If the exact same event can be simultaneously 'inclusive' or 'exclusive' (rather than unambiguously either one or the other), Polly is most likely required to engage in continual internal dialogues to reach decisions around what may be the most appropriate and/or inclusive course of action, rather than merely and passively implement external guidance on inclusive practices.

Advocacy or oppression?

In her seminal essay 'Can the subaltern speak?' Spivak (1988) writes about how, when we claim to speak up for those who are marginalised, we are often instead further marginalising them. By not listening to the 'subaltern', and speaking for them, we are merely articulating our subjective speculation and, in turn, perpetuating stereotypes of passivity and oppression. In explaining this, Spivak gives the powerful example of the tradition of immolating of widows, on a funeral pyre (sati), in parts of colonial India. By speaking out against this practice, she argues, Western colonialists saw themselves as liberating women from the tyranny of men. However, without talking to the widows themselves, the complexities behind sati remained unknown and the very simplistic notion of India as a regressive society (worthy of colonialisation) were perpetuated. Not too dissimilarly, it could be argued, the marginalisation of young people with SLD in schools is often disguised as 'advocacy'. Classroom practitioners may claim that Hafsa is 'enjoying' an activity, but the reality may be very different.

'Activist professionalism' and inclusive pedagogy

Sach's writings on 'activist professionalism' (2000, 2016) in teaching also give insight into Polly's dilemma. In her writings, Sachs contrasts 'activist professionalism' with the 'managerial professionalism' she found to be dominant within school systems across the globe. According to Sachs (2000), 'managerial professionalism' is a dogmatic ideology that associates effective practice with 'ritual' (p. 86) approaches that emulate those from the private sector. Managerial professionalism, she argues, also embeds individualism in teaching, through which teachers and schools tend to be viewed and managed in isolation. For Sachs, 'joint decision making and new ways of working together' (Sachs, 2000, p. 82) would be required to address dilemmas such as Polly's. Such 'joint decision making' would make Polly's dilemma a collective one, informed by multiple professional perspectives, rather than one which is largely carried by a single educator. Through Sachs' 'activist professionalism', therefore, 'difficult conversations' between individual teachers and pupils in schools become supported by wider dialogues beyond those conversations.

Under the managerial professionalism outlined by Sachs (Sachs, 2000), teacher planning might involve a core activity, devised with 'most' learners in mind, alongside alternatives for 'some' learners, such as an adapted task for the perceived 'less able' and an 'extension task' for the perceived more able. In contrast to this, however, Polly's RE lesson on terrorism gave everybody initial access to the same core task. She found, however, that Hafsa was struggling to engage with this core task in any meaningful way, making it tempting to go back to planning for 'most' and 'some' learners. However, quite often, Hafsa also struggled to access activities planned for 'some' learners who were perceived as 'less able'.

The research literature on the principle of Inclusive Pedagogy (e.g. Florian & Beaton, 2018; Florian & Black-Hawkins, 2012; Florian & Spratt, 2013) explores the nature of the professionalism required for teaching in diverse classrooms. Central to this research literature is the notion of 'craft knowledge', which has been defined as 'practical wisdom' (Florian & Beaton, 2018), cultivated by practitioners, through experience and reflection on experience. Through her encounters with Hafsa, and through reflecting on these experiences, there is scope for Polly to enhance her own professional craft knowledge and to use this in future encounters with future pupils. Much of the associated literature on the principle of Inclusive Pedagogy discusses a move away from planning for 'some' and 'most' learners to planning for 'everybody'(Florian & Linklater, 2010; Florian & Spratt, 2013; Spratt & Florian, 2015).

According to Spratt and Florian (2015), inclusive classroom practice involves getting the micro-culture of the classroom right through a recognition of how 'children grow through their interaction with others' (p. 90). Rather than think about 'some' and 'most' learners, they argue, teachers should instead think about creating positive dynamics within a lesson that support everyone's learning. For Polly's teaching of RE, this may involve addressing questions around the inclusion of Hafsa such as: Who could she be sat next to? How could a conversation between her and other students be initiated? Are there any images or artefacts I could present to open up a conversation? How can we most effectively work with her communication book to support her dialogues with peers? Such questions represent another fundamental shift – away from thinking about what pupils 'do' within a lesson, to the facilitation of the most effective dialogue and interaction for learning. This way of planning also represents a slight shift away from an exclusive preoccupation with our dialogues with learners, towards an appreciation of the value of the dialogues which learners have with one another.

Associations have been made between inclusive classroom practice and sociocultural perspectives on education. Daniels (2020), for example, explores the implications of the sociocultural theories of Vygotsky, for how we might conceptualise and plan for inclusion. According to Vygotsky, learning is social and occurs through meaningful communication. A Vygotskian approach to teacher planning, therefore, is likely to differ from alternative approaches that are instead influenced by the ideas of other twentieth-century psychologists such as Piaget (1896–1980) and Skinner (1904–90). Whereas a Vygotskian approach might involve facilitating conversations between learners, an approach to teaching Hafsa, influenced by Skinner, will instead be based on behaviourism, and may involve a reward system to support her with the things she finds difficult, and to follow defined classroom routines. Whereas a behaviourist approach may mean that Polly can avoid the chaos of frantically printing a picture of a peace dove for Hafsa to colour in, there is a danger that it can also circumnavigate difficult conversations which have incredible value. In schools where behaviourist approaches to working with pupils with SEND dominate, and there is a superficial appearance of efficacy, engaging in authentic and meaningful dialogues with learners arguably becomes increasingly difficult.

Conclusion

Polly ultimately did a lot of important work with Hafsa to support her to comprehend her grandfather's death. She spoke on the phone with Hafsa's mum. She also worked with Hafsa to create a shoebox altar, inspired by the tradition of displaying ofrendas in Mexico, to commemorate the day of the dead. This was something that did not feature in Polly's long-term planning; nor was it something that Polly had anticipated doing when delivering the first lesson of the RE unit on death. As a result of Polly's internal conversations, therefore, and engagement in a dilemma of possibility, a positive transformation in practice was inspired. Such a transformation seemed to be highly beneficial to Hafsa and her family. For teachers generally, having 'conversations with the situation', with an openness to change, is arguably likely to ultimately benefit young people and their families more generally, along with wider society.

Navigating the 'dilemma of possibility', therefore, involves confidence and overcoming self-doubt. It also involves a commitment to trying things out and having a go. Rouse (2008) writes about 'just doing it' in relation to inclusive education (p. 12). Rather than avoiding difficult conversations until we, one day, complete our quest for specialist-related skills, we need to instead take responsibility within the moment and step up whenever the situation we are in demands us to. In the author's experience, it is through our generic human qualities that the skills for difficult conversations tend to be found.

In many ways, it could be argued, it would be far easier for Polly not to have the difficult conversation with Hafsa. She could have avoided the discomfort of such sensitive dialogues and kept herself busy with her other pupils, until each hour, or each lesson, passed. Ultimately, however, Polly decided not to do this. Through dialogue with Hafsa, Polly found herself navigating the liminal space discussed by Bhabha (2004), to move herself beyond being merely the 'subject specialist', skilled with supporting high academic achievement in RE, and towards being 'The Inclusive Teacher', with a more holistic role in supporting pupils' overall development and well-being. The identification of a 'dilemma of possibility' from within Polly's story suggests that, when considering whether certain topics of conversation are inappropriate or off limits for particular pupils, we need to look beyond the 'dilemma of difference' written Norwich (2019) and focus on any doubts we might have around whether we 'should' or 'can' have these difficult conversations.

References

Bhabha, H. K. (2004). *The location of culture*. Routledge.

Black-Hawkins, K., & Florian, L. (2012). Classroom teachers craft knowledge of their inclusive practice. *Teachers and Teaching: Theory and Practice*, *18*(5), pp. 567–84. doi: 10.1080/13540602.2012.709732.

Buber, M. (1958). *I and Thou*. T & T Clarke.

Carpenter, B., Brooks, T., Cockbill, B., Fotheringham, J., & Rawson, H. (2011). *Complex Learning Difficulties and Disabilities Research Project: Final Report*: Specialist Schools and Academies Trust, London, http://complexld.ssatrust.org.uk.

Crowther, S., Ironside, P., Spence, D., & Smythe, L. (2017). Crafting stories in hermeneutic phenomenology research: A methodological device. *Qualitative Health Research*, *27*(6), pp. 826–35.

Daniels, H. (2020). Vygotsky and inclusion. In P. Hick, R. Kershner, & P. Farrell (Eds.). *Psychology for inclusive education* (pp. 36–49). Routledge.

Department of Education and Science (1978). *Special Educational Needs: Report of the Committee of Enquiry into the Education of Handicapped Children and Young People (The Warnock Report)*. Her Majesty's Stationery Office.

Florian, L. (2012). Preparing teachers to work in inclusive classrooms: Key lessons for the professional development of teacher educators from Scotland's inclusive practice project. *Journal of Teacher Education*, *63*(4), pp. 275–85. doi: 10.1177/0022487112447112.

Florian, L. (2014). What counts as evidence of inclusive education? *European Journal of Special Needs Education*, *29*(3), pp. 286–94. doi: 10.1080/08856257.2014.933551.

Florian, L., & Beaton, M. (2018). Inclusive pedagogy in action: getting it right for every child. *International Journal of Inclusive Education*, *22*(8), pp. 870–84. doi: 10.1080/13603116.2017.1412513.

Florian, L., & Linklater, H. (2010). Preparing teachers for inclusive education: using inclusive pedagogy to enhance teaching and learning for all. *Cambridge Journal of Education*, *40*(4), pp. 369–86.

Florian, L., & Spratt, J. (2013). Enacting inclusion: A framework for interrogating inclusive practice. *European Journal of Special Needs Education*, *28*(2), pp. 119–35, doi: 10.1080/08856257.2013.778111.

Forster, S. (2010). Age-appropriateness: Enabler or barrier to a good life for people with profound and multiple disabilities? *Journal of Intellectual and Developmental Disability*, *35*(2), pp. 129–31. doi: 10.3109/13668251003694606.

Graham, L. J., & Slee, R. (2008). An illusory interiority: Interrogating the discourse/s of inclusion. *Educational Philosophy and Theory*, *40*(2), pp. 277–93. doi: 10.1111/j.1469-5812.2007.00331.

Imray, P., & Hinchcliffe, V. (2012). Not fit for purpose: A call for separate and distinct pedagogies as part of a national framework for those with severe and profound learning difficulties. *Support for Learning*, *27*(4), pp. 150–7. doi: 10.1111/1467-9604.12002.

Lacey, P. (2011). A profound challenge: How to develop a curriculum for pupils with PMLD, https://senmagazine.co.uk/content/education/57/designing-a-curriculum-for-pmld-a-profound-challenge/.

McCray, A. D., Vaughn, S., & Neal, L. V. I. (2001). Not all students learn to read by third grade: Middle school students speak out about their reading disabilities. *Journal of Special Education*, *35*, p. 1. doi: 10.1177/002246690103500103.

Noddings, N. (2012). The caring relation in teaching. *Oxford Review of Education*, *38*(6), pp. 771–81.

Noddings, N. (2013) *Caring: A relational approach to ethics and moral education*. University of California Press.

Norwich, B. (2019). From the Warnock Report (1978) to an education framework commission: A novel contemporary approach to educational policy making for pupils with special educational needs/disabilities. *Frontiers in Education*, *4*, p. 72. doi: 10.3389/feduc.2019.00072.

Rouse, M. (2008). Developing inclusive practice: A role for teachers and teacher education. *Education in the North*, *16*(1), pp. 1–20.

Sachs, J. (2000). The activist professional. *Journal of Educational Change*, *1*, pp. 77–94.

Sachs, J. (2016). Teacher professionalism: Why are we still talking about it? *Teachers and Teaching: Theory and Practice*, *22*(4), pp. 413–25. doi: 10.1080/13540602.2015.1082732.

Schon, D. A. (2016). *The Reflective Practitioner: How Professionals Think in Action*. Routledge.

Shurr, J., & Kromer, G. (2018). Picture plus discussion with partners: peer centred literacy supports for students with significant disabilities. *International Journal of Developmental Disabilities*, *64*, pp. 4–5. doi: 10.1080/20473869.2017.1312060.

Spivak, G. C. (1988). Can the subaltern speak? *Marxism and the Interpretation of Culture*. University of Illinois Press.

Spratt, J., & Florian, L. (2015) Inclusive pedagogy: From learning to action. Supporting each individual in the context of 'everybody'. *Teaching and Teacher Education*, *49*, pp. 89–96. doi: 10.1016/j.tate.2015.03.006.

Standards and Testing Agency (2020). *The Engagement Model: Guidance for maintained schools, academies (including free schools) and local authorities*. https://dera.ioe.ac.uk//id/eprint/36323.

Wolfensberger, W. (1994). The growing threat to the lives of handicapped people in the context of modernistic values [1]. *Disability & Society*, *9*(3), 395–413.

5

Co-Production between Parents and Special Educational Needs Coordinators (SENCOs) – A Route to Transform Working Together

Lorna Hughes

Introduction

This chapter explores the potential of co-production for partnership working between parents and carers of children and young people with Special Educational Needs and/or Disability (SEND) and Special Educational Needs Coordinators (SENCOs) and how this way of working can open some conversations that might be considered difficult for both sides. SENCOs manage inclusion and support for children with SEND in schools and so the working relationship between parents and carers (referred to in this chapter as parents) and SENCOs can include a range of interactions and ways of working. This could include simple information sharing regarding support in place in school to more complex interactions, such as completing a referral together for external support for a child. The levels of participation from stakeholders will vary dependent upon the situation and activities being addressed in school. Some tasks will require parents and SENCOs to work collaboratively, whereas others may be more routine in nature. The process related to Education, Health and Care Plans (EHCPs) should involve the participation of parents alongside professionals (e.g. SENCOs, Educational Psychologists, Speech and Language Therapists) in decision-making, and so it is expected that it would include an opportunity for close working relationships which could provide the basis for co-production to take place. EHCPs have been the source of difficult conversations for many families and professionals because 'navigating the SEND system and alternative provision is not a positive experience for children, young people and their families' (DfE/DoHSC, 2022, p. 10). In too many cases these situations are not managed well, 'since the reforms, the number of appeals to the Tribunal has more than doubled (rising by 111% between 2013/14 and 2020/21)' (Bryant, Parish, & Kulawik, 2022). The Special Educational Needs and Disability (SEND) and Alternative Provision (AP) Improvement Plan (DfE/DoHSC, 2023) is set to address these challenges; however, the plans are gradual and include 'the next steps in a multi-year programme' (2023, p. 18). Therefore, ensuring dialogue between parents and professionals is managed well going forward is vitally important for all involved. This chapter includes a specific focus on the conversations surrounding children with EHCPs to explore opportunities for co-production as a route to transform working together.

The aims of the chapter are to:

1. Consider how engaging in difficult conversations relates to developing approaches involving co-production.
2. Foreground how difficult conversations can uncover and address potential barriers such as differences in values or power relations.
3. Explore what is required for difficult conversations to transform practice.

To meet these aims, I will discuss how a values-based approach aligns to ethics of care (Noddings, 2012) as central to nurturing difficult conversations. Understanding each other is central to ethics of care, and dialogue is essential to facilitate this understanding because 'we learn more about the other, and we need this knowledge to act effectively as carers' (Noddings, 2012, p. 238). Identifying barriers that impact on building relationships is important to enable addressing issues such as disempowerment, discrimination, dominant hierarchical structures and a lack of trust or sense of psychological safety. Through conversations, our awareness and compassion for others grow and enable us to look at our own values and beliefs through a different lens which can then lead to transformation of our thinking (Mannix, 2021; Noddings, 2012). Furthermore, fostering an open mind and being non-judgemental lead to inclusion and enables social justice positions to be adopted (Cahn, 2004).

Osborn and Canfor-Dumas (2018) foreground how we talk and listen to each other as the basis for everything we do and call for a talking revolution to improve how we communicate. They refer to the three pains which hinder effective communication; this includes, personal pain, group pain and societal pain. This chapter focuses on the challenge of group pain, when belonging to a group where communication is ineffective can negatively impact on the ways we communicate and work together. Osborn and Canfor-Dumas (2018, p. 8) propose 'creative conversation' as a model for eliciting a fundamental shift in communication. This model and the underlying principles and practices will be referred to in this chapter in relation to ways in which difficult conversations between parents and SENCOs could be viewed to support a more effective approach in the current SEND system.

The process related to EHCPs and policy background

The Children and Families Act (2014) and the associated SEND reforms in England introduced EHCPs which require statutory needs assessment to be undertaken by the local authority for children and young people with the most complex and significant needs, should this be deemed necessary. This legislative change intended a greater emphasis on aspirations and outcomes for learners, and increased focus on participation of children and parents in decision-making. The inclusion of all stakeholders as active and collaborative participants in the process of applying for, gaining and reviewing an EHCP was a key change in the legislation, and as a result, increased duties on professionals for implementation of more person-centred practices (see Figure 5.1). This shift created a notion that through practices that are participatory in nature, the views and values of children and families will be foregrounded, rather than overlooked while others make decisions for them. Therefore, communication became central to the EHCP process and could be considered to be a vehicle to promote positive engagement and working relationships in facilitating co-production as a participatory approach to partnerships.

Despite the proposed ethos of the SEND reforms in England aiming for an improved system with parents as co-producers – a structure that would build parental confidence in the system and reduce the number of EHCPs (DfE, 2011) – it has had the opposite effect with EHCPs increasing (Marsh & Howatson, 2020) and little evidence of collaborative ways of working in practice (Boddison & Soan, 2022). Finding the right spaces and conditions for dialogue to take place as part of the EHCP process is challenging because the SEND system continues to echo aspects of historic criticisms; these challenges include: the processes being overly complex or bureaucratic, inconsistent allocation of resources, lack of information and parents having to fight for support (Adams et al., 2018; DfE/DoHSC, 2022; DfE/DoHSC, 2023; HoCEC, 2019; NAO, 2019; Norwich, 2019; Sales and Vincent, 2018). It is often the case that the SENCOs and the parents demonstrate a great deal of good will and commitment in working together to secure the best outcomes for children, and they do place the child as centre of their

Statutory timescales for EHC needs assessment and EHC plan development

```
                    ┌─────────────────────────────────┐
                    │ Request for assessment/child or  │
                    │ young person brought to local    │
                    │ authority's (LA's) attention     │
                    └─────────────────────────────────┘
                                    │
                    ┌───────────────┴───────────────┐
              Yes   │  LA decides whether to         │  No
          ┌─────────│  conduct EHC needs assessment  │─────────┐
          │         └───────────────────────────────┘          │
          ▼                                                    ▼
 ┌──────────────────────┐                      ┌──────────────────────────┐
 │ LA notifies parent/  │                      │ LA notifies parents/     │
 │ young person of      │                      │ young person of decision │
 │ decision within a    │                      │ and right to appeal      │
 │ maximum of 6 weeks   │                      │ within a maximum of 6    │
 │ from request for     │                      │ weeks from request for   │
 │ assessment           │                      │ assessment               │
 └──────────────────────┘                      └──────────────────────────┘
          │
          ▼
 ┌──────────────────────┐
 │ LA gathers           │
 │ information for EHC  │
 │ assessment           │
 └──────────────────────┘
          │
          ▼
              ┌───────────────────────────┐
         Yes  │ LA decides whether an EHC │  No
       ┌──────│ plan is needed            │──────┐
       │      └───────────────────────────┘      │
       ▼                                         ▼
 ┌──────────────────────┐              ┌────────────────────┐
 │ LA drafts plan and   │              │ LA notifies        │
 │ sends it to parents/ │              │ parents/young      │
 │ young person         │              │ person of decision │
 └──────────────────────┘              │ and right to       │
       │                               │ appeal within a    │
       ▼                               │ maximum of 16      │
 ┌──────────────────────┐              │ weeks from request │
 │ Parents/young person │              │ for assessment     │
 │ has 15 calendar days │              └────────────────────┘
 │ to comment/express a │
 │ preference for an    │
 │ educational          │
 │ institution and      │
 │ should also seek     │
 │ agreement of a       │
 │ personal budget      │
 └──────────────────────┘
       │
       ▼
 ┌──────────────────────┐
 │ LA must consult      │
 │ governing body,      │
 │ principal or         │
 │ proprietor of the    │
 │ educational          │
 │ institution before   │
 │ naming them in the   │
 │ EHC plan. The        │
 │ institution should   │
 │ respond within 15    │
 │ calendar days        │
 └──────────────────────┘
       │
       ▼
 ┌──────────────────────┐
 │ Following            │
 │ consultation with    │
 │ the parent/young     │
 │ person, the draft    │
 │ plan is amended      │
 │ where needed and     │
 │ issued. (LA notifies │
 │ parent/young person  │
 │ of rights to         │
 │ appeal.)             │
 └──────────────────────┘
```

Left margin: At every stage, child and their parent and/or young person is involved fully, their views and wishes taken into account

Right margin (dashed box): On-going LA information gathering – where an LA requests co-operation of a body in securing information and advice, the body must comply within 6 weeks

Right margin: Maximum time for whole process to be completed is 20 weeks

Figure 5.1 Overview of the EHCP timescales and development when a request is made (DfE/DoH, 2015, p. 154).

planning and discussions (Armstrong, 1995; Curran et al., 2017; Lamb, 2009). However, external systemic factors are likely to hinder working relationships because they create complex conditions in which the parents and SENCOs are communicating. For example, the inconsistency over the allocation of resources could elicit a sense of unfairness and inequality on both the parents' and the SENCOs' part; it could cause confusion and frustration leading to heightened emotions that might impact on communication. In such a challenging context, it is vital to consider ways to address these persistent issues together through effective communication and participatory approaches. The SENCO tends to be the first point of contact in the school, and they hold a key position in relation to overseeing EHCPs. Therefore, although there might be a number of professionals involved in supporting a child and family, the relationship and conversations between the parent and SENCO are critical as they are frequent and often pivotal to the decisions that are being made.

The government's (DfE/DoHSC, 2023) plans for new National Standards for SEND reinforce the need for co-production in the system. The green paper proposed the introduction of 'consistent standards on co-production with children, young people, parents and carers' (DfE/DoHSC, 2022, p. 28). Yet, implementing consistent standards across all settings may require a change in thinking and practice because systemic and cultural aspects will need to be addressed (Lamb, 2009; NAO, 2019). This is why 'difficult conversations' are inescapable to support a move in mindsets and culture to a values-based approach to address these long-term and entrenched barriers evident in the SEND systems that hinder co-production experienced by parents and SENCOs.

> ## Pause for reflection
>
> - Based on your understanding of the policy context, what do you think are some of the factors which might be contributing to parents and SENCOs having to engage in conversations that might be considered as 'difficult'?

What is co-production?

There are different levels of participation in decision-making. Arnstein's (1969) ladder of participation has been used to conceptualise adults' increasing involvement in decision-making from the non-participatory model through to tokenism and then citizen control at the top of the ladder. Co-production could be considered at the higher levels of participation based on this model. It is important to look at ways we engage with others and consider if all stakeholders really are fully involved in decision-making, or if the engagement is situated at a lower level and, therefore, hinders opportunity for real influence or choice. Roper, Grey and Cadogan (2018, p. 1) claim that 'co-production goes beyond traditional consumer participation models' and identify a range of stages that are required to involve participants fully to effect co-production. This includes co-planning, co-design, co-evaluation and co-delivery which illustrate the investment required for this way of working. Co-production needs to pervade all aspects of working together so that it is an embedded approach rather than just inviting participation at specific stages of a process of decision-making. Essentially, they view co-production as requiring 'consumers [to be] involved in, or leading, defining the problem, designing and delivering the solution, and evaluating the outcome, either with professionals or independently' (Roper, Grey, & Cadogan, 2018, p. 2). It is clear this takes significant investment on the part of parents and on the part of professionals; it is not a simple transactional process and there may be different levels at which parents and professionals can or wish to participate. Co-production is therefore quite complex and not a static concept or process that can just be adopted without building conditions for it to happen. It will require genuine investment from all parties and a sensitive approach to how it is managed and implemented in practice. In some cases, this will require shifting mindsets and changes in culture as the parents are placed more centrally in the process. This highlights how fundamental building and maintaining effective communication and therefore working relationships are to enabling such a committed approach.

How do difficult conversations relate to co-production?

In some ways difficult conversations and co-production are interconnected. Difficult conversations between parents and SENCOs can happen without the requirement for co-production. However, co-production will not be implemented effectively without 'difficult conversations' taking place because a change in practice and mindset will pose challenges to both sides of the partnership. In fact, Stone, Patton and Heen (1999, p. xii) argue that successful implementation of change 'eventually *requires* people to have difficult conversations'. Acknowledgement of how best to manage these conversations may help to lay the foundations or strengthen conditions for effective co-production. Embedding practices that foster co-production, including valuing the difficult conversations that will take place, may improve relationships and open honest conversations because 'people who are willing and able to "stick through the hard parts" emerge with a stronger sense of trust in each other *and* the relationship' (Stone, Patton & Heen, 1999 p. xi). These stronger relationships can support improved conditions of trust and transparency for co-production to take place and for decision-making processes to be family-centred.

There has been a great deal of ineffective communication and breakdown in working relationships and confidence in the SEND system, which has impacted on parental trust and working relationships with professionals (DfE/DoHSC, 2022; Lamb, 2009). The EHCP process can be very challenging, which often involves managing very sensitive emotional situations (Coughlin & Sethares, 2017; Oliver & Barnes, 2012). This will undoubtedly include challenging conversations taking place. Yet, how these are managed can make all the difference to the nature of the partnership. One way to address these difficult conversations could be by opening up 'creative conversations', which I discuss next.

> **Pause for reflection**
>
> - How often do you consider the underlying values that underpin your conversations? Are any of those values embedded in social justice?

Osborn and Canfor-Dumas (2018, p. 9) refer to 'personal responsibility', 'openness' and 'creativity' as the three principles of 'creative conversation' to transform pains experienced by ineffective or even detrimental communication. The first principle of 'personal responsibility' aims at examining our attitudes to ourselves and considering the impact of our interactions on the outcomes. We are all active agents in the conversations, so we hold a level of influence. Valuing ourselves is just as important as valuing others, which is the second principle: 'openness'. Cahn (2004) highlights the necessity to underpin practice with a 'social justice' perspective. Without this '[w]e can't succeed because we can't get the participation we need from the very people we are trying to help' (Cahn, 2004, p. 21). At its core, the social justice approach would stop the devaluation of individuals and cycles of dependency. If the social justice principle is embedded in practice it would serve to address subordination, exploitation and discrimination. This focus on social justice illustrates the importance of the values-based approach in taking forward changes in practice which need appropriate implementation, such as investment in time, relationships and appropriate training for those involved. This echoes the third principle of 'creativity', which highlights the possibility of creative conversations to result in something worthwhile and of value (Osborn & Canfor-Dumas, 2018).

Current issues and barriers to co-production involve a range of factors which are further compounded by the complexities within the current SEND system. Co-production can be demanding enough to adopt due to the higher levels of commitment required, without the external influences and challenges that parents and SENCOs face. Two aspects explored within this chapter include understanding different values and managing the imbalance of power within working relationships, which I explore next.

Different values and how to address this in practice

Values are not easy to define – they are rooted in social, cultural and contextual factors as well as individuals' personal experiences and belief systems. Therefore, the beliefs held by individuals may differ over time or in different situations. Even when we may perceive values as being shared, for example, the shared values of a community, they do not always represent a homogeneous group due to individual differences. This can be quite significantly different from others in a shared group, or it could present as internal conflict whereby personal and group values might diverge. A 'values'-based approach could therefore be seen as challenging; however, it is the acknowledgement of this diversity and difference of values that is crucial even if understanding or agreeing with others' values may not always be possible. Thistlethwaite (2012) argues that it is when our values come into conflict that they become visible, and this happens when difficult conversations take place. It is crucial that our differing values are made 'visible' and that we can share our views in a safe space where all are free from fear of prosecution. The alternative is that values are invisible to the other party and therefore we will never know or be able to emphasise with each other, and worse, it can lead to dissatisfaction, frustration and further barriers to working together. Engaging in, what might often turn out to be a 'difficult conversation', can uncover and address these potential differences in values so that communication can then be more open and honest.

Trust is central to working together and dialogue is fundamental in building these trusting relationships. Lamb (2009, p. 40) noted that '[g]ood, honest and open communication is key to the development of positive working relationships and requires practitioners who listen to parents and are trusted by them'. Mistrust and lack of clear open communication and information have led to seriously detrimental outcomes in the current system. For example, children are excluded or withdrawn from education because appropriate provisions and support are not in place. Even when values differ, stakeholders need to feel safe and confident in the system in which they are operating and that this will lead to positive outcomes for their children's education and well-being.

Building trusting, open, working relationships for co-production to take place, therefore, requires time and investment. However, workload demands upon SENCOs are restrictive and place pressures on them which undoubtedly impacts the time they can allocate for working with parents. Curran et al. (2020, p. 4) call for protected time to allow SENCOs to be able to 'work with, and advocate for, children, young people, and their families'. Much of the SENCOs' role is administrative – the report noted that SENCOs identified almost three quarters of their time was taken up on paperwork processes related to EHCPs and evidence for referrals for local authorities. Therefore, shifting the focus from paperwork-based processes to valuing time and space for building and maintaining relationships is fundamental to enable co-production to happen.

Pause for reflection

- Why might parents' and SENCOs' beliefs and values differ? Could you write five differing examples that you have come across or could envisage?

Balancing what might be different values within the decision-making process for EHCPs could be challenging. For example, in some cases, children may be assigned a specialist provision through their EHCP, but will need to continue to attend their mainstream school until a place becomes available. This situation requires the parents and SENCOs to work together to meet the child's needs as best as they can until the appropriate provision is in place, but it can be challenging for parents if they know that the provision is not appropriate. It can also be challenging for the SENCOs because they will have a finite resource available to draw on. How this is managed by the parents and SENCOs and how well they can work together will influence the outcomes for the child. The responsibility often falls on the individuals directly involved to ensure the right support is implemented in practice. Furthermore, these situations are often imbued with 'difficult conversations' where sensitive matters need to be communicated and potentially undesirable messages delivered.

Importantly, parents are not a homogeneous group and undoubtedly will encompass a full diversity across society including different classes, educational backgrounds and socio-economic status. Factors such as this will influence the level and type of interaction required as parents work with SENCOs in managing EHCPs for their children (Soan, 2017). Parents require different levels of support which is dependent upon their individual circumstances, and this level of support required limits access to the system if it is not addressed adequately. For example, some parents may find the EHCP process so complex that they are not able to participate in making decisions. This process is paperwork-heavy and so parents who may have literacy difficulties could be disempowered or unable to contribute effectively if they are required to fill out forms. Likewise, professionals will vary considerably. There may be a commonality in their shared roles and or responsibilities, but their needs and the level of support they require will be diverse, as will their own backgrounds, values and beliefs. Their level of experience and training could affect their knowledge of the process and how they can support parents in co-production. Therefore, appropriate training in developing the skills of listening (Mannix, 2021) and the skills of expression (Stone, Patton & Heen, 1999) is required. This takes time and investment, but the outcome can be so much more rewarding when working with families and children. Transformation is more likely to occur when relationships are valued and those engaged in the dialogue have the skills to question in a caring environment. When this is fostered, the positive relationships often continue even beyond school and parents can become powerful advocates for the school.

Consequently, how parents and SENCOs perceive each other can influence their interactions and the effectiveness of processes such as managing EHCPs. Successful working relationships demand mutual trust and openness. Elwyn (2020, p. 4) refers to shared decision-making as a way to 'meet the need for values that most people hold dear, namely respect, trust, and agency, as we navigate some of the most difficult decisions in life'. In some cases, managing EHCPs involves difficult life decisions and ultimately difficult conversations, yet bringing these more challenging or conflicting values to the fore would foster openness in shared decision-making. Osborn and Canfor-Dumas (2018, p. 52) refer to the need for psychological safety in order to engage in conversations where there may be difficult decisions to make. They note that when conversation 'transgresses our values' we can close off and even become angry. They argue that the basic physical, emotional and mental needs will influence engagement and if we feel under threat then this can impact relationships. They pose the issue of the pain involved in impotently listening to a 'verbal attack on something we value or someone we really care about' (Osborn & Canfor-Dumas, 2018, p. 52). Although it is essential to recognise differences and conflict, it is important to recognise that it takes courage to listen to what is uncomfortable and to also try to recognise and understand the position of someone's opposing views and values. Acknowledgement that there will be difficult conversations and ways to manage the challenges can enable improved relationships. Ignoring the challenges will ultimately lead to the deterioration of the relationship and possibly withdrawal from the process entirely. Therefore, exploring how dialogue can support a collaborative approach and the benefits this can bring may, to some extent, address the persistent barriers and inequalities in the current system.

Imbalance in power and how to address this in practice

Cahn (2004, p. 22) referred to co-production as signalling a 'shift in status from subordination to some kind of parity'. He acknowledges that there is some ambiguity on how equal the standing is of those in the partnership which raises a question over levels of power in these relationships. Mannix (2021, p. 22) claims that 'a conversation works best when the power balance is as even as it can be'. Unfortunately, power differentials can be hidden and deep-rooted in past practices and hierarchical systems, with the same approaches and conversations happening over time. Even something quite basic such as meetings being set in school hours can be limiting to a working family who may find it difficult to attend. It is therefore important to adopt practices that illuminate power imbalances to raise awareness for both parents and SENCOs in order to positively influence mindsets, future conversations and therefore ways of working collaboratively.

Ensuring we adopt a culture that promotes a values-based approach may address the imbalance of power that occurs in conversations or where we aim to implement co-production. The power of an individual over another means there will always be a differential, and this can vary depending upon the time context and situation; in reality, it is unlikely that total equality will be achieved. However, partnership working will ultimately require the stakeholders to reach a consensus to lead to a viable outcome, and so managing these variations in power for each of the stakeholders is important to address. Not addressing power differentials may serve to hinder co-production because it obstructs ethics of care that leads to separations that induce 'the dualisms exploiter/exploited, oppressor/oppressed, moral agent/object, and so on' (Noddings, 2012, p. 236).

It is important to acknowledge that power relations extend beyond parents and SENCOs and will also include the local authority and the state. Despite empowering parents through legislation, it is the local authority that 'must determine whether it may be necessary for special educational provision to be made for the child or young person in accordance with an EHC plan' (Children and Families Act, 2014, p. 30). This power imbalance illustrates how both parents and SENCOs could be constrained. The power differentials evident in the current system serve to polarise those involved rather than providing a level basis for shared decision-making to take place. Even professionals with the best intentions may be restricted by the macro-influences within the state system. If conversations do not happen at the local authority level, it can thwart working relationships. For example, Boddison & Soan (2022) refer to difficulties that arise from co-production when there is tension in state policy and procedures. Parents have 'increased capacity for decision-making (DfE, 2011) whilst education professionals are limited in their flexibility as they have to follow prescribed LA procedures' (DfE, 2022, p. 99). Parents and SENCOs may therefore be constrained by the system because even when they have an effective working relationship, the control at the local authority level affects decision-making and the allocation of resources, arguably placing those navigating the system as ultimately being subordinate to the state. The green paper called for 'co-production embedded at every level of the SEND system' (DfE/DoHSC, 2022, p. 66) which must also include the state if successful practices are to be adopted and embedded going forward.

Parents need to feel the school, professionals and state have the best interest of their child at the fore. Too often this is not the case. Recent proposals highlight the need in the system to restore families' trust and 'confidence that their children will get the right support, in the right place, at the right time' (DfE/DoHSC, 2023, p. 5). However, what is concerning is that for too long now 'parents are not "in the know" and for some, the law may not even appear to exist' (HoCEC, 2019, p. 87). Vincent (2000, p. 32) refers to the common perception of parents' relationships with professionals as being 'positioned as [a] subordinate, less powerful group'. With the assumed position of society as generally passive, it may be the case that the majority of parents are passive in the approach to managing EHCPs. If the default position is passivity, then possibly the only way parents and SENCOs are able to engage with the system, where their voice is heard and valued, is by stepping out of this position of passivity. If this is the case, it is important to consider if this is an action all parents are able or willing to enact.

The socio-economic and education level of parents have been identified as influencing factors in decision-making processes (Reay, 2012). Parents who are able to draw on social, economic and cultural capital to effect some change, even if this is at an individual level, may be in a better position to take control of the aforementioned difficult conversations. This requirement for specialist knowledge and social capital is recognised in the current system (HoCEC, 2019, p. 87) as well as the issue that parents 'without significant personal or social capital, therefore, face significant disadvantage'. Furthermore, Sales and Vincent's (2018, pp. 67–8) findings identified that professionals were concerned 'that outcomes of the process do not necessarily reflect the child's needs but rather are influenced by factors such as the extent to which the child is considered "high profile", the ability of a parent to advocate on behalf of a child, and concerns about how the provision will be funded'.

It is therefore crucial that this disparity in social capital is addressed so all parents are able to engage in conversations that are meaningful and result in an equitable way forward. 'Understanding' is one key practice that Osborn and Canfor-Dumas (2018) refer to as underpinning their three key principles for 'creative conversation' to take place. This is essentially valuing what the speaker has to say as a basis of the conversations that take place and could be argued would serve to counter rigid power structures as a barrier to communication. Osborn and Canfor-Dumas (2018, p. 93) note that the 'power in any conversation lies with the listener – and even more with the understander'. This really highlights how truly knowing and understanding others in the conversation provides a strong values-based approach. In practice, this takes time and significant investment, but the benefits of SENCOs and parents really knowing and understanding each other would lay foundations for effective co-production. In turn, this approach would improve the system because 'the best performing SEND systems are those with a consistent focus on co-production' (DfE/DoHSC, 2022, p. 75).

Pause for reflection

- If socio-economic status and level of education influences access to and the ability to engage in difficult conversations, what can professionals do to provide a more equitable approach when they meet with parents?
- Rather than holding 'traditional meetings', list different ways we can communicate which might be more suited to inclusive practices.

How can parents and SENCOs nurture themselves through 'difficult conversations'?

Engaging in 'difficult conversations' can be very challenging and emotionally driven for both parents and SENCOs. Mannix (2021, p. 136) highlights the importance of seeing our own care and compassion as just as important as the care and compassion we provide for others because '[b]ringing ourselves to sit beside another person's deep distress can make us sad and leave us feeling drained'. Mannix (2021) outlined ways in which to take care of ourselves as well as others in our conversations, and these include:

- Accept without judging – listening without judgement is essential. Allowing others to explain a situation can provide an opportunity for gaining clarity or developing a new perspective.
- Be open-minded – there may be gaps or misunderstandings but we need to know how it appears to the other person as the basis for dialogue. It is essential to be able to listen and understand that differences do not need to be closed down.
- Having self-awareness – being aware of our own position, our emotions, thoughts, behaviours and potential biases will help us to keep balanced as we engage in dialogue.
- Listening to the voice within – listening to our inner voice is important for our well-being, although we need to be as critical of our own voice or position as we would while listening to advice from others.
- Practicing 'tenderness' in our conversations – recognising that what is being shared could be painful and will require sensitivity and respect in how we respond.
- Give away the power – helping people find their own solutions will empower them rather than trying to offer to fix situations. This is central to co-production.
- Self-care – understanding that we are worthy of care and compassion. We need to allow space for reflection and acknowledge when we need support.

Conclusions

Difficult conversations can be a way to resolve dilemmas and move towards a better future. Dialogue is essential for democracy through the inclusion of a range of perspectives from different backgrounds. We need to embrace diversity and individual cultures and beliefs if we are to contribute to a more just society. Yet, not everyone will be in the position to enter into 'difficult conversations'. It is important to realise that 'difficult conversations do not just *involve* feelings; they are at the core *about* feelings' (Stone, Patton and Heen, 1999, p. 13). Understanding this endeavour is progressive and may take time before conversations can take place to support richer and more ethical positions involving compassion and empathy. We need to be 'tender' in our approach (Mannix, 2021, p. 37).

Gastil (2014, p. 129) refers to shifting the focus away from policy and procedure and concentrating on dialogue and understanding each other better. This can mitigate some of the challenges related to difficult decision-making and provides the opportunity for improved communication to take place. Furthermore, Gastil (2014, p. 131) claims that this will force 'a democratic group to worry less about its decision-making tasks and focus instead on better understanding and appreciating its members, their personal histories, life aspirations, and ways of seeing the world'. This aligns with a values-based approach to facilitate co-production, but the current SEND system is too often laden with bureaucracy which hinders placing people at the centre (DfE/DoHSC, 2023).

Systemic issues within SEND will continue to be a challenge because the systems and processes are not likely to change quickly, despite the calls for review (HoCEC, 2019; NAO, 2019) and the recent plans for change (DfE/DoHSC, 2023). These political and economic challenges impact opportunities for parents and SENCOs to work together and effect co-production. Too often, even lower levels of participation are not consistently being applied, and as a result, both parents' and SENCOs' voices are being suppressed. If there is a true commitment to embedding co-production as a 'fundamental principle of the SEND system' (DfE/DoHSC, 2022, p. 29), then investment is required to transform the practice. At the heart of the change is dialogue; as Osborn and Canfor-Dumas (2018, p. 61) note this has been 'described as "thinking together" and "interthinking" – a form of interaction that creates a "safe space" in which we can express emotions, explore ideas, examine options and work out solutions (co-create) without fear of negative judgement.' Therefore, parents and SENCOs acknowledging that there are wider influences and factors that may be outside the realms of their influence will help to recognise what can be managed and achieved and may provide them with more solidarity and influence when working collaboratively.

Both parents and SENCOs can be susceptible to feelings of defensiveness or threat when there is conflict over values. For example, parents may see the issuing of an EHCP as resulting in the right provisions for their child, but in reality, this is not always the case because the SENCO may not be able to access further resources or support. Managing these points of tension is important to avoid a breakdown in working relationships. Our dialogue requires a repertoire of skills in how to manage conversations and relationships skilfully. Awareness of and training in difficult conversations would support managing this more effectively and would hopefully serve to increase trust. Likewise, co-production can be the vehicle that, through its value-based nature, offers a platform where those 'difficult conversations' can be enwrapped in empathy, understanding, and creativity.

We need to understand that developing co-production as a way of working is a process and not a destination where we will easily arrive. We may always be in the process of working towards increasing co-production. On occasions, we might inadvertently upset or misunderstand others. However, if at the core, we are placing the person as the centre in our interactions and practice then when these instances happen, we are better placed to draw on the strength of a trusting open relationship to address and repair misunderstandings. Taking the first steps towards changing practice to value what can come from 'difficult conversations' rather than avoid them can lead us all towards improved ways of working in the longer term.

References

Adams, L., Tindle, A., Basran, S., Dobie, S., & Thomson, D. (2018). *Health and care plans: A qualitative investigation into service user experiences of the planning process.* Research report London, Department for Education.

Armstrong, D. (1995). *Power and partnership in education: Parents, children and special educational Needs.* Routledge.

Arnstein, S. R. (1969). A ladder of citizen participation. *Journal of the American Institute of Planners, 35*(4), pp. 216–224.

Boddison, A., & Soan, S. (2022). The Coproduction Illusion: considering the relative success rates and efficiency rates of securing an Education, Health and Care plan when requested by families or education professionals. *Journal of Research in Special Educational Needs, 22*(2), pp. 91–104.

Bryant, B., Parish, N., & Kulawik, K. (2022). *Agreeing to disagree? Research into arrangements for avoiding disagreements and resolving disputes in the SEND system in England* Retrieved 1/2/23, from https://static1.squarespace.com/static/5ce55a5ad4c5c500016855ee/t/6221ee346c97bb4c0c754891/1646390841226/220222_LGA_SEND+disputes_report_FINAL.pdf.

Cahn, E. (2004). *No more throw-away people: The co-production imperative 2nd edn.* Essential Books.

Children and Families Act (2014). Retrieved 21 March 2022, from http://www.legislation.gov.uk/ukpga/2014/6/contents/enacted.

Coughlin, M. B., & Sethares, K. A. (2017). Chronic sorrow in parents of children with a chronic illness or disability: An integrative literature review. *Journal of Pediatric Nursing, 37*, pp. 108–16.

Curran, H., Moloney, H., Heavey, A., & Boddison, A. (2020). *The time is now: Addressing missed opportunities for Special Educational Needs Support and Coordination in our schools* Retrieved 1 November 2022, from https://www.bathspa.ac.uk/media/bathspaacuk/education-/research/senco-workload/National-SENCO-Workload-Survey-Report-Jan-2020.pdf.

Curran, H., Mortimore, T., & Riddell, R. (2017). Special Educational Needs and Disabilities reforms 2014: SENCO's perspectives of the first six months. *British Journal of Special Educational Needs, 44*(1), pp. 46–64.

Department for Education (2011). *Support and aspiration: A new approach to special educational needs and disability – Consultation.* TSO.

Department for Education / Department of Health (2015). *Special Educational Needs and Disability Code of Practice: 0–25 Years.* Retrieved 21 March 2021, from https://www.gov.uk/government/publications/send-code-of-practice-0-to-25.

Department for Education / Department of Health and Social Care (2022). *SEND Review: Right support, Right place, Right time. Available from: SEND review: Right support, right place, right time.* Retrieved 20 June 2022, from https://www.gov.uk/government/consultations/send-review-right-support-right-place-right-time.

Department for Education / Department of Health and Social Care (2023). *Special Educational Needs and Disabilities (SEND) and Alternative Provision (AP) Improvement Plan: Right Support, Right Place, Right Time.* Retrieved 12 March 2022, from: SEND and alternative provision improvement plan – GOV.UK (www.gov.uk).

Elwyn, G. (2020). Shared decision-making: What is the work? *Patient Education and Counseling, 104*(7), pp. 1591–5.

Fulford, K. W. M. (2004). Ten principles of values-based medicine. In J. Radden (Ed.). *The Philosophy of Psychiatry: A Companion* (pp. 205–34). Oxford University Press.

Gastil, J. (2014). *Democracy in small groups: Participation, decision-making and communication (Second Edn).* Library of Congress Cataloging-in-Publication Data.

House of Commons Education Committee (2019). *Special educational needs and disabilities.* House of Commons. First Report of Session 2019–20.

Lamb, B. (2009). *Lamb Inquiry: Special Educational Needs and Parental Confidence* Retrieved 15 October 2022, from https://dera.ioe.ac.uk/9042/1/Lamb%20Inquiry%20Review%20of%20SEN%20and%20Disability%20Information.pdf.

Mannix, K. (2021). *Listen: How to find the words for tender conversations.* William Collins.

Marsh, A. J., & Howatson, K. (2020). Education, health and care plans and tribunals in England: A statistical tale from 2019. *British Educational Research Journal, 46*(3), pp. 574–92.

National Audit Office (2019). *Support for pupils with special educational needs and disabilities in England*. Retrieved 12 December 2022, from https://www.nao.org.uk/report/support-for-pupils-with-special-educational-needs-and-disabilities/.

Noddings, N. (2012). *Philosophy of education 3rd edn*. Westview Press.

Norwich, B. (2019, July). From the Warnock report (1978) to an education framework commission: A novel contemporary approach to educational policy making for pupils with special educational needs/disabilities. In *Frontiers in Education* (Vol. 4, p. 72). Frontiers Media SA.

Oliver, M., & Barnes, C. (2012). *The New politics of disablement*. Palgrave Macmillan.

Osborn, P., & Canfor-Dumas, E. (2018). *The talking revolution: How creative conversation can change the world*. Port Meadow Press.

Reay, D. (2012). What would a socially just education system look like?: saving the minnows from the pike. *Journal of Education Policy*, 27(5), pp. 587–99.

Roper, C., Grey, F., & Cadogan, E. (2018) *Co-production Putting principles into practice in mental health contexts*. Retrieved 21 March 2022, from https://healthsciences.unimelb.edu.au/__data/assets/pdf_file/0007/3392215/Co-production_putting-principles-into-practice.pdf.

Sales, N., & Vincent, K. (2018). Strengths and limitations of the Education, Health and Care plan process from a range of professional and family perspectives. *British Journal of Special Education*, 45(1), pp. 61–80.

Soan, S. (2017). *The SENCO essential manual*. Open University Press.

Stone, Patton, & Heen (1999). *Difficult conversations: How to discuss what matters most*. Viking Penguin.

Thistlethwaite, J. E. (2012). *Values-based interprofessional collaborative practice*. Cambridge University Press.

Vincent, C. (2000). *Including parents? Education, citizenship and parental agency*. Open University Press.

Part Two

'Difficult Conversations' in Higher Education

6

Using a Community of Philosophical Inquiry Approach to Explore Race and Inequality in Higher Education Contexts

Fufy Demissie

Introduction

It is widely acknowledged that the death of George Floyd disrupted the status quo about race and equity across all levels of education (Ebbinghaus & Huang, 2022). Calls for racial equity and research evidence that had been previously ignored (Gillborn et al., 2016) suddenly gained prominence, whilst previously marginalised students and staff of colour found their voice. As a result, universities had no choice but to urgently review their policies and practices and their previous approaches to 'dealing' with the race issue in their institutions.

The changed emphasis on institutional and structural barriers was a welcome shift (Parveen, 2021). Rather than changing individuals (e.g. through unconscious bias training), the focus was now on removing barriers to issues such as access to elite universities and decolonising the curriculum (OfS, 2021)). However, while the recognition of institutional racism was welcome, it seemed to underplay the reality that individuals' beliefs and attitudes underpin and frame the structures that impact on students' educational experiences (Walker et al., 2023). In other words, universities' responses generally lacked (in the UK at least), any significant focus on facilitating opportunities for individuals to critically reflect on their assumptions and beliefs about the complex issue of race and its impact on students, institutions and society.

This gap in the policy discourse seems like a missed opportunity. As a trained facilitator of critical dialogue, my motivation for writing this chapter was to examine whether opportunities to engage in difficult conversations about race through a carefully structured methodology (Community of Philosophical

Inquiry) can create spaces for genuine reflection and enquiry. My approach to the 'problem' is underpinned by the notion that if meaningful change is what we seek, difficult conversations with our colleagues and students are vital (Dawson, 2015). It is a perspective that is informed by dialogue as a process of self-realisation, a way of raising awareness of internalised beliefs (Freire, 1973) and emotional discomfort as a precursor for meaningful reflection and transformation (Ahmed, 2018; Stone, et al., 2011).

The chapter begins with a brief historical background on racism before exploring current debates around anti-racist policies in higher education contexts. This is followed by a focus on issues around nurturing the anti-racist educator and the necessity of difficult conversations to support individuals' journey from the fear zone to the transformation zone (Kendi, 2019). The Community of Philosophical Inquiry methodology is described and proposed as an approach to nurturing the anti-racist educator, before descriptions of philosophical enquiries on the topics of labels and responsibility. The chapter concludes by reflecting on the strengths and limitations of CoPI and the challenges of transformative change.

This chapter will:

- Explore the debates around institutions' approach to addressing race and equity in HE
- Consider why 'difficult conversations' are needed to address race and equality in higher education
- Describe the Community of Philosophical Inquiry (CoPI) approach and its potential as a methodology for difficult conversations
- Use case studies to contextualise reflections on the CoPI methodology and the challenges of transformative change in the context of race and equity in higher education contexts.

The historical context

In contrast to the United States, where the enduring racial tensions have galvanised far-reaching policies and practices to address racism, UK higher education institutions are relative late comers (Law, 2017). An early catalyst for change was the McPherson's report that drew attention to the 'collective failure' of institutions to embed policies and practices (in areas such as admissions, curriculum and assessment) to tackle unequal educational and life outcomes (Rollock, 2009). For all public institutions, including universities, the subsequent Race Relations Act (Amendment) (2000) and the Equality Act (2010) enshrined legal accountability and external scrutiny of race equality policies and practices. As a result, universities were given a positive duty to promote difference and diversity.

But despite extensive research and advocacy (such as Centre for ethnicity and racism at the University of Leeds), universities were slow to respond to this legislation (Law, 2017). The evidence continues to show the ongoing detrimental effect of race on minoritised groups' mental and physical well-being, progress and achievements (Loke, 2015). That is, these students were less likely to be admitted to elite universities, awarded good degrees, or to be offered jobs, while HE staffs' mental well-being and career prospects were similarly affected (Law, 2017). The BLM movement put a searing spotlight on these realities that led some universities to embrace closer scrutiny of their policies and practices to tackle racism (AdvanceHE, n.d.).

Current debates about institutional responses to race and equity in higher education

In response to the government's accountability agendas (OfS, 2021), UK universities have prioritised improved access and participation in higher education for under-represented groups (including ethnicity). Whether this has led to more under-represented groups attending university is contested, but critics also argue that there is insufficient focus on student attainment once they are at university (Harrison & Waller, 2017). Until recently, another flagship policy for many universities was the provision of unconscious bias training for university staff. Unconscious bias is when our implicit beliefs and the world influence our expectations of others (e.g. female South Asian heritage students) and unknowingly affect the judgments we make about them (e.g. that they would not volunteer to become class representative) (Dee & Gershenson, 2017).

Critics have nonetheless argued that in many cases, these training courses have little or no effect and, in some cases, reinforce existing biases (Parveen, 2021). In part, this was due to the stand-alone nature of these events (much like health and safety courses), and the lack of sufficient preparation or follow-up sessions to evaluate or embed the learning gained. Campaigners have also pointed out that this policy is flawed because it implies that the problem lies with individual academics rather than the institutions to address racism in universities (Noon, 2018). In other words, unconscious bias training does not tackle issues such as admission procedures, grading, assessment practices, curriculum and promotion criteria that discriminate against people of colour.

One outcome of the BLM protests is that universities as well as students and staff have become increasingly conscious of the pervasive nature of institutional racism. Consequently, attention is now more focused on the institution rather than the individual, evident in the adoption of the Race Equality Charter by some universities. The Race Equality Charter aims to embed long-term institutional culture change that avoids a deficit model of the individual and acknowledges the impact of institutional racism (AdvanceHE, n.d.). It is a voluntary body where member institutions submit evidence to gain recognition for their anti-racist policies and practices.

The race equality charter addresses many of the shortcomings of historical policies and practices. Changing the focus from the individual to the institution is welcome because it acknowledges the structural nature of racism and identifies universities' responsibilities (AdvanceHE, n.d.; Arday & Mirza, 2018; Law, 2017). Thus, post-BLM initiatives have ranged from creating senior leadership posts for diversity to leadership courses for staff from minority backgrounds. While these initiatives are encouraging, they imply a deficit perspective that the lack of minorities in senior leadership positions is because minorities lack the right skills and confidence. This might be partially true in some cases, but tellingly, there has not been a similar focus on high-ranking university staff to improve their knowledge and understanding of institutional racism. The point here is that the issue is not just about minorities addressing minorities' issues with self-confidence; it is also about educating senior leaders about the institutional barriers.

> ## Pause for reflection
>
> Recall the events and reactions to George Floyd's murder in 2020:
> - What kinds of thoughts and feelings did you experience?
> - What was your institution's response?
> - Have you noticed any changes in institutional policy and your perspectives about racism?

Nurturing the anti-racist educator

Race is a complex, emotive and ever-present phenomenon that plays out differently in our daily lives. This is because *white* or *non-white*, everyone has a racialised identity based on unequal power and consequences

(Smithsonian, n.d.). Some recoil from the word racism itself; interpreting it as harsh and unsettling (Gillborn et al., 2016), while others vehemently reject the idea that racism has any meaningful impact on people's lives. Minoritised groups, on the other hand, continue to experience its pervasive effect on their own and their communities' educational and life outcomes. Additionally, tensions are ever-present about the use of words, e.g. *The N word* and their perceived meanings and implications. For example, at one time, the acronym BAEM (Black and Asian Ethnic Minority) was used indiscriminately for all non-white individuals, but it is now considered to be outdated, divisive and potentially discriminatory to some marginilised groups that might not fit into the BAME label (Mistlin, 2021).

A commitment to anti-racist practice is hard without engaging with the complexities and challenges of race and racism. Additionally, it requires a clear understanding of the history of racism, and its influences on society (Seidl, 2007). For example, one would need some understanding of the (mis) representation of influential people of colour in history (such as the little-known fact of black Roman emperors) to better understand the calls for decolonising the curriculum. This engagement also means undertaking a process of self-examination about one's beliefs and attitudes in dialogue with others (Gooden et al., 2018). But as Dlamini (2002) argues, there are limited opportunities in education to dissect and analyse these powerful concepts despite the impact that they have on educators and their students. For anti-racist practice to flourish, therefore, individuals need to be better informed about race and racism, but also be committed to examining their beliefs and assumptions to facilitate progress to the 'growth zone' (see Table 6.1).

Difficult conversations as a conduit for anti-racist thinking and action

Conversations about race are vital for understanding racism's impact on society and on the Academy (Miller-Klienhenz et al., 2021). These conversations can highlight preconceived ideas and assumptions and provide alternative interpretations and perspectives on contested terms and topics that can lead to critical consciousness (Miller-Kleinhenz et al., 2021; Watt, 2007). Moreover, they enable us to listen to alternative perspectives and to develop our knowledge and understanding.

However, such conversations are inherently 'difficult'. They are difficult because they challenge dearly held beliefs and values such as who counts as 'British'.

Additionally, they can awaken potentially conflicting views of beliefs or values about social justice issues (D'Andrea & Daniels, 2007), and require individual transformation involving a 'structural change in the way we see ourselves and our relationships' (Mezirow, 1978, p. 100). For example, individuals may dispute the basis of racism and its impact, resulting in fear, uncertainty and even anger, particularly when the conversation encourages the exploration of privilege (D'Andrea & Daniels, 2007). Others may worry about voicing uncertainties and fears, upsetting their peers by saying the wrong thing, or showing limited knowledge of the issues (Gooden & O'Doherty, 2015). In the right context, however, conversations about race can facilitate progress from the 'fear' zone to the 'learning' and 'transformation' zone, where the individual becomes progressively better informed about racism and prepared to take anti-racist action (Kendi, 2019).

So far, the discussion has outlined how the spotlight on institutional racism shifted institutions' focus from the individual to institutions' policies and activities to tackle racism in HE. However, I have also argued that this shift could, unwittingly, 'throw the baby out with the bath water' by undermining the focus on individuals' praxis of anti-racism through 'difficult conversations' about race. In the following section, I outline a methodology for difficult conversations with examples to illustrate its potential for facilitating personal growth and transformation.

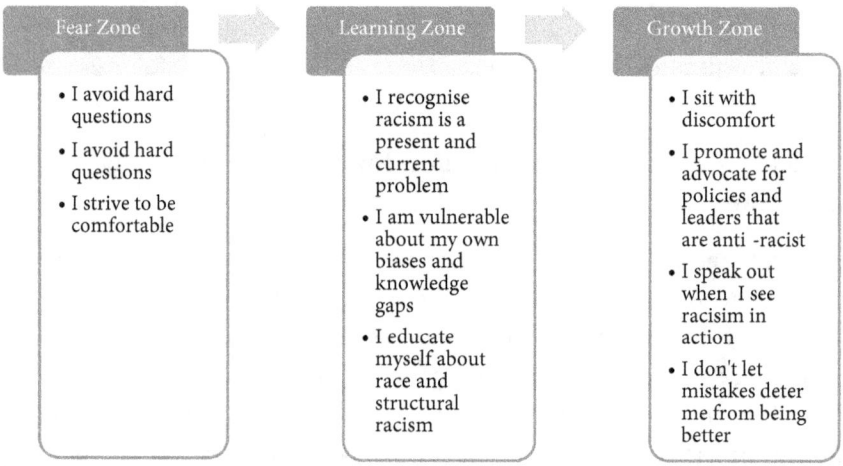

Figure 6.1 Becoming anti-racist behaviour. Adapted from www.SurgeryRedesign.com.

> **Pause for reflection**
> - Have you ever taken part in a conversation about race with friends or colleagues?
> - If not, what would you like to explore and examine?

The Community of Philosophical Inquiry (CoPI)

When the exchange of ideas and opinions is done in a respectful way there is at the very least, the possibility of empathy and at best a shift in one's perspective (Lipman, 2003). As outlined already, the topic of race and equity is complex, but discussion and interaction with others can be potentially transformative. The Community of Philosophical Enquiry (CoPI) draws on the Philosophy of Children (P4C) pedagogy that Matthew Lipman established to develop pupils' thinking. CoPI is underpinned by inquiry and dialogue that is conducted amongst a community of participants (Lipman, 2003). Importantly, the participants must 'buy into' the idea that beliefs and assumptions will be questioned, reasons must be given and evaluated, and clarification given and provided. In other words, it requires openness and willingness to be 'moved by good reasons' (Lipman, 2003; Splitter & Sharp, 1995).

CoPI is unique because, unlike other approaches to facilitate dialogue and discussion, it gives equal value to the caring, collaborative and critical and creative dimensions of thinking. Therefore, the role of the facilitator is central to this process, as she/he must ensure that the community of enquiry operates at its optimum level. Thus, the facilitator actively encourages the participants to state and justify their views and question their own and others' assumptions (Splitter & Sharp, 1995).

The role of the facilitator also extends to building the caring and collaborative dimension of dialogue. Through co-constructing the ground rules and the use of ice-breaker activities, the facilitator strives to minimise the 'threat to the self' and to build and embed trusting relationships. However, it is worth noting that the facilitator is not a neutral voice. Her/his world view and biases can inadvertently influence the ground rules, selection of stimuli, and the direction of the dialogue (Chetty & Suissa, 2016). Thus, while using the CoPI approach is an improvement on many fronts, it is not necessarily unproblematic; vigilance is therefore still needed to ensure that CoPI provides a genuine and authentic space for 'difficult' conversations in the context of a challenging topic such as race. In the following section, I outline how, in the aftermath of the BLM protests, a group of educators used CoPI to engage in 'difficult conversations' about race and equity in education.

Difficult conversations about race – a case study of CoPI in practice

During and after the BLM protests, I was approached by a colleague to facilitate CoPI enquiries relating to the topical issues of the day. Six early childhood educators took part in a self-initiated series of enquiries (4) over the course of a year. The participants were motivated by a desire to be accountable to their students, educate themselves about racism and explore practical actions they could take to address some of the issues in their own classrooms. In the following, I focus on two enquiries. After describing the two enquiries, I will reflect on how the approach provided a dialogic space to tackle difficult conversations about identity and responsibility, and an enabling environment for authentic interactions that highlighted its potential for learning and transformation.

Enquiry 1

Prior to the meeting date, the participants were sent a journal article entitled: Categorisation and minoritisation by Selvarajah et al. (2020). The article explored some of the dilemmas in categorising and labelling non-white groups. The authors argue that the term 'Minoritised' is better way to categorize students because it 'describe(s) intersectional forms of discrimination, and acknowledge the active processes involved in differential allocations of power, resources and ultimately health' (p. 1).

After discussing a summary of the article, the facilitator invited the participants to share their first thoughts and impressions. A common first response centred on the problematic nature of labels in terms of identity imposition on others (e.g. ethnic minority) and the effect they have on individuals. Typical comments revolved around the difference between self-chosen and imposed acronyms. Thus, a person of colour was considered by some as a more positive label than acronyms such as BAME. Others raised the significance of who is doing the categorisation so that some terms that are deemed offensive when a white person uses them may not have the same effect when used by a member of the marginalised community.

The next stage was to explore possible questions for the discussion. The following questions were proposed:

1. How do you, in early childhood, understand children's and families' multiple identities in an educational culture of capitalist capitalisation?
2. How do you understand multiple identities in a culture of capitalist/neoliberalist categorisation? (e.g. having to categorise children as EAL when they have multiple identities)
3. Why are some categorisations ok and some are not?

Most of the participants voted for question 3 and were invited to share their initial responses to the question. Initially, their responses explored the contexts in which categorisation were acceptable and when they were not. This led to a conclusion that, categorising is unproblematic in everyday life, e.g. categorising objects in supermarkets, but not when they are imposed on human beings. As the dialogue progressed, more concrete examples were also offered in relation to experiences, for example, of the conflicts in defining one's social class when one's education and life opportunities sharply differ from childhood friends and families. The dialogue seemed to highlight the untested assumptions that underpin labels and categories, offering a route to, perhaps, empathy towards people who are labelled as Black, or BAME.

By the end, a consensus was beginning to emerge that categorisation could be a problematic concept. For example, being labelled in a specific way, whether in terms of health or racial background, could facilitate additional support. Indeed, some organisations now offer targeted leadership development programmes. The discussion concluded with participants sharing their last thoughts on the question, leading the group to reflect on the power of language, i.e. in terms of what categorisation does in terms of social justice, and an emerging awareness of how categorisation can impact on their students' identities. The discussion led some to reflect on how they intuitively categorise their students without questioning their assumptions and the impact this may have on their students and the learning experiences offered.

Pause for reflection

- What questions would you wish to explore in relation to the issue of categorisation and labelling of individuals?
- Think about labels for a moment, what do you think is more important in your view? Self-chosen or assigned labels?

Enquiry 2

The stimulus for the enquiry was a series of statements that the participants were invited to categorise (Table 6.1).

After briefly considering the statements, the participants were invited to:

- Group the elements – and give reasons.
- Consider what kind of categories they used.
- Make connections between different elements – and give reasons.
- Decide which statement was the odd one out and to give reasons.
- Share any other comments/responses.

Based on this activity, the participants identified the following concepts as pertinent to the stimuli: *responsibility, silence, agency, power and lived experience*, before generating the following questions:

1. *How can we build collective responsibility to become an anti-racist institution?*
2. *How can we bridge the gap from non-racist to anti-racist?*
3. *Which should come first, collective or individual responsibility?*

Table 6.1 Stimulus for Enquiry 2.

1. Examining the historical roots and contemporary manifestations of racial prejudice and discrimination.
2. Exploring the influence of race and culture on one's own personal and professional attitudes and behaviour.
3. Identifying appropriate anti-racist resources to incorporate into the curriculum in different subject areas.
4. Identifying and counteracting bias and stereotyping in learning material.
5. Dealing with racial tensions and conflicts.
6. Identifying appropriate anti-racist resources to incorporate into the curriculum in different subject areas.
7. Developing new approaches to teaching using varying cognitive approaches to diverse learning styles.
8. Identifying appropriate assessment and placement procedures and practices.
9. Assessing the hidden curriculum and making it more inclusive and reflective of all students' experiences.
10. Ensuring that personnel policies and practices are consistent with equity goals and that they provide managers with the knowledge and skills to implement equity programs.

The participants voted for Question 1: *How can we build collective responsibility to become an anti-racist institution?* Compared to Enquiry 1, the stimulus was more personal and perhaps 'difficult' because it included examples of individual anti-racist action. The initial thoughts seemed to converge on institutional/collective practices as more important than individual actions, implying that institutional policies should facilitate individuals to act. However, as the dialogue progressed, the participants began to question the consensus. However, as the dialogue progressed, the participants began to question how effective the institutional policies can be if individuals do not partake in institutional initiatives activities that promote anti-racist practices.

The dialogue developed further when the group began to explore the concept of 'responsibility'. There were suggestions that responsibility at the individual and at the institutional level may be different. Individuals have responsibility to 'educate themselves and implement anti-racist practices', but at the same time institutions have a responsibility to prioritise anti-racist policies and create environments that support individuals to work towards racial justice in education, such as time and resources. The enquiry led to the following insights: the problematic nature of responsibility, the implications for individual and collective responsibility, and the interdependence between individual and collective responsibility.

> **Pause for reflection**
>
> - What question would like to explore in relation to individual and collective responsibility for nurturing anti-racist cultures?
> - Think about 'responsibility' for a moment: How important is what individuals do in developing anti-racist cultures? What are your reasons?

From the fear zone to the growth zone

The realisation of anti-racist policies is highly dependent on the extent to which individuals operate at the growth zone (see Figure 6.1). The growth zone is characterised by a readiness to speak out when encountering racism, be able to sit with discomfort, promote and advocate policies that are anti-racist and actively educate others about the effects of racism (Kendi, 2019). On reflection, I would argue that in Enquiries 1 and 2, there were discernible moments of relating to the *learning zone*. In Enquiry 1, we were able to explore the limits and possibilities of categorisation, and the conditions and criteria when categorisation might be ok, e.g. in relation to highlighting inequalities or protecting minoritised groups. This dialogue led to important insights about how our words reflect and extend power in ways that we only partially understand (Lupia & Norton, 2017).

Similarly, the questions of personal and institutional responsibility triggered reflections about individuals' roles and actions in promoting transformative change. The introduction of concepts such as *individual*, *collective* and *responsibility* forced the group to engage with the question at a deeper and more personal level. By changing the discussion from '*what can we do?*' to '*what are my individual responsibilities?*' the participants began to examine their beliefs, knowledge, assumptions and actions. It is true that questioning and potentially transforming deeply held beliefs and attitudes is no easy matter, as our identities are inextricably linked to how we see the world (Mezirow, 1978). However, given the readiness by the participants to question their assumptions and beliefs as well as the status-quo, it seems that opportunities for self-examination (as exemplified in this chapter) could be an important starting point and perhaps, an essential pre-requisite to re-envision the world and build individuals' confidence to engage in anti-racist action (Gooden et al., 2018; Mezirow, 1991).

Reflections on CoPI

Miller-Klienhenz et al.'s (2021) approach to instigate conversations about race in academia echoes some aspects of the CoPI approach. For example, staff were encouraged to select their own objectives for the course, operated under the principles of trust, agreed that it's okay to be uncomfortable, and committed to active listening and empathy, and a commitment to becoming agents of change. As a result, the majority felt they developed the confidence and courage to engage in these conversations with colleagues and felt better prepared to facilitate and partake in these discussions in the future.

In a similar way, CoPI enabled the participants to make progress in their knowledge and understanding of some key issues in race and equity in education. Philosophical thinking enabled the participants to explore key concepts such as '*responsibility*', provide examples and counterexamples (of acceptable and unacceptable categorisation), explore distinctions (responsibility means different things at collective and institutional levels) and pose thought-provoking questions (*are categories and identities the same?*). At the same time, caring and collaborative thinking were evident in the way participants took turns, were respectful to each other, listened to each other, and built on each other's ideas. Indeed, a common consensus was that CoPI enabled an authentic space to 'think out loud' and to consider alternative perspectives and learn from each other. The participants acknowledged fear of saying the wrong thing or upsetting someone was a considerable barrier to 'difficult conversations'. Additionally, while stimuli were provocative, they allowed discussion of challenging ideas.

As stated earlier, ground rules (such as *be respectful of others' views*) are commonly adopted to establish a 'safe space' so that individuals feel they can express their views without fear of judgment or conflict (Hardiman et al., 2007). However, though the notion of a 'safe space' is well-established, it is a contested concept. In relation to ground rules such as 'agree to disagree', for instance, Arao & Clemens argue that 'safe spaces' can 'conflate safety with comfort' (2013, p. 143) and question whether it is reasonable to expect safety in dialogues around social justice. For example, some participants may feel pressured to sidestep 'difficult conversations', e.g. through refraining from sharing their lived experiences of racism, or challenging the status quo. In contrast, the idea of brave spaces is an environment where 'participants feel able to be honest, candid, self-disclosing' (Ali, 2017; Stanlick, 2015, p. 117). Therefore, I consider the space that we created and occupied in the enquiries as a 'brave space'.

As a context for undertaking difficult conversations, CoPI offers many advantages. The dialogue is driven by the participants' interests and questions so that they are more likely to be invested in the discussions. The approach has a clear structure with clear expectations about the participants' and facilitator's roles (SAPERE, 2010) which is likely to minimise the 'threat to the self' and encourage participation (Rodgers & Freiberg, 1970). Moreover, there is a shared understanding of the underlying principles of creative, critical, collaborative and caring thinking (SAPERE, 2010) that encourages participants to 'creatively hold tension' rather than avoid complexity (Stanlick, 2015). Thus, inherent in CoPI is an acknowledgement of liminality in relation to truth and knowing (Bhabha, 2004; Lipman, 2003) and a commitment to a community of inquiry (SAPERE, 2010; Turner, 2012). CoPI, therefore, offers a valuable methodology for 'difficult conversations'. However, it is still worth noting that deliberative approaches such as CoPI are not a panacea to all 'difficult conversations' (Lupia & Norton, 2017). It is uncertain whether the outcomes are meaningful and sustainable as we do not know if the participants' reflections and insights (as in the enquiries highlighted earlier) necessarily lead them to reassess their beliefs and future actions.

Conclusion

Transformative and meaningful change in how universities tackle overt, implicit and structural racism is highly dependent on the individuals who work in these institutions. But given the complexities and the challenges of anti-racist praxis, individuals need spaces for self-examination and opportunities to develop their knowledge and understanding of issues related to race and equity. It is through challenging and difficult conversations with others that we begin to develop meaningful self-knowledge about ourselves and problematic concepts such as power, identity and equity. The 'difficulty' of these conversations, however, necessitates trusting and safe spaces where critical discussions can flourish. The Community of Philosophical Inquiry (CoPI), with its emphasis on the caring critical, collaborative creative thinking offers one possibility for meaningful self-examination within a supportive challenging collaborative context. To conclude, without attention to individual transformation, institutional policies, on their own, are unlikely to result in sustainable and transformative change. Universities, therefore, have a duty to actively promote spaces for 'difficult conversations' about the racial dimension of teaching, learning and being in academia.

References

AdvanceHE https://www.advance-he.ac.uk/equality-charters/race-equality-charter. Retrieved 21 December 2022, from www.advancehe.ac.uk.

Ahmed, S. K. (2018). *Being the change. Lessons and strategies to teach social comprehension*. Heinemann.

Ali, D. (2017). Safe spaces and brave spaces. *NASPA Research and Policy Institute, 2*, pp. 1–13.

Arao, B., & Clemens, K. (2013). From safe spaces to brave spaces. In L. Landerman (Ed.). *The Art of Effective Facilitation: Reflections from Social Justice Educators* (pp. 135–50). Stylus Publishing.

Arday, J., & Mirza, H. S. (Eds.) (2018). *Dismantling race in higher education: Racism, whiteness and decolonising the academy*. Palgrave Macmillan.

Bhabha, H. K. (2004). *The location of culture*. Routledge.

Chetty, D., & Suissa, J. (2016). 'No go areas': Racism and discomfort in the community of inquiry. In *The Routledge International Handbook of Philosophy for Children* (pp. 43–50). Routledge.

D'Andrea, M., & Daniels, J. (2007). Dealing with institutional racism on campus: Initiating difficult dialogues and social justice advocacy interventions. *College Student Affairs Journal, 26*(2), pp. 169–76.

Dawson, M. (2015). Sociology as conversation: Zygmunt Bauman's applied sociological hermeneutics. *Sociology, 49*(3), pp. 582–7.

Dee, T., & Gershenson, S. (2017). Unconscious Bias in the Classroom: Evidence and Opportunities. *Stanford Centre for Education Policy Analysis.* Retrieved December 2022.

Dlamini, S. N. (2002). From the other side of the desk: Notes on teaching about race when racialised. *Race Ethnicity and Education, 5*(1), pp. 51–66. https://doi.org/10.1080/13613320120117199.

Ebbinghaus, M., & Huang, S. (2022). Institutional consequences of the black lives matter movement: Towards diversity in elite education. *Political Studies Review, 21*(4), pp. 847–56. https://doi.org/10.1177/14789299221132428.

Equalities Act (2010). Retrieved 21 December 2022, from https://www.legislation.gov.uk/ukpga/2010/15/contents.

Freire, P. (1973). *Pedagogy of hope.* Routledge.

Gillborn, D., Rollock, N., Warmington, P., & Demack, S. (2016). Race, Racism and Education: inequality, resilience and reform in policy. *University of Birmingham.* Retrieved 21 December 2022 from www.efaidnbmnnnibpcajpcglclefindmkaj/https://soc-for-ed-studies.org.uk/wp-content/uploads/2019/02/GillbornD-et-al_Race-Racism-and-Education.pdf.

Gooden, M. A., & O'Doherty, A. (2015). Do you see what I see? Fostering aspiring leaders' racial awareness. *Urban Education, 50*(2), pp. 225–55. https://doi.org/10.1177/0042085914534273.

Gooden, M. A., Davis, B. W., Spikes, D. D., Hall, D. L., & Lee, L. (2018). Leaders changing how they act by changing how they think: Applying principles of an antiracist principal preparation program. *Teachers College Record, 120*(14), pp. 1–26. https://doi.org/10.1177/016146811812001409.

Hardiman, R., Jackson, B., & Griffin, P. (2007). Conceptual foundations for social justice education. In L. A. Bell, M. Adams, & P. Griffin (Eds.). *Teaching for Diversity and Social Justice.* 2nd ed. (pp. 35–66). Routledge.

Harrison, N., & Waller, R. (2017). Success and impact in widening participation policy: What works and how do we know? *Higher Education Policy, 30*(2), pp. 141–60. https://doi.org/10.1057/s41307-016-0020-x.

Kendi, I. X. (2019). *How to be an antiracist.* One world.

Law, I. (2017). Building the Anti-racist University, action and new agendas. *Race Ethnicity and Education, 20*(3), pp. 332–43. https://doi.org/10.1080/13613324.2016.1260232.

Lipman, M. (2003). Thinking in Education. Cambridge University Press.

Loke, G. (2015). Breaking the race inequality cycle in higher education: A change of focus is needed to break the statistical groundhog day. *Aiming Higher,* pp. 42–4. Retrieved 7 July 2022 from http://nectar.northampton.ac.uk/7264/1/Aiming%20Higher.pdf#page=44.

Lupia, A., & Norton, A. (2017). Inequality is always in the room: Language & power in deliberative democracy. *Daedalus, 146*(3), pp. 64–76. Retrieved 21 December 2022 from https://doi.org/10.1162/DAED_a_00447.

Mezirow, J. (1978). Perspective transformation. *Adult Education*, *28*(2), pp. 100–10.

Mezirow, J. (1991). *Transformative dimensions of adult learning*. Jossey-Bass.

Miller-Kleinhenz, J. M., Kuzmishin Nagy, A. B., Majewska, A. A., Adebayo Michael, A. O., Najmi, S. M., Nguyen, K. H., & Fonkoue, I. T. (2021). Let's talk about race: changing the conversations around race in academia. *Communications Biology*, *4*(1), pp. 1–6. https://doi.org/10.1038/s42003-021-02409-2.

Mistlin, A. (2021). So, the term BAME has had its day: What should replace it? Retrieved 21 December 2022, from https://www.theguardian.com/commentisfree/2021/apr/08/bame-britain-ethnic-minorities-acronym.

Noon, M. (2018). Pointless diversity training: Unconscious bias, new racism and agency. *Work, Employment and Society*, *32*(1), pp. 198–209. https://doi.org/10.1177/0950017017719841.

Office for Students (2021) *Regulatory advice 15: Monitoring and intervention: Guidance for providers registered with the office for students*. Retrieved 7 July 2021, from https://www.officeforstudents.org.uk/media/e65c2c7f-cd77-403e-a582-af7d6e1909f1/ra15-mint-guidance-update-october21.pdf.

Parveen, N. (2021). *Unconscious bias training alone will not stop discrimination critics say*. Retrieved 7 July 2021, from https://www.theguardian.com/money/2021/mar/02/unconscious-bias-training-alone-will-not-stop-discrimination-say-critics.

Race Relations Act (Amendment) (2000). Retrieved 21 December 2022, from https://www.legislation.gov.uk/ukpga/2000/34/contents.

Rogers, C. R., & Freiberg, H. J. (1970). *Freedom to learn*. Charles Merrill.

Rollock, N. (2009). *The Stephen Lawrence inquiry 10 years on*. Retrieved 21 December 2022, from www.runnymedetrust.org. Retrieved 9 May 2010.

Seidl, B. (2007). Working with communities to explore and personalize culturally relevant pedagogies: Push, double images, and raced talk. *Journal of Teacher Education*, *58*(2), pp. 168–83. https://DOI:10.1177/0022487106297845.

Selvarajah, S., Shannon, G., Muraya, K., Lasoye, S., Corona, S., Achiume, E.T., & Devakumar, D. (2020). Racism, the public health crisis we can no longer ignore. *The Lancet*, *395*(10242), pp. e112–e113. https://doi:10.1136/bmjgh-2020-004508.

Smithsonian (n.d.) *Talking about Race: Race and Racial Identity*. Retrieved 25 March 2023, from https://nmaahc.si.edu/learn/talking-about-race/topics/race-and-racial-identity.

Society for the Advancement of Philosophical Enquiry and Reflection in Education (SAPERE). Retrieved 7 July 2021, from www.sapere.org.uk.

Splitter, L. J., & Sharp, A. M. (1995). *Teaching for better thinking: The classroom community of inquiry*. Australian Council for Educational Research.

Stanlick, S. (2015). *Getting 'real' about transformation: The role of brave spaces in creating disorientation and transformation*. Michigan Publishing, University of Michigan Library.

Stone, D., Patton, B., & Heen, S. (2011). *Difficult conversations: How to discuss what matters most*. Portfolio Penguin.

Turner, E. (2012). *Communitas: The anthropology of collective joy*. Springer.

Walker, S., Bennett, I., Kettory, P., Pike, C., & Walker, L. (2023). 'Deep understanding' for anti-racist school transformation: School leaders' professional development in the context of Black Lives Matter. *The Curriculum Journal, 34*(1), pp. 156–72. DOI: 10.1002/curj.189.

Watt, S. K. (2007). Difficult dialogues, privilege and social justice: Uses of the Privileged Identity Exploration (PIE) model in student affairs practice. *College Student Affairs Journal, 26*(2), pp. 114–26.

Welton, A. D., Owens, D. R., & Zamani-Gallaher, E. M. (2018). Anti-racist change: A conceptual framework for educational institutions to take systemic action. *Teachers College Record, 120*(14), pp. 1–22. https://doi.org/10.1177/016146811812001402.

Challenging Hierarchical Barriers through Co-Creation of Curricula in HE: Students-Lecturers Reflection on Critical Dialogue

Elizabeth Collins and Hannah Wilson

Introduction

The increased integration of student voice in higher education (HE) has been steadily rising over the years as universities face the ever-growing challenge of recruiting students from a competitive pool of candidates (Freemen, 2016). Subsequently, student councils, forums and surveys have become a common place to provide students with the opportunity to have a say in how our universities operate (Bovill & Woolmer, 2019). However, the level of intervention students are afforded relies on the level to which academic staff are able and willing to engage (Bovill et al., 2011). There is a growing body of research suggesting that student involvement needs to and can go deeper than the current idea of student councils and surveys associated with student voice. Co-creation is one of the means to provide opportunities where students can work collaboratively with academic staff to design curricula, learning outcomes and pedagogical styles (Bovill et al., 2011). The benefit of such work is said to provide transformative learning opportunities for all involved, broadening the thinking of both academic staff and students (Healey et al., 2014).

With these co-creative principles in mind, we, as undergraduate students took the opportunity to work in collaboration with our lecturers to reimagine two already taught modules. Our group comprised of four students and two members of academic staff and we used a dialogic approach over three focused session. The modules were discussed openly in relation to content and delivery from both student and teacher perspectives. These conversations were difficult and, at times, uncomfortable as power dynamics and hierarchies were uncovered and brought out to the open. This kind of discomfort, however, leads to a greater understanding of partnerships that can be built within learning communities when power dynamics are acknowledged and addressed as illustrated in this chapter. Drawing on the work of Freire (1970), we discuss how difficult conversations about power dynamics between students and lecturers engaged in co-creation can lead to transformative realisations for both. It is our hope that this chapter will offer food for thought to both students and educators in HE and encourage them to reflect on their internalised beliefs and assumptions about their 'place' in education.

Teacher-student dialogue in the 'third space'

Freire (1970) discussed the paradox of student-teacher relationships in traditional educational structures, which are based upon students as recipients of knowledge and teachers as knowledge providers. This is referred to as the banking concept of education, in which the more educators can deposit 'wisdom' in their students, the more they are valued as a teacher (Freire, 1970). This paradox appears throughout the current structure within HE today, with performance indicators and assessment outcomes being valued over equitable caring education (Bovill, 2020). This phenomenon places lecturers in a position of power in which they become gatekeepers for what constitutes knowledge (Bovill et al., 2011). The hierarchy upheld by this system positions students as inferior to their knowledge providers. Both conscious and unconscious preservation of this hierarchy is in place to maintain the status quo; therefore, students become bystanders within their own education instead of active participants.

The student body in HE is often a diverse group of individuals with different lived experiences. Yet, upon arrival in HE classrooms, their identities are often partly homogenised and assumed (Griffiths et al., 2018). As institutions seek to become more socially just by attracting a more diverse range of students, we argue that a more democratic education should also be sought in order to reflect the diversity of student bodies, while striving for a more equitable caring education. However, the challenge that arises from encouraging a more diverse student body lies in the provision of inclusive teaching that champions differences among individuals. Freire (1970) suggested that a move towards problem-posing education could provide an alternative to the banking concept, as it utilises differing identities and experiences as an aid to education. Through problem-posing education, teachers may gain different perspectives to inform more inclusive teaching practices. For example, dialogic education incorporates collaborative knowledge sharing and less rote learning techniques, which therefore lends itself to a more inclusive style of education as it becomes more dynamic (Wegerif, 2006). Contrary to the banking model of education, engaging with collaborative knowledge sharing requires people as individuals, comprised of their own stories, identity and experiences, to bring themselves to the forefront. It was through our own experiences of co-creation, that these aspects of ourselves were brought into the conversation and used to frame our perspectives on the modules taught. However, bringing personal aspects of oneself to conversation means making yourself vulnerable to the judgements of others; yet it is such vulnerability that leads to a greater connection between academia and lived experiences of students and lecturers. This openness is required not only by students but by academic staff, who in most cases will need to take the lead on this way of being to demonstrate the link between experience and academic narratives (hooks, 1994).

Community of Philosophical Inquiry (COPI), which was used as the framework for co-creation within our research project, may be considered a form of problem-posing education (Lipman, 2003). COPI develops individuals' dialogic reasoning skills by encouraging questioning of a provided stimulus (Topping & Trickey, 2007). To encourage effective questioning, COPI nurtures caring, creative and critical development of questions (Lipman, 2003). Throughout the whole process of COPI, students and staff are equals, with staff acting more as facilitators within the process than directors, and value is placed on the process of thinking, not just getting answers right (Resnick *et al.*, 2018). All enquiries following the COPI structure must start by laying ground rules for expected behaviour during the enquiry: in our project these were co-constructed among the group to provide the opportunity for all to direct the values we would be governed by. Aligning expectations helped to create a respectful community atmosphere for the conversation to take place and helped to remove some of the aspects that make conversations challenging. For example, agreement of a phrase to use if your opinion differed from that which had already been said. Pre-agreement of such terms meant we were able to speak honestly without internal barriers, opening up a 'third space' where students and academic staff felt able to engage in open dialogue.

Lubicz-Nawrocka (2019) describes the third space in education as a specific setting with 'shared responsibility, equity, reciprocity and empathy' (Lubicz-Nawrocka, 2019, p. 39). It was noticed within the third space we created that the student-to-teacher relationship evolved into more of a partnership. These new partnerships between students and academic staff allowed for a more honest dialogue to occur, compared with the previous relationship, and provided insight for both sides to broaden their understanding of the taught content and how it was relayed. These conversations challenged us as students to view HE from the alternative perspective of a lecturer providing the opportunity to see how their personal educational philosophies work within the HE structure. Through gaining an understanding of each person's position, we felt a more respectful partnership was built which allowed for more honest conversation. Such honesty also posed potential fear of negative repercussions; however, in our experience the respect and openness created through having such difficult conversations in the third space later transferred to the classroom through more thoughtful and respectful conversations with both our peers and the academic staff.

> ## Pause for reflection
>
> - How can reciprocal student-teacher relationships be built during teaching time to enable open dialogue between stakeholders?

Reaching the third space where honest and meaningful dialogue could be shared between students and academic staff was not a quick process. The sessions were originally intended to be an hour but all three exceeded this time as it felt like the surface had only been scratched after the initial hour. This may demonstrate the time investment required to build the partnership relationships that enable meaningful and potentially difficult conversations to take place (Bovill, 2020). The time and performative constraints placed upon staff make it challenging to commit to engaging with students in this way and may therefore be a limiting factor for both staff and students (Bovill, 2020; Bovill *et al.*, 2011). Our research took place in addition to the usual teaching commitments of the academic staff and lecture time of the students over the summer break. Consequently, co-creation requires a strong commitment to the ideals of democratic education from all parties to get involved.

The power dynamics and hierarchies at play in higher education

> As someone ... you know, not everyone has that thing within them to challenge authority which is what K and A [the tutors] would represent in that situation. That is a really big thing, for me sitting here as an undergraduate student and say,

'Sorry Dr ...,I think you have got this wrong'. I think there is a big power, sort of, relationship there, you know, it takes quite something for you to feel that strongly about – Participant D

The concept of students challenging the authority of academic staff's decisions became a prominent fixture of our discussions within the project. We concluded that the varying levels to which decisions could be challenged were influenced by the student's perception of themselves as undergraduates being lower down the academic hierarchy in comparison with their titled lecturers. As demonstrated by the extract above, lecturers are seen to represent the authority over students, who fear the consequences of their actions in class. As lecturers assess students' work personally, it can sometimes feel to the student that they 'choose' if we pass or fail. Such detachment from one's own grades demonstrates the passive student identity created by the banking concept of education as students perceive education as something that happens to them, not something in which they are involved (Healey *et al.*, 2014). This makes the concept of co-creation challenging to students as, by the time they reach HE, they have spent years occupying the passive student role and therefore may not know how to contribute towards their learning (Lubicz-Nawrocka & Bovill, 2021). The fear and embarrassment felt by getting it wrong in front of an authority figure may quell any thoughts of input, even when students are asked directly to do so. Likewise, co-creation felt 'unusual' in that our voice was sought after and our views were weighted equally to those of our lecturers. As we adopted this different, and somewhat uncomfortable, way of co-creating our learning environment, we experienced a dynamic process where knowledge transmission became a two-way process between all parties (Bovill, 2011; Healey *et al.*, 2014). The hierarchy in place made this change uncomfortable and required working through as part of the conversation. Once we had identified that we felt the impact of the hierarchies at play within our academic course team, we were able to address it through a discussion acknowledging the academic staff's relative powers within the hierarchy. The result of this understanding meant our previously more passive student identities evolved into a more agentic form.

Moving away from passive identities can be difficult for students, and it is argued that more needs to be done to enhance student empowerment. The concept of student empowerment also emerged from our data in relation to the impact of the student voice. For example, throughout the project, we questioned the 'usefulness' of our feedback and input on our own studies since we never knew how our feedback affected the development of the learning materials or communities. We argue that perhaps we did not feel empowered to provide feedback at the time of delivery of these modules and so we were unable to receive that benefit. Looking at empowerment as a term in itself, it may reveal a direct demonstration of the perceived control lecturers hold and can, therefore, choose to share with students (Young & Jerome, 2020). Student empowerment is often viewed as an overwhelmingly positive concept rooted in liberation from oppressive forces. However, we question the impact of such empowerment narratives on students, as such freedom positions the problem within the student, excusing the overall domineering structures from their part in subjugation (Hicks & Lloyd, 2021). Moreover, when viewed in combination with other student voice protocols, such as student councils, the formalisation of ways in which students can provide feedback may be further disempowering to some (Healey *et al.*, 2014; Lubicz-Nawrocka, 2017). Some students may prefer to speak directly with academic staff for fear of 'getting staff in trouble' if they follow the official feedback procedure that is directed to senior members of the institution. Yet, others may prefer the degree of separation a formalised procedure brings, as it avoids the difficult conversation with their individual lecturer. The differing preferences demonstrate the complexity of determining what is empowering and for whom. In all versions of student voice, providing students with the agency to choose what empowers them allows for a shift in power to occur.

It is imperative to note that formalising student feedback procedures demonstrates a more corporate agenda of HE, placing students as consumers purchasing a product (Canning, 2017). As with the purchasing of any other product in consumerist societies, if they are subsequently unsatisfied with its contents, they are able to complain. This was particularly noticeable during the Covid-19 pandemic; when teaching moved online, value for money became a prominent storyline from a student perspective as it was suggested this was not the service that had been paid for (Pan, 2020). Although, in our case, co-creation provided the opportunity for students' voices to be heard and responded to in a collaborative way, some may see engaging with student voice from a consumerist perspective as keeping the customer happy. The consumerist stance may mean that some students feel more able to voice their opinions in order to receive a more tailored service towards their needs, and in the process become less passive in their learning, knowing they can change it (Cook-Sather, 2020). However, this commercialisation of education reinforces the banking concept of education where knowledge is viewed as something to be bought and which, as discussed, works mainly to maintain the status quo. Breaking this status quo requires an internal challenge of your own student identity and the way in which you view HE. Therefore, we encourage you to reflect on the following statements and questions.

> **Pause for reflection**
>
> The conflicting stances on HE as a consumerist endeavour creates a difficult conversation in itself: who is empowered by this view and who is disempowered by it? The discussion around the marketisation of HE is permeated with political and social stances on the world, and therefore can be uncomfortable to discuss with others. It evokes the need to reflect on how you see HE: Is it a product you are purchasing to further your own economic prosperity or is it a way to widen your understanding and open your mind to different thoughts and ideas? Undoubtedly your answer to this will inform your view of the hierarchy at play in HE. Furthermore, it is possible you may occupy the grey area between the two, respecting the current known hierarchy in the knowledge you could complain when required. The existence of this grey area also means the decision to attend a HE setting itself doesn't necessarily equate to the abandoning of passive student identities and actively engaging in HE. However, confronting these underlying assumptions can unlock a deeper level of enlightenment over our own learning experience, leading to a greater understanding of ourselves and our learning.

Partnerships in learning communities

I feel like you have always both been very easy to talk to from the beginning of our courses um, so I think I have felt like I could just talk to you about things without feeling like you are going to judge me or you are going to be like, no, you are not right or something like that. – Participant B

The concept of a trusting partnership became prevalent during the discussions on the content of the co-created modules in the project. Ultimately, it was clear that we as the participants would not receive the direct benefits of updated modules. Therefore, we placed our trust in the academic staff to take the feedback on board and implement it where possible. Furthermore, as the discussions took place in an open conversation there was no anonymity and, therefore, we had to trust whatever was discussed would not be held against us by the lecturers in future modules. The extract above demonstrates the foundation of this trust was built within the delivery of the module as the participant suggests it was their relationship with the lecturers, as people who you could talk to without fear of judgement that enabled them to get involved with the project. Consequently, to impact the learning materials and delivery of content, we must acknowledge the influence of the personal connections made within the diverse learning community that direct the possibility of honest and meaningful feedback.

The multiple relationships at play within diverse learning communities show the importance of cultivating a safe and comfortable learning environment (Bovill, 2020). Engaging with a learning community, that being both academic staff and other students, and feeling part of it is said to improve academic attainment (Healey *et al.*, 2014). Within our project, we aligned our learning values through the implementation of COPI and the construction of ground rules for conversation to ensure a safe space was created. However, performatively driven education makes learning communities more difficult to cultivate as competition is encouraged under the requirement for students to demonstrate their worth by regurgitating their 'banked' knowledge (Maguad, 2018). As such, only students that perform this way are validated, causing inequality and mistrust within the learning community. For us, through taking part in co-creation, our lecturers changed the dynamic of what was valued which allowed us to see each other as equals learning together rather than competitors. Furthermore, through this change, our lecturers became a more integral part of our learning community as opposed to external knowledge providers. Therefore, to bridge the divisions created by a culture of competition, academic staff need to take the lead on decentralising the perceived norm, inspiring us to move towards a collaborative learning philosophy, where we are valued and empowered as individuals.

As with the development of any partnership, trust is something that develops over time and needs to exist both ways (Healey *et al.*, 2014). The further down the path of co-creation you go, as the trust develops, the partnership deepens. In our experience, this creates a stronger learning community that transcends beyond the initial COPI and into the classroom. In our experience, previous engagement in expressing student voice on a university-wide scale through anonymised end-of-module feedback forms were poorly received as merely a tick-box exercise. We felt that the ambiguity of such forms with pre-set answers of 'strongly agree' to 'strongly disagree' were not a sign of students being heard, as the data the forms would produce could not accurately portray student's perception of a module (Brooman *et al.*, 2015). Within our research discussions, we collectively concluded that said forms discouraged us from engaging with feedback as it felt disingenuous and created a mistrust of the genuine desire for meaningful feedback.

During our discussions, the reason behind the participants' involvement came to the forefront. Unpicking motives can be an uneasy situation and the ensuing conversation may be difficult, but it is one that is imperative to the success of co-creation. Within our group, one reason stated for taking part was owing to the lack of opportunities for networking and experience to put on CVs due to remote learning. The motives behind students' willingness to engage with co-creation may impede the perception of their participation, therefore, requiring trust that, even if other motives are present, they do not impact their contribution to the project (Canning, 2017). Furthermore, it was clear that our lecturers leading the co-creation were keen advocates of the positive impact of the method which, consequently, created an expectation for us as students to provide something that was 'worthwhile' to fulfil their reasons for engaging in co-creation. Such narratives around taking part for personal gain on both sides may create a barrier to the formation of trusting partnerships between staff and students. However, through navigating the difficult conversation of motives for participation, further trust is built within the budding partnership between lecturers and students. Reflecting on our own experience of co-creation, it was our trust in the learning community created during our sessions that participation would be a positive step for all regardless of individual motives. Furthermore, the partaking in these difficult conversations allowed us to revisit our perception of the people we learn with, and the positive impact collaboration has to transform our own learning experiences.

Transformative nature of co-creation

> *Because I think that this has definitely changed the way that I would approach things in the future and sort of giving me more, I suppose belief, that actually if we have you for another module in level 6 or something that actually I could say to you, K, I think this was really great, but I didn't enjoy this or, like, and I feel like you'd actually want to hear it.* – Participant D

The experience of collaborative working partnerships between students and academic staff is suggested to be transformational for all involved. The benefits are said to provide an increased level of engagement from students, a positive impact on student self-worth as they feel validated by having their opinions heard, and the cultivation of employability skills (Lubicz-Nawrocka, 2019). Co-creation also allows students and academic staff to move beyond the traditional hierarchy discussed (Hutchings *et al.*, 2013). The transformation of this relationship means that the learning experiences for all involved can be improved as barriers, such as power dynamics, become less obtrusive.

A student who requires alternative means of communication, for example, may be more likely to voice this requirement within a partnership (Healey *et al.*, 2014), the outcome of which may be beneficial to themselves and others. Moreover, the dialogue that takes place to come to such arrangements allows students to develop their professional communication skills and reasoning skills within a caring environment. If education is to aid social justice, producing more critically conscious, communal-minded citizens will help; however, they need to be given the opportunity to cultivate dialogic reasoning. Such skills go beyond what is required by universities; dialogic reasoning and the ability to have potentially difficult conversations can be utilised in all other aspects of life while also increasing future employability prospects (Temple Clothier & Matheson, 2019).

The process of co-creation can also broaden the variety of voices heard within educational institutions. Universities have often been founded upon a very particular type of person: usually white, able-bodied, and middle class (Attridge, 2021). Despite recent moves towards widening participation of marginalised identities, these efforts may be ill-effective if the experience of being at university homogenises the student body to the previous 'norm' (Symonds, 2021). Providing the opportunity for more voices to be honestly heard may allow varying perspectives to be gained and responded to. The current view of knowledge means such perspectives are only viewed when passed on from the academic staff who, depending on their own positionality, might never have considered the experience of all their students (Canning, 2017). It is through this collection of perspectives in co-creation that a more inclusive, democratic education system may be cultivated.

A more democratic education may also aid a more democratic society (Sant, 2019). As students transform their thinking by gathering a variety of opinions, they develop a stronger sense of self and, thus, become more civic-minded citizens (Lubicz-Nawrocka, 2019). Furthermore, they develop a greater sense of empathy towards others who may experience the world differently and for whom the civic society is not currently easy to navigate (Hermsen *et al.*, 2017). Consequently, placing the emphasis on developing a more inclusive, empathetic community who can think critically and respectfully may alter the societal structures in which we live. The more people who take on this stance within our society, the more that the structures and systems which uphold the current norms may be critically investigated and demystified, enabling a cultural shift towards more equitable systems (Sant, 2019).

> **Pause for reflection**
> - Consider times when you critically analyse norms that exist in our society. What helps to shape your analysis?

Barriers to transformation through co-creation

So, then we are very aware of the fact that when we do give feedback, although as a lecturer or module lead, they may really agree with themselves, there is so many hoops they have to jump through, so it just seems like it is a token to give the feedback, but it is often too challenging to put in the practice or to change the module. – Participant C

In order to unlock the benefits co-creation has to offer in leading to transformative thinking, all stakeholders need to be willing to experience such transformation: without this willingness a barrier is created (Bovill *et al.*, 2011; Mercer-Mapstone & Mercer, 2018). This willingness, most likely, requires a level of dialogue to instigate this approach and to discuss the potential barriers – this dialogue can be difficult for both parts. Part of the difficulty in these conversations is the mind frame of those taking part: you need to be open to changing thoughts and developing on what you thought you knew. The enjoyment of learning comes from transcending the boundary between what is known and unknown (Mapstone-Mercer & Mercer, 2018). Consequently, when both students and staff alike escape the monotony of having a prescribed curriculum, the excitement generated becomes the key part.

The concept of transformation may not always be viewed positively as the development of thoughts and reconsideration of what you once believed can be deeply unsettling (Lumb & Bunn, 2021). Hence, for both students and academic staff, co-creation will strike a level of concern. Academic staff will need to relinquish some level of control over their teaching, and students may be anxious their words may be miscommunicated or misconstrued, resulting in disastrous effects later down the line. Part of our initial nervousness to take part in the project certainly stemmed from this mindset. Therefore, within our current structures, it will not be possible for co-creation to occur without academic staff taking the initial lead. The reluctance to make a move towards more democratic education may be partially rooted in the scrutiny of performance statistics, but also in resistance from the students to abandon their passive learner identities and to disrupt the status quo of current hierarchies. Structural changes, in the way 'good' students are regarded as those who can regurgitate the most banked knowledge to perform in standardised tests, may be required and, as such, this can feel overwhelming. Yet, on a fundamental level, the cultivation of a learning community that respects and humanises individuals may assist in the move away from passive learner identities towards a wider change. We suggest this wider change is possible through the navigation of difficult conversations in which the process of developing, challenging, and changing thoughts is valued over the outcome.

For a student to feel they have a seat at the metaphorical table, it is not only important that their voice is present, but also that it has power and is listened to (Cook-Sather, 2020). Structural inequalities that currently exist within institutions mean some voices are disproportionately listened to over others (Healey *et al.*, 2014). Depending on the type of co-creation being used, there is sometimes the need for a selection process to decide which students are able to participate in the partnership projects. This raises ethical considerations around how participation is determined. Moreover, even when it is left to the students to volunteer, those already engaged and thriving in HE may be more likely to contribute than those from marginalized groups or those with lower academic attainment (Bovill *et al.*, 2016). As such it is argued that this makes co-creation an elitist program which benefits those already at an advantage within HE settings (Cook-Sather, 2020). Therefore, for co-creation to be a truly inclusive strategy, these inequalities need to be considered to diversify the voices heard.

Concluding thoughts

This chapter furthers Freire's (1970) suggestion to move away from the banking concept of education towards more democratic problem-posing education, through the use of co-creation. We propose that using a more collaborative and creative technique to alter curricular would result in education becoming more transformative and inclusive for all. A key principle of this focuses on encouraging critical thinking within institutions, which may challenge the traditional ideas of the lecturer being the 'sage on the stage' (Bovill, 2020). Furthermore, critical thinking enables students to become more active and engaged within the learning community, meaning education ceases to be something that is done to them. We hope that such a move towards more critically conscious beings would bring about further social change within our societies, as students are not taught subject content in isolation of its real-world context. We propose that providing the time and space to engage in difficult conversations within HE can enable a third space in which social change can be experienced through the breaking down of hierarchical barriers. Inhabiting this third space can then allow further difficult conversations to flourish and deepen our own understanding of the purpose of HE and its structures and systems in which we operate.

Our experience of taking part in co-creation has transformed our thinking in many ways. First, the way we view knowledge, learning, and the purpose of higher education has changed. Our participation demonstrated to us the difference between knowledge as chunks of information passed down from lecturers to students and knowledge as an evolving process of the way in which we think. The project was not graded, nor did it require written engagement, and therefore did not feel like we were specifically 'learning' in the traditional 'gaining information' sense of the term which we had unknowingly adopted. Therefore, at the beginning, neither of us would have ever said we were taking part to gain 'knowledge', but merely an experience to take with us into our future practice. However, our engagement with the project and consequent reshaping of the relationship between ourselves and our lecturers meant, in further modules after the project, we felt more confident to speak up in class and provide our opinion or experience as this felt more validated than before. Knowing our lecturers valued us as individuals meant we felt less defined by the marks we had received from them previously and more confident in our own ability to learn. In this respect, the development of relationships created in the third space transcended the classroom.

Conversations between students and academic staff can be made uncomfortable by the traditional student and teacher positions that each person occupies, yet when these positions are moved away, the discussions become more meaningful and honest (Healey et al., 2014). Continual exposure to problem-posing education such as COPI has been demonstrated to improve engagement for both students and academic staff, even after regular sessions are stopped (Millet & Tapper, 2012). Having already trialled COPI within a session of our previously taught modules, when presented with the option to take part in this research project, the COPI method used for these sessions did not concern us as we were familiar with it already. Furthermore, the fears of potential difficult conversations that would arise through participation in the research were eased having already experienced the respectful nature of COPI.

While recognising the wealth of opportunity co-creation presents, the challenge of introducing it cannot be ignored. The approach academic staff take during the selection of students is an important aspect to the equality of co-creation. Without a transparent and fair selection process, the transformational benefits of co-creation are lost, as are the adjustments that can be made to the curriculum in order to be more inclusive and representative of the students' lived experiences (Cook-Sather, 2020). Within our own research project, there was no selection process but an open offer that was sent to all members of the cohort to sign up to the sessions. Yet, it should be considered that the four out of five who did respond to the invite were among the higher academic achievers in the cohort. While the recruitment process did not outwardly exclude anyone, the extent to which others felt able to participate may be questioned. The uptake of our project may confirm the idea that students with lower grades may feel like they have little to contribute to any additional projects as they feel lower down the classroom hierarchy (Cook-Sather, 2020). By having lower grades in a module, a student may feel they did not fully take or understand everything from the module, therefore impacting their desire to partake in the retrospective co-creation.

Pause for reflection

- How can we ensure the voices of students who may not consider themselves high achievers are included in co-creation?

Democratic education aims to be less about what the lecturers dictate and more about creating a learning community through the building of partnerships (Healey *et al.*, 2014). If HE is to provide opportunities for people to grow as individuals, not just as academics, institutions must consider the ways they are working towards this (Biesta, 2006). HE is uniquely placed with more flexible curriculums to adapt a more democratic equitable stance (Zawacki-Richter *et al.*, 2020). This suggests that with this adaptation, HE can pave the way for more equitable education which may eventually filter down to schools. Making a shift towards rehumanising the people behind the statistics within institutions requires a conscious consideration of one's own position, and acknowledgement of one's own privileges within said system. Therefore, to potentially make this shift, the most difficult conversation you may have is that of being honest with yourself.

References

Attridge, É. (2021). Understanding and managing identity: Working-class students at the University of Oxford. *Journal of Further and Higher Education*, 45(10), pp. 1–16. https://doi.org/10.1080/0309877x.2021.1985979.

Biesta, G. (2006). What's the point of lifelong learning if lifelong learning has no point? On the democratic deficit of policies for lifelong learning. *European Educational Research Journal*, 5(3–4), pp. 169–80. https://doi.org/10.2304/eerj.2006.5.3.169.

Bovill, C. (2020). Co-creation in learning and teaching: The case for a whole-class approach in higher education. *Higher Education*, 79(6), pp. 1023–37. https://doi.org/10.1007/s10734-019-00453-w.

Bovill, C., Cook-Sather, A., & Felten, P. (2011). Students as co-creators of teaching approaches, course design and curricula: Implications for academic developers. *International Journal of Academic Development*, 16(2), pp. 133–45. https://doi.org/10.1080/1360144X.2011.568690.

Bovill, C., Cook-Sather, A., Felten, P., Millard, L., & Moore-Cherry, N. (2016). Addressing potential challenges in co-creating learning and teaching: overcoming resistance, navigating institutional norms and ensuring inclusivity in student–staff partnerships. *Higher Education*, 71(2), pp. 195–208. https://doi.org/10.1007/s10734-015-9896-4.

Bovill, C., & Woolmer, C. (2019). How conceptualisations of curriculum in higher education influence student-staff co-creation in and of the curriculum. *Higher Education*, 78. https://doi.org/10.1007/s10734-018-0349-8.

Brooman, S., Darwent, S., & Pimor, A. (2015). The student voice in higher education curriculum design: is there value in listening? *Innovations in Education and Teaching International*, 52(6), pp. 663–74. https://doi.org/10.1080/14703297.2014.910128.

Canning, J. (2017). Conceptualising student voice in UK higher education: Four theoretical lenses. *Teaching in Higher Education*, 22(5), pp. 519–31. https://doi.org/10.1080/13562517.2016.1273207.

Cook-Sather, A. (2020). Respecting voices: How the co-creation of teaching and learning can support academic staff, underrepresented students, and equitable practices. *Higher Education*. https://doi.org/10.1007/s10734-019-00445-w.

Freeman, R. (2016). Is student voice necessarily empowering? Problematising student voice as a form of higher education governance. *Higher Education Research & Development*, 35(4), pp. 859–62.

Freire, P. (1970). *Pedagogy of the oppressed*. Bloomsbury Academic.

Griffiths, D. A., Inman, M., Rojas, H., & Williams, K. (2018). Transitioning student identity and sense of place: Future possibilities for assessment and development of student employability skills. *Studies in Higher Education*, 43(5), pp. 891–913. https://doi.org/10.1080/03075079.2018.1439719.

Healey, M., Flint, A., & Harrington, K. (2014). *Engagement through partnership: Students as partners in learning and teaching in higher education.* The Higher Education Academy.

Hermsen, T., Kuiper, T., Roelofs, F., & Van Wijchen, J. (2017). Without emotions, never a partnership! *International Journal for Students as Partners, 1*(2), pp. 1–5. https://doi.org/10.15173/ijsap.v1i2.3228.

Hicks, A., & Lloyd, A. (2020). Deconstructing information literacy discourse: Peeling back the layers in higher education. *Journal of Librarianship and Information Science, 53*(4), pp. 559–71.

Hicks, A., & Lloyd, A. (2021). Deconstructing information literacy discourse: Peeling back the layers in higher education. *Journal of Librarianship and Information Science, 53*(4), pp. 559–71.

hooks. (1994). *Teaching to transgress: Education as the Practice of Freedom.* Routledge.

Hutchings, C., Bartholowmew, N., & Reilly, O. (2013). Differential student engagement: lessons learned. In C. Nygaard, P. Bartholomew, L. Millard, & S. Brand (Eds.). *Student Engagement: Identity, Motivation and Community* (pp. 125–44). Libri Publishing.

Lipman, M. (2003). *Thinking in education.* 2nd Edition. Cambridge University Press.

Lubicz-Nawrocka, T. (2017). Co-creation of the curriculum: Challenging the status quo to embed partnership. *The Journal of Educational Innovation, Partnership and Change, 3*(2). https://doi.org/10.21100/jeipc.v3i2.529.

Lubicz-Nawrocka, T. M. (2019). 'More than just a student': How co-creation of the curriculum fosters third spaces in ways of working, identity, and impact. *International Journal for Students as Partners, 3*(1), pp. 34–49. https://doi.org/10.15173/ijsap.v3i1.3727.

Lubicz-Nawrocka, T., & Bovill, C. (2021). Do students experience transformation through co-creating curriculum in higher education? *Teaching in Higher Education,* pp. 1–17. https://doi.org/10.1080/13562517.2021.1928060.

Lumb, M., & Bunn, M. (2021). Dominant Higher education imaginaries: Forced perspectives, ontological limits and recognising the imaginers frame. In R. Brooks, & S. O'Shea (Eds.). *Reimagining the Higher Education Student* (pp. 114–32). Routledge.

Maguad, B. (2018). Managing the system of higher education: Competition or collaboration? *Education, 138*(3), pp. 229–38. https://doi.org/https://www.ingentaconnect.com/content/prin/ed/2018/00000138/00000003/art00003.

Mercer-Mapstone, L., & Mercer, G. (2018). A dialogue between partnership and feminism: deconstructing power and exclusion in higher education. *Teaching in Higher Education, 23*(1), pp. 137–43. https://doi.org/10.1080/13562517.2017.1391198.

Millet, S., & Tapper, A. (2012). Benefits of collaborative philosophical inquiry in schools. *Educational Philosophy and Theory, 44*(5), pp. 546–67. https://doi.org/10.1111/j.1469-5812.2010.00727.x.

Pan, S. (2020). COVID-19 and the neo-liberal paradigm in higher education: changing landscape. *Asian Education and Development Studies, 10*(2), pp. 332–35. https://doi.org/10.1108/aeds-06-2020-0129.

Resnick, L., Asterhan, C., Clarke, S., & Schnatz, F. (2018). Chapter 13 Next Generation Research in Dialogic Learning. In *The Wiley Handbook of Teaching and Learning* (pp. 323–38). John Wiley & Sons, Inc.

Sant, E. (2019). Democratic education: A theoretical review (2006–2017). *Review of Educational Research, 89*(5), pp. 655–96. https://doi.org/10.3102%2F0034654319862493.

Symonds, E. (2021). Reframing the 'Traditional Learner' into the 'Partner' in Higher Education. In R. Brooks, & S. O'Shea (Eds.). *Reimagining the Higher Education Student* (pp. 132–51). Routledge.

Temple Clothier, A., & Matheson, D. (2019). Using co-creation as a pedagogic method for the professional development of students undertaking a BA (Hons) in Education Studies. *Journal of Further and Higher Education, 43*(6), pp. 826–38. https://doi.org/10.1080/0309877x.2017.1409344.

Topping, K. J., & Trickey, S. (2007). Collaborative philosophical inquiry for schoolchildren: Cognitive gains at 2-year follow-up. *British Journal of Educational Psychology, 77*(4), pp. 787–96. https://doi.org/10.1348/000709907x193032.

Wegerif, R. (2006). Dialogic education: what is it and why do we need it? *Education Review, 19*(2), pp. 55–68.

Young, H., & Jerome, L. (2020). Student voice in higher education: Opening the loop. *British Educational Research Journal, 46*(3), pp. 688–705. https://doi.org/10.1002/berj.3603.

Zawacki-Richter, O., Conrad, D., Bozkurt, A., Aydin, C. H., Bedenlier, S., Jung, I., Stöter, J., Veletsianos, G., Blaschke, L. M., Bond, M., Broens, A., Bruhn, E., Dolch, C., Kalz, M., Kerres, M., Kondakci, Y., Marin, V., Mayrberger, K., Müskens, W., & Naidu, S. (2020). Elements of open education: An invitation to future research. *The International Review of Research in Open and Distributed Learning, 21*(3), pp. 319–34. https://doi.org/10.19173/irrodl.v21i3.4659.

8

Free Speech, Conversation and the 'Difficulty' of Academic Freedom

Seán Henry

Introduction

Academic freedom has received considerable media, political and scholarly attention in recent years. Often, the emphasis within these discourses has been on questions surrounding free speech, understood in terms of the rights of individuals to question, critisise and (in some instances) even offend others to resist the status quo and pursue 'truth'. What brings me to this chapter is an interest in the framing of academic freedom in these individualistic terms. I am interested in challenging the idea that academic freedom, so understood, inevitably resists the status quo. The basis for my claim lies in my observation that an individualistic framing of academic freedom fails to account for our shared relationships with one another, relationships that are arguably more 'difficult' in how they expose us to experiences that we may not wish to otherwise think about, for example, the experiences of those who are marginalised or disenfranchised. It is because of this that I develop in this chapter an alternative understanding of academic freedom, one premised less on free speech, and more on the notion of 'difficult conversations.'

In developing the need for this kind of perspective more fully, I draw your attention first to the following:

> This Government stands unequivocally on the side of free speech and academic freedom, on the side of liberty, and of the values of the Enlightenment.
> (Department for Education, 2021, p. 5)

These words feature in the foreword to a 2021 report entitled *Higher Education: Free Speech and Academic Freedom* by the then-Secretary of State for Education Gavin Williamson. In line with its 2019 manifesto commitments, the purpose of the report is to communicate the Conservative Government's plans to 'strengthen freedom of expression and academic freedom in higher education in England' (Department for Education, 2021, p. 7). Much of its content acts as a justification for the Higher Education (Freedom of Speech) Bill, which (at the time of writing, January 2023) has passed through both Houses of Parliament and is at the final amendment stages before Royal Assent.

What is distinctive about the report and Bill is their shared understanding of the importance of free speech for upholding the academic freedom of staff and students working and studying in higher education. Indeed, the report claims that significant historical changes (like advancements in women's Suffrage or gay rights) were made possible 'because of the strong liberal tradition of free debate' to be found in universities and higher education settings. A June 2022 letter by Michelle Donelan (the then-Minister of State for Higher and Further Education) to vice-chancellors of the higher education sector echoes many of the themes expressed in the report above. Like the report, Donelan foregrounds the obligation of higher education providers to create environments in which students and staff have the confidence to discuss and debate issues freely. She continues by implying that the involvement of higher education providers in schemes that seek to promote diversity on campuses and tackle social inequalities is an attack on the principles of free speech, given threats posed by so-called 'cancel culture'.

Two things about the above interest me. The first aspect that I find interesting in the Conservative Government's statements above is the *individualistic* understanding of freedom that they seem to rely on. Both the report and Donelan's letter tend to position 'freedom' as something that a student or academic individually possesses and exercises (through, for example, debate), rather than as something that is lived out through the shared nature of our relationships with others. Indeed, the Government's statements paint a picture of academic freedom as a solo act, limited to the lawful, free expression of one's own views, irrespective of the personal, social, and political consequences of doing so. Furthermore, they tend to forget that a student's or academic's exercise of free expression is dependent on the presence (immediate or otherwise) of others to be exercised to begin with. In this sense, the statements above lose sight of how the 'freedom' to express what one feels or thinks is made possible precisely *because* of one's shared interdependence with others, not despite it.

In a book about difficult conversations, my criticism of the government's individualistic understanding of academic freedom, with its emphasis on debate, is relevant. In my view, to think of academic freedom individualistically is to think of it as something separate from the difficulties we can all face when confronted by the experiences of (known and unknown) others, particularly those who might be structurally oppressed or marginalised because of their race, ethnicity, social class, sexuality, gender identity or disability. I would like to suggest that linking academic freedom to an individualistic account of free speech has the potential effect of quashing challenges to the status quo in higher education settings, despite the government's claims otherwise. In this sense, this chapter's criticism of understanding academic freedom individualistically is motivated by a commitment to *preserving* the 'difficulty' of difficult conversations, to taking seriously the challenge of connecting with marginalised others in ways that honour the freedoms we collectively share.

In setting about this task, I reflect in this chapter on the alternative value of *conversation* for reimagining academic freedom as an interdependent practice that faces, rather than denies, the difficulties of social injustice. I focus on conversations that are 'difficult', i.e., conversations that unsettle us in some way by challenging us to take the experiences of marginalised others seriously. Following this, I offer some thoughts for reflection, before appending the chapter with some activities practitioners in higher education settings (and further afield) can engage with for exploring these ideas with each other. But first, allow me to start by sharing with you a personal classroom experience I had that brought many of these issues into focus for me.

An experience from the classroom

In January 2021, I was lecturing at an Education Department in an Irish university. I was teaching a module called 'The Foundations of Educational Thinking', a module introducing undergraduate science education students to philosophical and sociological perspectives on education. The purpose of the module was to provide an opportunity for my students to engage with philosophical and sociological research in ways that would allow them to explore the extent to which education systems can contribute to the reproduction of structural classism, racism, sexism, homophobia, ableism, etc. A few weeks into the module, a conversation in class around Freirean critical pedagogy digressed into a debate on sexism in education, specifically in relation to the exclusion of women from STEM education and STEM fields. One male student in the class (who I pseudonymise as Michael) took exception to several claims made by his peers, arguing that sexism was not a structural problem in STEM fields today given the existence of gender quotas within research schemes, and the support many young women receive to advance in STEM (through, for example, school/university access channels).

The debate became heated, with many women in the class challenging Michael on his views, some vocally and others through the chat function of our virtual learning environment (classes were online at this point due to ongoing coronavirus restrictions). A week later, some of the women who challenged Michael lodged complaints to me against him, on the grounds that Michael had proceeded to make sexist comments about one of the women in a private social media group chat. An informal disciplinary process with colleagues followed, part of which involved me meeting with Michael to discuss what had happened and the context around it. During this discussion, Michael shared with me how he felt classroom spaces should be spaces where ideas can be rigorously debated, no matter how offensive or otherwise some ideas might be. Nonetheless, he verbally acknowledged the harm caused by his sexist social media comments and committed to apologising to the woman he had harassed.

Pause for reflection

- To what extent do you agree and/or disagree with Michael's understanding of classroom spaces?

The following week, to respond restoratively to these events, I worked with the class in compiling a group 'contract' of behaviour, where the group collaboratively drafted a document detailing their expectations for one another's conduct moving forward. Considering the events that had happened, many of the students stressed the importance of engaging respectfully with one another across their differences, avoiding name-calling and other discriminatory behaviours. Some of the students also mentioned the importance of creating a space where people could respectfully disagree with one another. All seemed well, until the very last class of the year, where students were sharing with each other their ideas for the end-of-semester assignment. Michael shared with the group that he planned to write his paper on misandry in education, with a particular focus on how education systems supposedly privilege girls and women at the expense of boys and men. Tired and weary, I quickly diverted the class discussion away from this terrain. A few hours after the session, however, I received an email from one of the other students in the class, who claimed that Michael's choice to write an essay on misandry in education was unacceptable, and that it betrayed an attitude that risked causing harm, not only to Michael's classmates but to Michael's future pupils of science. My (somewhat dismissive) response to my student was: it was Michael's academic freedom as a student to write about whatever topic he wished and that all student submissions would be graded vigorously against the criteria set for the assignment.

Several questions and themes arise for me in reflecting on this experience (and maybe for you too!), so it is not my intention to elaborate on them all here. One immediate point that comes to me, however, was the appeal I made to academic freedom as a response to my student's concerns. In framing Michael's academic freedom as a justification for his choice of topic, I fear I granted legitimacy to an individualistic understanding of academic freedom divorced from any sense of responsiveness to others or to the particularities of specific contexts. Indeed, the sexist events that had happened that semester were not separate from the theme of Michael's essay, and his choice to pursue it – perhaps a betrayed (I assume) effort either to reassert his initial defensiveness or to undermine the perspectives of those who initially lodged complaints against him. Irrespective of my assumptions, however, it was a provocative choice on Michael's part, and certainly not one that displayed any sense of receptiveness to the pain he had caused others, or to the recent history of his relationship with his peers. Furthermore, Michael seemed to have been changed very little (at least outwardly) by the events that had happened, which was interesting given his earlier lauding of debate as a necessary part of his university education.

Pause for reflection

- What do you think could have been done to elicit a different kind of response in Michael?
- Could another kind of approach have been more transformative?

Considering this experience, I am interested in exploring other ways of conceiving academic freedom, ways that are: (1) committed to building affirmative relations with marginalised others, and (2) enacted through practices that allow for more authentic transformation in others. It is in these terms that I turn to the idea of academic freedom as a conversational practice.

Academic freedom as a conversational practice

Conversation has been a recurring theme in philosophical perspectives on education for some time. Aislinn O'Donnell (2012), for instance, has positioned conversation as helpful for education in giving opportunities for people to think collectively with one another in educational spaces, in ways that build affirming and potentially transformative relationships between people of different perspectives. Sharon Todd (2015) has spoken about the benefits of conversational approaches to teaching in providing students with the chance to encounter the existential questions raised by difference. Kevin Williams and Patrick Williams (2017) have also written about conversation, seeing 'pedagogies of conversation' as valuable for challenging students to move away 'from individual and cultural mindsets' (p. 254), and opening them up 'to the challenge of better argument' (p. 262). Michael Oakeshott's (1962) concept of 'the conversation of mankind' has been taken up in similar terms, with many, like Hanan Alexander (2015) and David Bakhurst and Paul Fairfield (2016), understanding conversation as a metaphor for any kind of education committed to liberal learning and personal development. Therefore, reflecting on academic freedom as a conversational practice seems to echo many contemporary perspectives within educational thinking.

However, to think of academic freedom as a conversational practice first requires me to outline what I mean by *conversation* itself, and what value it brings to understanding academic freedom as an interdependent practice that faces the difficulty of social injustice. In outlining my meaning of conversation, I turn to the work of Emile Bojesen (2019), who understands conversation as a practice with some enduring effects on our understanding of what it means to engage with, and relate to, others.

What is conversation?

Emile Bojesen's (2019) account of conversation is valuable for this chapter in how he distances conversation from practices of debate (something which, you will recall, Michael valued as a key part of university life). For Bojesen, one unique feature of conversation is how conversation begins from 'conditions of infinity or strangeness'. This means that conversations are made possible because of their unknown quality. Put differently, conversations, unlike more formal engagements like debates, move in unpredictable directions because conversing parties typically 'go with the flow' with one another, sharing and responding to each other in a fluid and intuitive way, rather than in a way that is scripted or in a way that seeks to make one point of view or position 'win out' over another.

This unpredictable quality to conversation as a way of engaging with others is important for Bojesen because it resists efforts to annex the other within the domain of the 'I'. This means that when we converse with another person, we engage with them in order to hear what they have to say and to 'go with the flow' of the exchange between us, rather than treating the other person and their views as something to be merely studied, persuaded, recognised or identified with for my own gain or ego (2019, p. 655). Because of this 'go with the flow' quality, conversation is distinctive for 'the movement of thought' it allows for, which for Bojesen refers to how conversation (and, in particular, the language used in conversation) is characterised by ideas moving in unpredictable, non-linear, and potentially transgressive or even uncomfortable directions.

This movement of thought, where ideas unfold in unpredictable ways, is both characterised and enabled by the multiple possibilities and meanings found in the very language we use in conversing with others, something which Bojesen refers to as the 'sense of the infinite' in language. This 'infinite' quality to the language of conversation is significant for Bojesen in the effects it has on how we understand ourselves as human 'subjects', i.e., as selves in relationship to others in the world. He writes the following:

> Conversation ... can develop a subject but in a manner that destabilises its autonomy through the language that accommodates it. Conversation is radically decentring in the sense that the subject is formed through the movement of language. Rather than being able to possess language, the subject is possessed (or, perhaps, dispossessed) by language. Conversation forms but also deforms and dissolves identity, putting it always on the move. To find oneself in conversation is also to lose oneself in conversation. (p. 652)

There are many ideas being communicated in this passage, so before I break it down a little, I invite you to consider the following for reflection:

Pause for reflection

- Can you remember a conversation that played the dual role of allowing you to find yourself and lose yourself at the same time?
- What was it about that conversation that allowed you to be deeply engaged but also deeply moved or disturbed?

Returning to Bojesen, when Bojesen refers to the capacity of conversation to 'destabilise' the autonomy of the subject, he is referring to how conversation (with its multiple meanings and unpredictability) challenges the idea of the subject as an individualistic entity in control of its engagements with others. The unpredictability of conversation 'decentres' the subject; that is, it shows us that we are not at the centre of our worlds, and that our development as people is influenced just as much (if not, more) by the unpredictable effects that others have on us when we engage with them. In this sense, we cannot relate to others in purely individualistic terms, but are instead continuously and unpredictably 'moved' by others in our engagements with them. In this way, conversation shows us that we can never truly 'possess' or 'master' what we say: because of our interdependence with others, there are always factors in our exchanges that we cannot anticipate or determine. As I develop further in the next section, it is this that makes conversation difficult: through conversation, we encounter the limits of our own egos, as well as the obligations that come with being responsive to other people and their experiences.

For Bojesen, conversation's ability to 'dispossess' the subject challenges efforts to frame our exchanges in terms of what I myself might determine, desire, or seek to assert. As Todd (2013, p. 4) makes clear: 'Conversations are not just about speaking to each other, but about the nature of listening, of receiving, of being open to something or someone outside of myself'. Indeed, when we converse with others (for instance, in a classroom context or in the pub), we rarely know where we will 'end up', for the speech of the other can never be boxed within what I alone can anticipate or desire. From Bojesen's perspective, it is this 'infinite' or 'strange' quality of conversation that exposes who we are to new and untold possibilities and challenges, possibilities that can exceed and transform the limits of our social and political identities, positions, and differences. In this sense, conversations transform because their unpredictability has the potential to bring us in directions we cannot foresee.

What value does conversation bring to understanding academic freedom?

Having outlined some of the enduring features of conversation, I now return to the context I set out in the introduction and offer some thoughts on the value of understanding academic freedom as a conversational practice. For me, one of the main advantages to understanding academic freedom as a conversational practice is in how conversation creates spaces in which 'difficult knowledge' can be encountered.

The concept of 'difficult knowledge' is an important one for me to develop here (Britzman, 1998, 2013; Britzman & Pitt, 2004; Pitt & Britzman, 2003). In the context of educational research, the concept is often used to refer to pedagogical content that is traumatic or difficult to bear in some way, as well as to educational experiences that are potentially destabilising for staff and students (intellectually, psychologically, emotionally). In this way, knowledge can be difficult not only because of the content of the knowledge itself but also because of staff and students' engagements with, and relationship to, that content, and with one another (Boler & Zembylas, 2003; Bryan, 2016; Pitt & Britzman, 2003; Zembylas, 2014). Many of the authors referenced here support the idea of engaging students with difficult knowledge through so-called 'pedagogies of discomfort', as it is through such engagement, they argue, that the status quo can be challenged and structural change enabled (Boler, 2013). In a likewise fashion, conversations too can be difficult: in their unpredictability, they can expose us to experiences and perspectives that we would rather avoid.

At a superficial level, encountering difficult knowledge can be seen as similar to the framing of academic freedom with free speech offered by the Government and Donelan in the Introduction: in both cases, a commitment to challenging students is prioritised. What makes these accounts different, however, is the former's commitment to exposing students' difficulty or discomfort with the view to challenging our collective implication in unjust and exclusionary practices, like, for example, racism (Zembylas, 2022). In this sense, pedagogical engagements with difficult knowledge are valuable in their explicit commitment to undoing oppressive systems of power that marginalise the typically disenfranchised, something that an individualistic framing of academic freedom avoids, if not actively discourages (think of Donelan's letter!).

For me, it is the unpredictability of conversation, with its openness to the other, that renders it a worthwhile practice for exercising academic freedom, as it can create the spaces needed to honestly confront the realities of other's experiences ahead of one's own, however difficult such confrontation may be. In light of this difficulty, to limit academic freedom to an individualistic account of freedom of speech runs the risk of wrapping academics and students in cotton wool, cossetting them from the difficulties the most marginalised in our societies face.

Concluding reflection

As I reach the end of this chapter, I turn again to Michael. In many ways, Michael's behaviour can be read as a symptom of a certain way of understanding academic freedom: one characterised by a desire to argue one's point, to 'win' one's case, to re-assert one's ego, or to play Devil's advocate in a world where hypotheticals trump responsibility. Perhaps more generously, Michael's behaviour can also be read as a safeguard against the prospect that what one holds to be true and/or identifies with might, in fact, be wrong. I write this not to excuse Michael's sexism or to justify my own inadequate responses to it but rather to situate it (and incidents like it) within the context of a patriarchal academy that breeds defensiveness against vulnerability through performativity indicators, high-stakes testing, competitive grading practices and the like. If we are to nurture the conditions for people to engage in difficult conversations, perhaps we need to start by affirming an alternative vision of academic freedom, a freedom actualised less through a rugged, competitive, individualism (where some 'win' and others 'lose') and more through an attunement to our collective responsibilities, where we transform what is desired by us into what is desirable for others (Biesta, 2013).

Whereas some may seek to conflate academic freedom with the individualistic exercise of free speech, I suggest that a focus more on the quality of relationships necessary for conversation to happen is perhaps a more productive place from which to begin discussions on academic freedom. I engage in this shift of emphasis not to lose sight of the role free speech (or, indeed, any other kind of exchange) may or may not play in academic life but rather to bring to the fore those flesh-and-blood textures of academic life that might otherwise be flattened when academic freedom is framed solely in terms of an individual 'right' to be protected. Specifically, I have in mind those relationships between students and academics, and academics and administrators, etc., upon which our capacity to converse often depends, relationships of solidarity, curiosity, openness and humility, for example. In this respect, Judith Butler's work on academic freedom is instructive. Butler maintains that 'academic freedom implies a right to free inquiry within the academic institution, but also an obligation to preserve the institution as a site where free inquiry can and does take place' (2017, p. 857). In thinking about academic freedom with Butler, I foreground conversations, and the qualities of relationship needed to productively sustain them, in order to avoid reducing our interactions in the academy to mere footnotes to the exercise of free speech above all else. Indeed, the desire of Alexis Gibbs to move discourses around academic freedom away from 'the indulgence of speaking' to 'the exercise of listening' (2021, p. 22, p. 38) is instructive for facing the difficulty of academic work, and the kinds of conversations that enable it to flourish. In this sense, freedom of speech is easy, whereas conversation is something far more challenging.

Appendix: Practical activities to consider

The four activities below are offered as a way for readers to unpack more fully what might be meant by 'difficult conversations', and how these can relate to ideas like 'freedom of speech'. You can adapt these for use with academics, or practitioners in schools, youth work settings, etc. They have been designed so that they can be engage with collectively and consecutively, or individually. A slightly varied version of these can be found in the resource *Sharing the World: Educational Responses to Extremism*, to which I contributed (O'Donnell et al., 2022).

Activity 1: Mapping Difficult Conversations

1. Divide the cohort into small groups of three or four. You can also do this exercise on your own or with a small group.
2. Ask each person to recall an example of a difficult conversation that they have had in their lives as a practitioner. Invite each participant to write about this in a paragraph for themselves, before sharing in their groups.
3. Provide each group with a large piece of paper divided into four sections: 'Social', 'Cultural', 'Political' and 'Professional'.
4. Encourage each group to identify and reflect on the social, cultural, political and professional factors that rendered each of their recounted conversations 'difficult'. Encourage one member of each group to take notes under the appropriate sections on the page, to which the remaining group members can also contribute if they wish.
5. Using these notes as a guide, invite each group to produce two to three minute video clips (recorded on a mobile phone or laptop), where each group member provides an individual response to the theme of 'Difficult conversations'. If recording is not possible, this could alternatively take the form of short individual/group presentations to the entire group (presented through PowerPoint, or through more creative means, e.g. a roleplay 'talk show').

Tip: You might like to reflect on how to change the themes when working with young people.

Activity 2: Embodying Difficult Conversations

1. Divide the group into groups of four (different groups from Exercise 1 if possible).
2. Invite each group member to recount the difficult conversation they have had in a classroom/youth work setting again. Having listened to each member's story, invite the group to focus on one that they found to be collectively provocative or engaging.
3. With this story in mind, ask three group members to take on one of the following roles: 'Myself', "What I said", "What I heard" or "Others with me". Through their bodies, ask these group members to physically represent the relations between each in response to the question 'What made this difficult conversation difficult for you?' The fourth group member will be tasked with articulating the reasoning behind their 'embodied reflection' with the wider group.
4. Having spoken to and showcased their embodied reflections, each participant will then be asked to return to their groups and reconsider their previous arrangement in light of the discussions that proceeded at Step 3. They may also like to assign alternative labels to the roles, depending on their thinking.
5. The groups will showcase their embodied reflections again, with the fourth group member speaking to the changes that were made and why.
6. The exercise will conclude with a final, whole-group conversation around the question 'What makes difficult conversations difficult?'

Activity 3: Writing Difficult Conversations

1. Divide the group into groups of three or four. Provide each group with a large piece of paper (A0 or similar) and markers/pens.
2. Give the groups a question prompt pertaining to a 'difficult' issue (e.g. 'Is masculinity toxic?') You may also like the group to collectively generate and vote for their own question in response to a stimulus, or to choose from a series of optional questions.

3. Ask one member of each group to write the question prompt onto the large piece of paper.
4. With this question as a springboard, invite each group to engage in a 'written' conversation with each other on the page, where each group member responds in writing to the comments of the others. Encourage group members to respond in as casual a way as possible – participants can 'circle back' to points written at a previous point in the exercise, cross out and rephrase their earlier contributions if they wish, etc.
5. Conclude the exercise by inviting participants to compose an anonymous letter to their group members. In this letter, participants should reflect on the experience of engaging in the written conversations. They should identify ideas that were important to them, thoughts on what they found 'difficult' to think and write about, and any further questions the written conversation raised for them.
6. Place these letters in a 'letterbox' assigned to each group (a regular shoebox will do). Ask each participant to read aloud to their group a letter other than their own. You may like to do this immediately after the exercise, or a few days/weeks later, depending on the nature/topic of the conversations had.

Activity 4: Sustaining Difficult Conversations

1. Divide the group into groups of three or four. Provide each group with a large piece of paper (A0 or similar), along with various art and stationery supplies (pencils, pens, colours, paints, etc.).
2. Invite the group to depict an outline of a human body on the page. Alternatively, this could be included on the page in advance of the activity. Ask each group to consider the following questions:
   - If this body were a representation of a professional setting that sustained productive, difficult conversations, what would some of the different organs, limbs, and body parts stand for?
   - What would the 'blood' be? The skeleton? What kind of 'food' would this 'body' need?
   - What kinds of 'physical exercise' would it require?
   - What 'immune defences' would it need to cultivate, and against what kinds of disease?

References

Alexander, H. (2015). *Reimagining liberal education: Affiliation and inquiry in democratic schooling*. Bloomsbury Publishing.

Bakhurst, D., & Fairfield, P. (2016). *Education and conversation: Exploring Oakeshott's legacy*. Bloomsbury Publishing.

Biesta, G. (2013). *The beautiful risk of education*. Routledge.

Bojesen, E. (2019). Conversation as educational research. *Educational Philosophy and Theory*, 51(6), pp. 650–9.

Boler, M. (2013). Teaching for hope: The ethics of shattering worldviews. In V. Bozalek, B. Leibowitz, R. Carolissen, & M. Boler (Eds.). *Discerning Critical Hope in Educational Practices* (pp. 48–61). Routledge.

Boler, M., & Zembylas, M. (2003). Discomforting truths: The emotional terrain of understanding difference. In P. Trifonas (Ed.). *Pedagogies of Difference* (pp. 115–38). Routledge.

Britzman, D. P. (1998). *Lost subjects, contested objects: Toward a psychoanalytic inquiry of learning*. SUNY Press.

Britzman, D. P. (2013). Between psychoanalysis and pedagogy: Scenes of rapprochement and alienation. *Curriculum Inquiry*, 43(1), pp. 95–117.

Britzman, D. P., & Pitt, A. (2004). Pedagogy and clinical knowledge: Some psychoanalytic observations on losing and refinding significance. *JAC: A Journal of Composition Theory*, 24(2), pp. 353–74.

Bryan, A. (2016). The sociology classroom as a pedagogical site of discomfort: Difficult knowledge and the emotional dynamics of teaching and learning. *Irish Journal of Sociology*, 24(1), pp. 7–33.

Butler, J. (2017). Academic freedom and the critical task of the university. *Globalizations*, 14(6), pp. 857–61.

Department for Education (2021). *Higher education: Free speech and academic freedom*. Accessed June 2022. Available at https://www.gov.uk/government/publications/higher-education-free-speech-and-academic-freedom.

Donelan, M. (2022). *Letter from Michelle Donelan to higher education providers*. Accessed June 2022. Available at https://wonkhe.com/wp-content/wonkhe-uploads/2022/06/Letter-Regarding-Free-Speech-and-External-Assurance-Schemes-1.pdf.

Gibbs, A. (2021). A responsibility to seek the truth: Revisiting Averroe's decisive treatise for academic freedom's missing imperative. *Philosophy and Theory in Higher Education*, 3(1), pp. 21–40.

Oakeshott, M. (1962). *The voice of poetry and the conversation of mankind*. In: M. Oakeshott (Ed.). *Rationalism in Politics and Other Essays* (pp. 197–247). Liberty Fund INC International Concepts.

O'Donnell, A. (2012). Thinking-in-concert. *Ethics and Education*, 7(3), pp. 261–75.

O'Donnell, A., Malone, A., & Melaugh, B. (2022). *Sharing the World: Educational Responses to Extremism*. Accessed June 2022. Available at https://edurad.eu/courses/module-1-sharing-the-world-educational-responses-to-extremism/.

Pitt, A., & Britzman, D. (2003). Speculations on qualities of difficult knowledge in teaching and learning: an experiment in psychoanalytic research. *International Journal of Qualitative Studies in Education*, 16(6), pp. 755–76.

Standish, P. (2016). A turn in conversation. In D. Bakhurst, & P. Fairfield (Eds.). *Education and Conversation: Exploring Oakeshott's legacy* (pp. 111–26). Bloomsbury Publishing.

Todd, S. (2013). *Difficult Conversations, or the Difficult Task of Facing Humanity*. Presentation given as part of the *Impossible Conversations* Series. National College of Art and Design. Dublin, 9th April 2013. Accessed June 2022. Available at https://www.hughlane.ie/phocadownload/exhibitions/cummins_conversation%203%20fin-26.pdf.

Todd, S. (2015). Creating transformative spaces in education: Facing humanity, facing violence. *Philosophical Inquiry in Education*, 23(1), pp. 53–61.

Williams, K., & Williams, P. (2017). Lessons from a master: Montaigne's pedagogy of conversation. *Educational Philosophy and Theory*, 49(3), pp. 253–63.

Zembylas, M. (2014). Theorizing 'difficult knowledge' in the aftermath of the 'affective turn': Implications for curriculum and pedagogy in handling traumatic representations. *Curriculum Inquiry*, 44(3), pp. 390–412.

Zembylas, M. (2022). Post-truth as difficult knowledge: fostering affective solidarity in anti-racist education. *Pedagogy, Culture & Society*, 30(3), pp. 295–310.

'Engaging Educators in Conversation on Our Climate and Ecological Emergency'

Elena Lengthorn

Introduction

I am sorry.

I am truly, deeply, sorry.

Sorry, that we find ourselves in a position where this chapter, a chapter about difficult conversations on our global climate and ecological emergency, needs to be created, needs to be read and needs to become your action. Nobody grew up planning for this, a future of flooding, increased extreme weather events, drought and food shortage. Does anyone want this? Did anyone choose this? I am sorry that, individually and collectively, we are now facing an existential crisis. A crisis that will impact the entire human population directly, through extreme heat, floods, fire or by their accompanying energy shortages and food insecurity.

I am also stubbornly optimistic and feel empowered to be able to convey these messages here to invite you to reflect on your own impact and place in this crisis. This reflection, whether a difficult conversation with the self or with others will, most likely, require some shifts in thinking and allowing yourself to 'sit in the uncomfortable' (Bhabha, 2004). Now is the time, like no other, to leave our conversational comfort zones and talk about protecting humanity.

We have, according to Professor Lewis Dartnell (2018, p. 2), 'replaced nature as the dominant environmental force on earth'. He reminds us that our urban centres, alongside our industrial and mining activities, have profound and lasting effects. Effects that have moved us beyond the stability of the Holocene and into a new geological epoch: the Anthropocene – an age during which humans shape the climate and the environment, recasting the landscape and causing widespread extinctions.

Despite fifteen years at the environmental education chalkface it was not until I read Bendell's 'Navigating Climate Tragedy' paper (2018) that I felt the true weight of our difficult future. The article is compelling, examining issues of:

1. The speed of change moving much faster than climate predictions.
2. The non-linearity of these changes and the climate tipping points that are already active leading to 'runaway change'.
3. The projections of six degrees of warming under our current emissions pathway.
4. The observed phenomena already being more extreme than climate prediction models forecast, e.g. storms, droughts, floods, fires.

I was, like other readers, shaken viscerally while reading this article, while also feeling a deep sense of resonance with my own experiences as an environmental educator. And this is why I aim to use this space to connect us to the need to urgently open a climate reality dialogue with ourselves, our peers and wider community, and equip us with the tools to do so. I will journey with you through a brief outline of the major policies worldwide that target our urgent need for societal change in relation to ecological emergency. I will discuss the intricacies of the language used in conversations about climate change and how these, often difficult, conversations are imperative for all of us, to embark on in addressing our climate and ecological emergency, particularly within the education system.

Policies for climate change action

The largest climate-related agreement, with collaboration across 193 countries, are the United Nations' 17 Sustainable Development Goals (UN, 2015), with their 169 strategic sub-targets towards ending poverty, tackling inequality and combating climate change. The first state level declarations of climate emergency emerged in the UK (BBC, 2019), and followed since by a further 39 countries, 2,319 jurisdictions and local governments (covering 1 billion people), who have added their declarations (Climate Emergency Declarations, 2023). However, despite the UK joining this commitment in 2015 there was little movement in the educational landscape until the publication of the Sustainability and Climate Change (S&CC) strategy paper (DfE, 2022a). But Covid-19, a global pandemic in our time of environmental degradation and the associated resultant increase in the risk of pandemics, has had a considerable impact on moving the climate emergency agenda forward.

The S&CC paper (DfE, 2022a), a strategy for the UK education and children's services systems, recognises the vital role that education plays in creating a better, sustainable, future for children and in tackling global heating. The first of its five action areas is Climate Education, which includes two key strategies: A youth Climate Leader Award and A Virtual National Education Nature Park. The hard work in the creation of this strategy has been recognised but the paper has also been criticised for not going far or fast enough (Dunlop & Rushton, 2022; NGA, 2022; Sustainable Food Trust, 2022). These limited efforts of current interventions to fulfil the Sustainable Goals are also echoed in the words of Antonio Guterres in his video introduction to the launch of the latest Intergovernmental Panel on Climate Change (IPCC):

> The jury has reached a verdict and it is damning. This report of the Intergovernmental Panel on Climate Change is a litany of broken climate promises. It is a file of shame, cataloguing the empty pledges that put us firmly on track towards an unliveable world. (Guterres, 2022)

Guterres (2022) shares the catastrophic nature of our inaction, reminding us of the irreversible climate impacts that we are perilously close to and urges for the need to cut emissions radically, by 45 per cent, within the decade. Urgent and effective conversations are needed and are essential to adapt to and survive these changes (Stone et al., 2011), and I now turn to some of those difficult conversations within the climate change debate.

Difficult conversations about climate change capitalism

Dunlop and Rushton (2022b) draw our attention to the inherent tension between capitalism and climate change and thereby a teachers' perception that climate education can be a risky activity (anti-capitalism having been designated an extreme stance, subject to The Prevent Duty (Home Office, 2015)). Dunlop and Rushton (2022b) suggest that this 'extreme' framing discourages teachers and pupils from having opportunities to 'challenge economic models that contribute to continued climate change and climate injustice' (Dunlop & Rushton, 2022b, p. 10). They further highlight the depoliticising effect of the DfE Sustainability and Climate Change strategy, as it places additional demands on the education system without an enabling policy environment.

This unsynchronised setup might appear to be aiming at 'doing something' while not addressing the systemic problem (Dunlop & Rushton, 2022b) and therefore delaying the onset of the difficult conversations and action towards the transformative change that is necessary.

Ahmed (2018, p. 45) recognises that in difficult conversations we 'carry the weight of the moments when we're not able to do all that we'd hoped' – this weight seems inevitable in climate education conversations considering the policy deficit. Beyond this, an even broader invitation to converse on education in climate and ecological emergency (CEE) comes from the issue of safeguarding. Rackley (2023) invites us to regard our changing climate as a consideration for educators in keeping learners safe, from mental health issues like eco-anxiety to responding to climate-related events like flooding. All educators have a responsibility for safeguarding and for providing a safe environment, yet our school safeguarding policies do not reflect these risks.

These conversations are difficult for two key reasons: the climate emergency is a 'super wicked problem' with multiple, complex, causes. It is variable, has socially unjust and unpredictable impacts and uncertain solutions (Saab, 2019); climate change is intrinsically linked to existential themes at a range of scales, from the individual to entire nations, and in severity, from impacts on well-being to being life-threatening (Huggel et al., 2022). Friere (1970) identified the uncomfortable in difficult conversations in the threat to hierarchies and identities and we can argue that the climate conversations are difficult in exploring the threat to our very survival, without which we 'sleepwalk into climate catastrophe' (UN, 2022). This raises the question: What uncomfortable conversations are needed for schools to incorporate responses to this crisis in their policies? And I will try to outline some of the ways this question can be addressed through opening climate conversations within the education.

The role of educators

Educators are carrying, not for the first time, a mighty societal responsibility to prepare young people for an uncertain future. However, Teach the Future (2021) revealed that 92 per cent of 7600 interviewed teachers do not feel confident teaching about climate crisis due to inadequate training. Likewise, two-thirds of secondary school teacher-participants in another Teach the Future (2022) survey claimed that climate change is not embedded in a meaningful way in their curriculum, though 9/10 participants recognise its relevance in their subject area.

Despite these barriers, Howard-Jones et al.'s (2021) research reveals that 73.3 per cent of the teachers they surveyed are already directly teaching or engaging students in conversation on climate change. Moreover, teacher respondents did not consider climate change activities for social change too political, with a preference for individual advocacy for secondary-aged pupils and family participation preferred for primary-age pupils. Many educators are already on board and eager to embed climate conversations within and beyond their classrooms. The UK Government commitment to the SDGs specifically includes a target on climate education (SDG 13.3) focussed on: 'awareness-raising and human and institutional capacity on climate change mitigation, adaptation, impact reduction and early warning' (UN, 2015). There is also a direct link to the role of teachers in their responsibility to educate for a sustainable future (SDG 4.7):

> By 2030, ensure that all learners acquire the knowledge and skills needed to promote sustainable development, including, among others, through education for sustainable development and sustainable lifestyles, human rights, gender equality, promotion of a culture of peace and non-violence, global citizenship and appreciation of cultural diversity and of culture's contribution to sustainable development. (UN, 2015)

The UK is therefore, as a United Nations member state, responsible for the realisation of these targets, with all sectors having a role in their delivery. Nonetheless, some teachers remain reticent to explore ways to embed some elements of climate education, finding the topic too political and fearing potential accusations of personal bias with regard to social activism (McLaverty, 2022). The publication of the new 'Political Impartiality in Schools' guide (DfE, 2022b) reinforces the importance of a partisan position, of presenting topics with a balanced representation of opposing views, and, perhaps unsurprisingly, it was met with some fierce debate. Some have argued that that the government is attempting to ban discussion of certain topics and control *woke* teachers, while others argue that it clarifies teachers' legal responsibilities in relation to the Education Act, Equality Act, Prevent Duty and the Human Rights Act (Worth, 2022).

Partiality (unfair bias) was cited in the 2007 case of *Dimmock v The Secretary of State for Education and Skills*, when the plaintiff sought to ban the use of Al Gore's *An Inconvenient Truth*' film for educational purposes. The S&CC strategy argues that the scientific facts of climate change itself are not a political issue, but that there is a political debate about the best ways to address it and advises that this needs to be done in line with the new guidance (DfE, 2022a). But what does this mean exactly? What does this look like? Will this hinder the difficult climate conversations we need to be opening? The next section is devoted to a critical discussion about these questions.

Safe spaces to address 'the uncomfortable' of climate conversations

Moving our CEE into our psyche and our ways of being can start simply by making the issue part of our everyday conversation. This section will explore some of the challenges to opening this dialogue, alongside the importance of doing so and some potential strategies. Project Drawdown (Hawken, 2017), the most comprehensive plan proposed to reverse global warming, acknowledges that the language of climate change can be confusing because it consists of specialised scientific language, acronyms and jargon that can repulse and disorient the unenlightened reader. Their project aims to engage a broad audience and 'bridge the climate communication gap' (Hawken, 2017, p. xiii) by making their work as accessible as possible, debunking confusing terminology, e.g. 'negative emissions', and avoiding the language of conflict. Another obstacle in terminology can be militarised climate crisis phrases like 'the war on climate' and 'combatting climate change'. These phrases adopt the language of fighting and battle frame climate change as an enemy to mankind, whereas, in reality, we are the creators of this changed climate and adapting our language to reflect that might help people to move into acceptance and, hopefully, action.

Carr and Bendell (2021) remind us that Bendell's (2018) viral paper was an invitation to begin a global conversation and suggest that group processes can be productive in ways of relating to difficult information, the emotions associated with them, and our interconnectedness. Furthermore, Carr and Bendell (2021) explore the essential role of facilitation in providing a space to explore our climate fears and uncertainty that can also provide a place for building the stamina that is required to remain present with these challenging issues and difficult emotions. It is important to recognise the discomfort as necessary for social transformation to occur (Ball, 2017). At the same time, we need to pay attention to the mental and relational habits that keep us stuck in behaviours of oppression and destruction to ourselves, others and the environment; these could include imagined separateness, dominant individualistic ideas or an illusion of separation from the natural world (Carr & Bendell, 2021). To revert these habits and behaviours and enable our actions to become more attuned to our connectedness with the natural world, a critical dialogue needs to take place, ideally with non-judgemental, empathetic and curious conversational skills, the characteristics that Lipman (2003) recognises as acquired rather than innate, therefore in need of cultivation.

A fundamental part of facilitating these difficult conversations is containment, understood generally as keeping something harmful under control. In the context of conversations on climate and ecological crisis it refers to creating a safe physical and emotional space, a liminal space of unknowns, to experience and express the uncomfortable emotions relating to this existential crisis. Carr and Bendell (2021) highlight two containment aspects for consideration: external/hard, and internal/soft. Externally, it includes the physical structures of the context, from accessibility to comfort, to the administration of joining and developing knowledge and expectations of the processes. Internally, it includes the characteristics of the facilitator, their empathy, presence and consistency.

However, this 'safe space' also poses challenges in the containment processes, one being the inherent risk of exploring the crisis: loss of livelihoods, food insecurity and sense of meaning and our historical actions to sustain these things having caused the harm (Carr & Bendell, 2021). Furthermore, the danger of a single story of the safe space, when in reality it is a subjective experience shaped by our lived experiences and dominant cultures. Therefore, we should consider an ethic of care in how we approach climate conversations through two containment processes, caring for and preparing the participants both physically and emotionally (Carr & Bendell, 2021). Ideas on how to ensure this caring approach to self and others are explored next.

Addressing the barriers to 'difficult conversations' about climate change

The heating effect of atmospheric carbon dioxide and water vapour was discovered by Eunice Foote in 1856 and we've been more acutely aware of the threat of climate change for over three decades. Since Hansen's testimony to the US Senate in 1988 on the relationship between greenhouse gases, observed warming and climate impacts, a series of campaigns of deliberate misinformation by vested interests (Brulle, 2018) have created a polarisation of public opinion and lessened the likelihood of essential climate conversations taking place. In this section I will explore some of the recognised barriers and strategies to approaching climate dialogue, specifically with educators.

Awareness of the 'defences' towards conversations about climate change

Stoknes (2017) describes five inner defences that need to be overcome to support effective climate communications:

1. Distance – having a sense that these issues are happening in a different time and place, in distant places, not in their own communities, and in the future not in their own time.
2. Doom – the habituation and desensitisation to difficult climate disaster reporting, leading to 'apocalypse' fatigue and subsequent avoidance of the topic.
3. Dissonance – the feeling of an inner discomfort, arising hypocritical feelings, developing justifications for our climate negative behaviours and delay tactics.
4. Denial – being aware of difficult knowledge but living and acting as if we don't know (sometimes reinforced within our communities).
5. Identity – our cultural identify can override the climate science facts.

Self-support

Pihkala (2020) recommends that environmental educators should first take actions to support themselves (in the form of self-reflection), after which they are better equipped to help their learners develop their own emotional stamina and resilience. The Climate Psychology Alliance (CPA), with their focus on adaptation (acceptance of climate crisis and modifying our ways of being) in the face of climate crisis, is an excellent starting point for practitioners seeking to support themselves, from guidance on emotional work and reflexivity, to training and therapeutic support.

Addressing eco-anxiety

Eco-anxiety is described by Pihkala (2020) as a 'rapidly growing phenomenon' (broadly understood as anxiety about the climate crisis) which is having an impact on well-being around the globe but most particularly young people, who are experiencing solastalgia and climate grief (Lawrence et al., 2021). Furthermore, Lawrence et al. (2021) highlight a relationship between increased suicide rates and increased temperatures, as well as severe distress following extreme weather. A level of resilience and familiarity is required to support educators in facing up to the challenge of CEE teaching (Pikhala, 2020). To increase resilience and familiarity with this subject, self-conversation and reflection can be cultivated. This might come in the form of a creative outlet like the 'Letters to the Earth' project, and their invitation to grapple with the future of our planet in the form of a written communication to the Earth – an opportunity to process what is happening to the world and creating something to share fears, frustrations, passion and, sometimes, hope. This project provides online group resources, community and education toolkits and also collates the letters in an online resource gallery. They've also published a book of the letters with a poignant introduction from Emma Thompson where she argues that 'All humans know somewhere deep – somewhere like our spinal chords, somewhere we are not used to communicating with – that our planet is suffering' (2021, p. 1). Thompson also depicts the paradox of how we are on our own *and* together at the same time, while we must act because 'the ruling powers will not do enough to alter the course of this terrifying history' (p. 3).

To support educators in this exploration of eco-anxiety, organisational and peer support could enable teachers to manage their own difficult emotions, as well as develop their own emotional skills to use in their work, from validating these emotions to creative activities to consider them more deeply (Pikhala, 2020).

Pause for reflection

- How do you feel about the state of our environment? What was the most recent climate related news story you heard? How did it make you feel?
- You could share your reflections in a 'Letter to the Earth' here https://www.letterstotheearth.com/ and express your frustrations, fears, love or hope.

Scales of conversation – starting with the self

Lertzman (2019) suggests that we need to be attuned to adapt and collaborate. This attunement is part of the journey from eco-anxiety to action, exploring it as feeling understood and accepted for where we are in our CEE journey, without being judged or shamed (Lertzman, 2019). Attunement starts with the individual, with our own connection to our emotions, exploring our feelings through our realisations of our CEE, a sense of permission to be who we are through these difficult truths whilst also remaining curious about our experiences (Lertzman, 2019). Lertzman (2019) recommends leading with attunement by acknowledging our difficult climate reality, by sharing our own fears and lack of answers – creating a sphere of liminality (Bhabha, 2004).

Moving beyond the self

The next level of climate communication might come in the form of peer-to-peer interactions. Stoknes (2017) shares this level of 'social' response as his first solution to transforming apocalypse fatigue through brain friendly climate communication, highlighting that these social interactions can create a new normal in attitudes and behaviours, e.g. the peer effects of climate related decision-making in the spread of solar panels within neighbourhoods (Barton, Wenz, & Levermann, 2021). These difficult conversations, outside the self, can begin to break down the distance, dissonance and denial elements of our apocalypse fatigue but may be met with resistance. It is challenging and emotional to explore our CEE. It is, therefore, important to stay mindful of the social, economic and emotional positions of our conversation partners and avoid blaming, judging and criticising.

Scaling up climate conversations: Wider community

Stoknes (2017) suggests that our individual solutions are insufficient to solving our predicament. We must move beyond our own actions and ruminations to unite our understanding and efforts. This crisis is global and requires, according to David Attenborough (2021), in his address to the UN Security Council, 'unparalleled levels of global cooperation'. Community or workplace interactions with this difficult and urgent topic can be addressed collectively through the process of people's assembly, which involve democratic gatherings, freely open to participation, to address issues of importance – in this case our CEE.

The UK government held a Citizen's Assembly in early 2020 – a process whereby randomised citizens are chosen to learn about, deliberate on and make recommendations about an issue, e.g. on our climate crisis. The subsequent report, The Path to Net Zero (2020), outlines how this civic sortition (a lottery-based method for selecting citizens) believe how the UK should be working towards its zero emissions target. It includes over fifty recommendations for ten areas of our lives, from travel to heating our homes. However, it is ultimately still up to our elected officials as to whether the recommendations are followed and implemented.

This process inspired the pilot of an online climate assembly with a small group of secondary school teachers in Worcestershire, West Midlands, UK.

The Saturday event, held on World Environment Day (and important to note, at the weekend due to teachers not being able to take time out of a Covid-19-deprived timetable), included input from expert witnesses on local climate impacts, e.g. flooding, food security, wildlife, mental health and physical health. The localisation of the input was aimed at overcoming the geographical and temporal dissonance that is frequently felt about the climate crisis. The selection of topics was based on feedback from audiences at BERA and Advance HE Sustainability conference workshops, who were asked to share which climate issues they felt were of most relevance for teachers in their professional capacity. After each stimulus input from the contributors, a social discussion was built into the process with facilitated e-breakout spaces to discuss the impact on attendees, inviting crucial self-reflection, as well as exploring the implications for their personal and professional roles.

Consequently, Lengthorn and Asbury (2021) shared that attendees reported a benefit from having an increased local understanding of the climate impacts in terms of their confidence to teach about these topics but also in talking to their colleagues. Additional benefits included collaborations that extended from the day with attending teachers making links with each other and the local experts to develop cross-institutional eco-actions. As a result, an innovative twelve-hour enhancement activity for training secondary teachers at the University of Worcester entitled 'Education in Climate Emergency' was developed as well as a subsequent further pilot with informal educators, adult volunteers and young leaders from the Scout Association, as part of the Climate Emergency work of Scouts Hereford and Worcester (Scouts H&W, 2022). This, again, led to the development of a community of practice and eco-action collaborations across volunteer sections and groups. The assembly process can be harnessed at a range of scales, from single classrooms, to year groups, or whole organisations and communities, to initiate these difficult conversations about our climate reality and act as the much needed galvanising force and psychological support that is crucial as we face this crisis.

Pause for reflection

Could you plan a community assembly event in your own context (your classroom, a social group or with family) to discuss collective knowledge of the impact of the climate crisis locally and potential actions?

Inclusive communication for urgent adaptation

Phillips (2021) advocates for communication on adaptation and provides the following reasons to move these conversations forward:

1. If adaptation conversations are not undertaken, they will struggle to climb the agenda of powerful decision-makers globally.
2. If adaptation is not on the agenda many will suffer and perish or be forced into maladaptive responses.
3. If adaptation is low on the agenda then those with means may adapt with little accountability, scrutiny and in self-centred rather than community-centred ways.
4. Even those adapting in socially responsible and just ways may maladapt if they haven't had access to training, information and good-practice.
5. A lack of conversation about adaptation by the climate movement risks adoption of the narrative by other movements with the potential for unjust, unwanted, outcomes.

Phillips (2021) reminds us that the voices of those already enduring the difficult consequences of climate change, a situation that most of those people are not responsible for, are being ignored and marginalised and that a lack of conversation will enable the powerful to focus on their own adaptations. It is imperative, therefore, that we acknowledge this and use our own power and privilege to undertake climate crisis conversations and explore climate justice.

A variety of organisations are now offering support for urgent climate dialogue. Client Earth, an environmental law charity with a specialist approach to tackling climate change and defending wildlife, have created a useful publication to help us all speak up for the planet, a 'Guide to Having Climate Conversations' (2022). It includes five straightforward suggestions, developed with their legal and policy experts, to help us all find the confidence to speak up on this 'emotionally charged' topic (Client Earth, 2022, p. 2). These include:

1. Ask open questions to explore what conversation participants care about and believe, call attention to an increased understanding of the participants values enabling a more meaningful conversation.
2. Reframing the issue by connecting climate issues to themes that resonate, e.g. economy, nature, health.

3. Tell convincing stories, using a classic setup, problem and resolution narrative. We relate more easily to experiences and stories than statistics.
4. Know and include the facts.
5. Remain calm and remember that every single conversation counts!

It's crucial, as we broaden and deepen our climate emergency dialogue, that we ensure it is accessible to everyone. The International Disability Alliance (2022, p. 2) research into provisions for people with disabilities identifies a further barrier in suggesting that people with disabilities are being systematically ignored when it comes to the climate crisis, with only 35 of the 192 parties subject to the UN Paris accord referring to people with disabilities in their nationally determined contributions and only 45 referring to people with disabilities in any national policies or programmes for adaptation.

The UK, unfortunately, had been cited as an example of a nation that has not taken account of disabled people's needs in its climate plans. People with disabilities are more vulnerable to climate impacts and are already facing more danger in extreme events e.g. stranded wheelchair users during Hurricane Katrina in 2005 and again during Hurricane Sandy in 2012. Activists like Elizabeth Yeampierre, co-chair of the Climate Justice Alliance, have long been focused on the links between climate change and racial injustice, but our world is only just waking up to the connections between race, privilege and climate justice. Perhaps the first step to addressing this is to acknowledge the intersectional nature of our existential crisis, that there will be no environmental justice without solidarity, disability justice, racial justice and transitional justice (Greenpeace, 2022).

Self-care of the facilitator

Lerztman (2017, p. 3) argues that stories and narratives about climate change are powerful and the most effective way to enable people to react and respond to our climate reality is by 'having conversations'. However, it's essential to acknowledge the impact these conversations can have on the facilitator. The Deep Adaptation process, developed by Carr & Bendell (2021), takes this into consideration by encouraging an acknowledgement of the emotional load to facilitators and participants, via their practice of co-hosting the facilitation, always pairing (or more) people and encouraging 'careful & honest attention' is given between and within them, so as not to diminish their ability to navigate the space and support participants.

Carr and Bendell (2021) seek to remind us that it's not about making the process more comfortable, an impossible task in the face of societal collapse, but rather facilitating the discomfort in this liminal space of emotional transition as we move to fully understanding, both individually and collectively, in the process of decentralising our 'norms' to inspire reflection (Cherry, 2021) and adapt. Wray (2022) reminds us that what we talk about speaks to how much we care about it, and if we're not talking about the climate crisis in our personal or professional lives then we are not giving it importance. She cites a conversation with Caroline Hickman, founder of the Climate Psychology Alliance, when Wray questioned building comfort into her approach to facilitating climate conversations and heard from Hickman that perhaps, instead, we need to get better at sitting with the discomfort.

Our choice of climate language obviously shapes the difficult conversations we need to administer through this discomfort, and Wray (2022) connects us to the evolution of climate language from 'global warming', which she suggests proved too divisive to secure consensus, and 'climate change' which isn't explicit about the heating threat and was adopted at the time of the first UN climate change assessment. Wray (2022) suggests that we need to engage intellectually and emotionally to integrate the dark climate reality into our lives without a breakdown, the opposite response to our instinct to become stressed, defensive and blameful. This perhaps starts with our own emotional education and can then permeate into our professional and community responsibilities. This education can begin with the consideration of instigating conversations about the climate crisis while building the awareness that:

1. it can be difficult to contain emotions that arise in yourself and others on this issue and requires practice;
2. a cycle of silence is perpetuated if we don't open these conversations;
3. neither using only positive storytelling, nor shaming from a moral high-ground, are effective communication tools;
4. flexibility of thought and emotional intelligence is required to activate change;
5. adults must first self-regulate their own difficult emotions in order to be able to help children manage their own and that essential intergenerational communication about our crisis requires 'special care and age-appropriate honesty' Wray (2022, p. 202).

Conclusion

This chapter has highlighted several barriers to initiating and embedding difficult climate conversations in our personal and professional lives, but the risk of not doing so is, quite literally, catastrophic. The UNEP (2022, p. XV) are championing nothing short of a global system transformation, acknowledging that a step-by-step approach is no longer viable, that the window on limiting heating to 1.5° C is closing rapidly and requires a 45 per cent emissions reduction by 2030. The science is unequivocal and we ignore it at our peril. Those that will suffer most are those with the least capacity to act, our children. We, dear reader, have the capacity, the privilege, the opportunity and an ethical responsibility to advocate for them. I implore each of you to urgently take up this challenge, to initiate and accelerate these crucial conversations, and to do so with an ethos of kindness and compassion, in the spirit of being good ancestors to our unborn future.

When I tried to explain the premise of this chapter to my son, aged 13, he asked me, 'How do we start these conversations?' My response, for us all: 'Darling, we must start them with ourselves, in exploring our own values of nature, community, of livelihood, of health and privilege. When we are strong enough, we must then extend our climate conversation circle to our friends and families and then expand again to our colleagues and communities. Perhaps by adopting an assembly process that uses local examples, we can help overcome dissonance and move people to action. The most important thing is that we start them now.'

Pause for reflection

Who do you feel comfortable talking to about our climate reality?
Who do you feel uncomfortable talking to about it? Know that whoever they are, they probably feel uncomfortable too and would appreciate someone else breaking the spell of their defences.

References

Ahmed, S. K. (2018). *Being the change. Lessons and strategies to teach social comprehension*. Heinemann.

Attenborough, D. (2021). *Address to the UN Security council* [web streamed]. United Nations. 23 February.

Ball, S. J. (2017). School politics, teachers' careers and educational change: A case study of becoming a comprehensive school. In *Education and Social Change* (pp. 29–61). Routledge.

Barton-Henry, K., Wenz, L., & Levermann, A. (2021). *Decay radius of climate decision for solar panels in the city of Fresno, USA*. Sci Rep, *11*, pp. 8571. Nature https://www.nature.com/articles/s41598-021-87714-w#citeas.

BBC (2019). *UK Parliament declares climate change emergency*. BBC News Online 1st May. BBC https://www.bbc.co.uk/news/uk-politics-48126677.

Bendell, J. (2018). *Deep adaptation: A map for navigating climate tragedy*. University of Cumbria. https://insight.cumbria.ac.uk/id/eprint/4166/.

Bhabha, H. K. (2004). *The location of culture*. Routledge.

Brulle, R. (2018). *30 years ago global warming became front-page news – And both Republicans and Democrats took it seriously. The Conversation*. https://theconversation.com/30-years-ago-global-warming-became-front-page-news-and-both-republicans-and-democrats-took-it-seriously-97658.

Carr, K., & Bendell, J. (2021). *Facilitating Deep Adaptation: Enabling More Loving Conversations about Our Predicament*. In J. Bendell, & R. Read (Eds.). *Deep Adaptation: Navigating the Realities of Climate Chaos* (p. 175). Polity.

Cherry, L. (2021). *Conversations that make a difference for children and young people: Relationship-focused practice from the frontline*. Routledge.

Client Earth (2022). *Speak up for the Planet: Your guide to having climate change conversations*. Client Earth. https://www.action.clientearth.org/speak-our-planet.

Climate Assembly UK (2020). *The path to net zero: Climate assembly UK full report*. UK Parliament. https://www.climateassembly.uk/report/.

Climate Emergency Declarations (2023). *Climate emergency declarations in 2,319 jurisdictions and local governments cover 1 billion citizens. Climate Emergency Declaration*. https://climateemergencydeclaration.org/climate-emergency-declarations-cover-15-million-citizens/.

Dartnell, L. (2018). *Origin: How the Earth made us*. Penguin, Random House.

DfE (2022a). *Sustainability and Climate Change: a strategy for the education and children's services system*. https://www.gov.uk/government/publications/sustainability-and-climate-change-strategy/sustainability-and-climate-change-a-strategy-for-the-education-and-childrens-services-systems.

DfE (2022b). *Political Impartiality in Schools*. UK Government. https://www.gov.uk/government/publications/political-impartiality-in-schools/political-impartiality-in-schools.

Dunlop, & Rushton, E. A. C. (2022). The place of education in the government's draft sustainability and climate change strategy. *British Educational Research Association Blog*. BERA. https://www.bera.ac.uk/blog/the-place-of-education-in-the-governments-draft-sustainability-and-climate-change-strategy.

Dunlop, L., & Rushton, E. (2022a). *Opinion: The sustainability & climate change strategy for schools doesn't match what students want*. UCL News. https://www.ucl.ac.uk/

news/2022/may/opinion-sustainability-climate-change-strategy-schools-doesnt-match-what-students-want.

Dunlop, L., & Rushton, E. A. C. (2022b). Putting climate change at the heart of education: Is England's strategy a placebo for policy? *British Educational Research Journal, 00*, pp. 1–19. https://doi.org/10.1002/berj.3816.

Elstub, S., Farrell, D. M., Carrick, J., & Mockler, P. (2021). *Evaluation of Climate Assembly UK. Newcastle*: Newcastle University. https://eprints.ncl.ac.uk/file_store/production/277537/A3EE1B3A-B9F3-4F79-A2BB-9BAE82090FE6.pdf.

Freire, P. (1970). *Pedagogy of the oppressed*. Routledge.

Global Action Plan (2020). *Climate Anxiety an introduction for teachers. Global Action Plan*. London: Our Lives. Our Planet. https://www.transform-our-world.org/files/climate_anxiety_-_an_introduction_for_teachers.pdf.

Greenpeace (2022). *Confronting injustice Racism and the environmental emergency*. Greenpeace. https://www.greenpeace.org.uk/wp-content/uploads/2022/07/Confronting-Injustice-Report_2022.pdf.

Guterres, A. (2022). *Video message by UN Secretary General at the WGIII AR6 press conference*. IPCC. https://www.youtube.com/watch?v=EaZRvli9fgQ.

Harvey, F. (2022). *Disabled people are being 'systematically ignored' on climate crisis, says study*. The Guardian. https://www.theguardian.com/environment/2022/jun/10/disabled-people-systematically-ignored-climate-crisis-study?CMP=Share_iOSApp_Other.

Hawken, P. (2017). *Project Drawdown: The most comprehensive plan ever proposed to reverse global warming*. Penguin Books, Random House.

Hickman, C., Marks, E., Pihkala, P., Clayton, S., Lewandowski, R.E., Mayall, E.E., Wray, B., Mellor, C., & van Susteren, L. (2021). Climate anxiety in children and young people and their beliefs about government responses to climate change: A global survey. *The Lancet Planetary Health, 5*(12), pp. e863–e873. https://www.thelancet.com/action/showPdf?pii=S2542-5196%2821%2900278-3.

Home Office (2015). *Statutory guidance: Prevent duty guidance*. UK Government. https://www.gov.uk/government/publications/prevent-duty-guidance.

Howard-Jones, P., Sands, D., & Fenton-Jones, F. (2021). The views of teachers in England on an action-oriented climate change curriculum. *Environmental Education Research, 27*(11), pp. 1660–80. https://doi.org/10.1080/13504622.2021.1937576.

Huggel, C., Bouwer, L. M., Juhola, S., Mechler, R., Muccione, V., Orlove, B., & Walimann-Helmer, I. (2022). The existential risk space of climate change. *Climatic Change, 174*, p. 8. https://doi.org/10.1007/s10584-022-03430-y.

Intergovernmental Panel on Climate Change (IPCC) (2022). AR6 Climate Change 2022: *Mitigation of Climate Change*. IPCC. https://www.ipcc.ch/report/sixth-assessment-report-working-group-3/.

International Disability Alliance (2022). *Status Report on Disability Inclusion in National Climate Commitments and Policies*. Canada: McGill Centre for Human Rights and Legal Pluralism. https://www.internationaldisabilityalliance.org/sites/default/files/drcc_status_report_english_0.pdf.

Lawrence, E., Thompson, R., Gianluca, F., & Jennings, N. (2021). *The impact of climate change on mental health and emotional wellbeing: current evidence and implications for policy and practice.* Grantham Institute. Imperial College. https://spiral.imperial.ac.uk/bitstream/10044/1/88568/9/3343%20Climate%20change%20and%20mental%20health%20BP36_v6.pdf.

Lengthorn, E., & Asbury, M. (2021). Worcester educator climate assembly: Promoting sustainability leadership through participation. A community approach to education in climate emergency. *Discover Sustainability, 2*(1), pp. 1–23. https://link.springer.com/article/10.1007/s43621-021-00053-8.

Lertzman, R. (2017). *Tackling apathy and denial.* Climate 2020. https://www.climate2020.org.uk/wp-content/uploads/2017/09/LERTZMAN_CLIMATE2020.pdf.

Lertzman, R. (2019). *How to turn climate anxiety into action.* TEDWomen. https://www.ted.com/talks/renee_lertzman_how_to_turn_climate_anxiety_into_action?language=en.

Lipman, M. (2003). *Thinking in Education.* Cambridge University Press.

McLaverty, J. (2022). *Are schools facing a squeeze on social activism and debate?* OXFAM. https://views-voices.oxfam.org.uk/2022/07/are-schools-facing-a-squeeze-on-social-justice-activism-and-debate/.

NGA (2022). *NGA's response to DfE's Sustainability and Climate Change Strategy.* National Governance Association. https://www.nga.org.uk/News/NGA-News/April-2022/NGA-s-response-to-DfE-s-Sustainability-and-Climate.aspx.

Phillips, M. (2021). *Great Adaptations: In the Shadow of Climate Crisis.* Arkbound.

Pihkala, P. (2020). Eco-Anxiety and Environmental Education. *Sustainability, 12*(23), DOI: 10.3390/su122310149. https://www.researchgate.net/publication/346732307_Eco-Anxiety_and_Environmental_Education.

Rackley, K. (2023, September, 23). *Climate change – A safeguarding issue?* Geogramblings.com https://geogramblings.com/2020/09/23/climate-change-a-safeguarding-issue/.

Saab, A. (2019). *Climate change: The super wicked problem of climate change action.* Geneva Graduate Institute. https://www.graduateinstitute.ch/communications/news/super-wicked-problem-climate-change-action#:~:text=Climate%20change%20is%20a%20%E2%80%9Csuper,might%20well%20cause%20further%20problems.

Scouts Hereford and Worcester (2022). *Climate assembly and workshop day.* Scours H&W. https://www.scoutshw.org.uk/declaration-of-climate-emergency.

Stoknes, P. (2017). *How to transform apocalypse fatigue into action on global warming.* TED Global. NYC,USA https://www.ted.com/talks/per_espen_stoknes_how_to_transform_apocalypse_fatigue_into_action_on_global_warming?language=en.

Stone, D., Heen, S., & Patton, B. (2011). *Difficult conversations: How to discuss what matters most.* Penguin.

Sustainable Food Trust (2022). *Has the DfE's Sustainability and Climate Change Strategy really addressed the problems we face.* Sustainable Food Trust. https://sustainablefoodtrust.org/news-views/sustainability-and-climate-change-strategy/.

Teach the Future (2021). *Teaching the Future.* Teach the Future. https://www.teachthefuture.uk/teacher-research.

Teach the Future (2022). *Research with teachers in England on climate education and the curriculum.* Teach the Future. https://uploads-ssl.webflow.com/6008334066c47be740656954/61e6b5bc02d87c41dcb45951_20220113_Teach%20the%20Future_climate%20education%20-%20Overall%20summary%20report.pdf.

Thompson, E. (2021). *Letters to the Earth – Introduction.* Harper Collins.

UNEP (2022). *The Closing Window: Climate crisis calls for rapid transformation of societies. Emissions Gap Report 2022.* United Nations Environmental Program. https://www.unep.org/resources/emissions-gap-report-2022.

United Nations (2015). *Do you know all 17 SDGs?* United Nations Department of Economic and Social Affairs. https://sdgs.un.org/goals.

United Nations (2022). *UN News: UN chief warns against 'sleepwalking into climate catastrophe' United Nations.* https://news.un.org/en/story/2022/03/1114322#:~:text=With%20the%20planet%20warming%20by,from%20these%20levels%20of%20chaos.%E2%80%9D.

Van Kessel, C. (2020). Teaching the Climate Crisis: Existential Considerations. *Journal of Curriculum Studies Research, 2*(1), pp. 129–45.

Worth, D. (2022). *Impartiality guidance: What do schools need to know?* Times Educational Supplement magazine. Retrieved 14th March 2023, from https://www.tes.com/magazine/analysis/general/impartiality-guidance-what-do-schools-need-know.

Wray, B. (2022). *Generation Dread: Finding Purpose in an Age of Climate Crisis.* Penguin, Random House.

Part Three

'Difficult Conversations' in the Research Context

10

(Looking) Behind the Mask: How Difficult Conversations in Research Can Illuminate the Complex Inner Worlds of the Teacher and the Researcher

Sally Hinchliff

Introduction

This chapter is about how *difficult conversations* with teachers have emerged as a leitmotif in my ongoing doctoral research: how they fascinate me, intrigue me, concern me and leave me with more questions than when I began! I focus on a recent pilot study which employed a narrative life history approach (Goodson, 2013) to explore how teachers navigate their educational beliefs and values in their work. I am interested in all actors in these research conversations: both the teachers (my two participants) and the researcher (myself), and I aim to capture these voices as faithfully as I can. Throughout the chapter, I will apply two lenses: one which explores teachers' individual and unique stories, and another which considers the researcher in relation to the stories told to them and the conversations that they are a part of. My intention is to uncover what difficulty 'looks like and feels like' for both parties and how it shapes their particular experiences. At the same time, I am interested in how in this confrontation with difficulty, as researchers and as teachers, we might gain new insights which can transform our thinking and practice: for example, for both researcher and the researched the knowledge to ensure an ethics of care in such sensitive territory. And, for the teacher/participant, the opportunity to find a voice to imagine the kind of classroom where they might flourish.

Drawing on this problematic notion and what for me has become a truly fascinating research context, the aims of the chapter are threefold: (1) to examine how research conversations can unravel 'hidden' and potentially difficult aspects of teachers' identity, (2) to articulate the challenges of research dialogue for the researcher who seeks to understand the difficulty embodied within teachers' professional roles and identities and (3) to explore whether creating liminal spaces for dialogue about teachers' inner conflicts can be transformative.

Reflecting on these aims, it is clear that they seek to answer questions about relationships: relationships between teacher and their work, between researcher and participant, and how these relationships and the difficulty which permeates them might be transformed to help both researcher and teacher to flourish.

Relationships are of course about connections (Palmer, 1997), and at this introductory stage I want to be transparent about my belief in the *connectedness* of researcher and researched. This belief foregrounds all my thinking, and as I will go on to argue, it is precisely through this connectedness as a researcher listening to my participants' life stories that I have begun to uncover and to understand teacher difficulty. And yet, at the same time, it cannot be denied that this process of uncovering difficult stories has been problematic: both methodologically and emotionally, for both sides. In this way, I have come to see the shared stories of my life history research encounters as both a gift and a burden! This, 'dark and light' of narrative, is a tension which is central to my study and has, at times, been difficult to navigate, but it is precisely this need to grapple with difficulty which has moved me to want to write about it and to share my thoughts with others. For difficulty, I have come to see, is intriguing in its very complexity, and moreover, where is the challenge or indeed the benefit in writing about and reflecting upon something in the social world which is straightforward and already 'known'? I also strongly feel that for this chapter to be beneficial for the reader, they must feel that they too can make a connection with the researcher and with the teacher/participant becoming 'selves-in-relation' (Doucet & Mauthner, 2008, p. 402) and finding resonance in the stories told, and the problems posed. In sum, I want this chapter to be meaningful whether you are a teacher, a researcher or indeed someone like me who floats between these two identities. My hope is that what I have to say will be a catalyst for more reflection, more wondering, and more conversations – difficult or otherwise.

Naming the difficulty: For teacher and for researcher

The difficulty of difficulty: Before going any further, it is apparent to me that we can have no meaningful shared understanding of difficult conversations and their potential to disrupt and to transform, unless I articulate the nature of that difficulty as I have perceived it. To do just this, drawing on my doctoral research, I will now set out what I have come to understand as *difficulty* from the perspective of the teacher-participant *and* from my perspective as the researcher.

To be clear, I have found the task of defining and writing difficulty far from easy. My supposition is that whether we are a teacher or a researcher of teachers, difficulty and difficult conversations make us feel vulnerable, a view borne out in a plethora of research studies and theorisation (see for example Claxton, 1989; Eaude, 2012; Kelchtermanns, 1993, 2005; Moore, 2006). And indeed, why should we expect to feel at ease with a topic which is likely to disrupt our already complicated professional lives, which might question orthodoxies, or even lead us to question ourselves and our relationships with others? How many of us, be it in the classroom or in the fieldwork, seek out this conscious uncovering and new self-awareness? My sense is that we are much more likely to dissemble, to put on our 'game face' (don the mask), so that difficulty is pushed down beneath the surface of the conversation. Difficulty is, therefore, I argue, intrinsically challenging for researcher and researched: it is uncomfortable for a teacher to speak of and therefore hard for the researcher to capture. And, woven into this complex picture, is the additional challenge of how the researcher deals with the difficulty which confronts them as they consume the stories of others. *And yet*, and this is axiomatic to everything I will share in this chapter, I am convinced that difficulty is *worth* uncovering, however elusive it may be. From my pilot study research experience, I know that difficulty is perceptible, that it is relatable. It may take time to unearth it, but my experience is that researcher and participant can work together to identify difficult experiences and learn about themselves through this process of discovery. This elusive yet uncannily present phenomenon of difficulty brings to mind the writing of feminist writer/researcher Andrea Doucet. In her analytical framework, Doucet (2007) is interested in the 'ghosts' which haunt our professional work, the 'shadow [of] others which are present in our stories' (p. 74). Doucet's metaphor resonates. I have seen how difficulty casts a shadow, that it weaves in and out of the stories told to me by teachers, all the time complicating the task of the researcher. Acknowledging the elusive, unpindownable nature of difficulty, it is important to try to define the properties of the difficult conversation, as experienced by researcher and researched, so that we have a framework to help us identify them. My framework for difficulty is as follows:

For the teacher:

1. How they navigate conflict between their educational values and those of the educational institution where they work.

2. How they experience the relationships with others in their institution (with adults and with children) in the light of conflicting perceptions of the role of the teacher in the school.
3. How they navigate a curriculum which they perceive to be inappropriate for the needs of their pupils.
4. How all of the above impact on their identity, emotional wellbeing, and agency.

And, for the researcher:

1. How they might navigate difficult conversations with sensitivity, ensuring that they maintain an ethics of care (Josselson, 1996).
2. How they resolve the ethical tension inherent in encouraging participants to unveil difficult experiences, some of which may be troubling, or even distressing.
3. How they might ensure that they show *themselves* compassion as a researcher (Sirois and Rowse, 2016). For example, if they are troubled by the context and content of a difficult conversation, how do they process this response which be the product of personal past trauma?
4. The extent to which they can take off their own mask and share their concerns, and vulnerabilities. In deciding to remove the mask do they jeopardize the research encounter, or enhance it?

Reviewing these layers of difficulty for teacher and researcher, it is clear that encountering difficulty in research is challenging. But then neither party is a stranger to difficulty. Both teachers and researchers constantly negotiate complex personal and professional terrain in their work – their actions are ethically and emotionally charged (Bibby, 2011; Hammersley-Fletcher, 2015; Kelchtermans, 2005; Moore, 2006; Sayer, 2011); therefore, difficulty it could be said 'goes with the territory'. With this in mind, I now shine a light on the ethical, emotional and methodological challenges of my own study. To involve you, the reader, in the dilemma which I faced along the way, you will find 'pauses for reflection' and, here, I invite you to be troubled, puzzled and intrigued by some of the issues which have emerged for me in this confrontation with difficult conversations and to consider what you might do presented with similar conundrums.

Part 1: 'In the grip of the story' (Goldin, 2019, p. 512): The interplay between difficulty, storytelling and researching through story

The researcher's story: Confronting one's difficult past

As Peter Clough expresses so perfectly, 'We never come innocent to a research task' (2002, p. 17), and as good a place as any to begin in interrogating my own researcher experience of difficulty must be with an exploration of my researcher positionality. Without doubt, my central research question – *How do teachers navigate the enactment of their educational beliefs and values in their work?* – is, in the words of the veteran life history researchers Goodson and Sikes, 'knottily entangled' (2001, p. 15) with my own troubled teacher biography. To give some context, as a teacher I often felt diminished and undervalued; more often than not, these damaging feelings often were the product of difficult conversations, for example where I had tried (and failed) to defend a teaching strategy which I felt was right for the children in my class, opposing the one which had been imposed. I recall that these conversations took courage and level of self-belief which I did not always possess. They left me feeling vulnerable and exposed. These are clearly difficult memories, and, over a decade later when I began to research with teachers and heard of their own experiences of discord and dissonance, I had the realisation that I was still 'haunted' by my teacher past (Doucet, 2007), that it framed not only my past experience as a teacher but also my current positionality as a researcher. Furthermore, and with no small degree of sadness, I also realized that I had not dealt with this profoundly difficult and destabilising past experience. I had not found closure. Looking back, I see now that my 'escape' from the distress of the school classroom to the relative calm of initial teacher education (ITE) had only postponed me having to confront my past. I tentatively began to broach this confrontation with difficulty through my masters study into the emotional dimension of training to teach and I am now embracing it head on in my doctoral journey.

In the next section on researching with teachers using a life history methodology, I will share how I found a way to reflect upon and to articulate the difficulty that I encountered in the process of the exploration of others' stories. But, for now, suffice to say that I have an inextricable personal/professional connection with my doctoral study, to the extent that without this difficult professional past and a need to make sense of it, I doubt that I would have chosen this particular research focus, or indeed be writing this chapter!

So, returning to the aims of the chapter, with its focus on the challenges of the research dialogue and of uncovering and defining difficulty within research conversations, I ponder over the question of how much does my researcher entanglement with the classroom hinder or enhance the study. My provisional position, as I am only in the foothills of my research, is that this personal connection is enhancing and illuminating. My first-hand experience of difficulty, of feeling diminished, silenced and vulnerable, has helped me to be an empathetic researcher (Ellis, 2007; Josselson, 1996) and to practise an ethics of care. I have empathy as I have taught in similar classrooms to those which my participants describe. I have experienced the joy and the pain of that teacher experience. I have stood in their shoes, lived their difficulty and tried (and sometimes failed) to engage in the difficult conversations with other colleagues, seeking to make things better, to challenge, to confront. However, what I have also discovered (and I will go on to exemplify this discovery with examples from my data analysis) is that my response to elements of the teachers' stories was, at times, almost visceral, to the extent that I began to wonder if it was damaging. This leads me to argue that as researchers of difficulty we must exercise self-care, and that it comes primarily through making space for deep, reflexive thinking about the content of those stories/research encounters which upset, move and destabilise us (Gilligan, 2015; Gilligan & Eddy, 2017; Mauthner & Doucet, 2007, 2008; Tolman & Head, 2021). I would go as far to say that my own reflection has brought with it some of the closure which I have unknowingly been seeking. It may have taken more than a decade, but finally, I am starting to make sense of my own teacher past and the difficulty embedded within it. This, I feel in itself, represents a kind of transformation, a coming to terms with earlier struggle, and an utterly unexpected gift of researching with teachers. Greene (1995, p. 20) articulates this transformation for me so well

> A reflective grasp of our life stories and of our ongoing quests, that reaches beyond where we have been, depends on our ability to remember things past. It is against the backdrop of those remembered things, and those funded meanings to which they gave rise, that we grasp and understand what is now going on around us.

I feel sad for my former self, a young teacher who did not really understand what was happening around her, who felt she had no voice. I wish that there had been a space for her to feel safe and be heard, to transform her difficulty into something positive. Having uncovered my own teacher biography through research with others, I advocate for the importance of creating a safe space in schools where teachers might share difficult experiences with one another, and through these encounters find solidarity, kinship and possibly new understandings of themselves and their situation. In the third section of this chapter, I will say more of how this liminal space (Thomassen, 2009) might be built and what it might empower.

> ## Pause for reflection
>
> - As researchers of the social world and recognising that as researchers we too are part of the world which we seek to better understand (Dean, 2017) how easy is it to escape the 'ghosts' of our professional/ personal pasts?
> - Do we need to acknowledge these and swiftly move on, or are they in fact a driver for our research? If they are indeed so central to our enquiry, do they need to be written into it? (what Fine calls 'writing the self' (Denzin & Lincoln, 2002, p. 107).

The Teacher's story: Narrative research as a gateway to understanding teacher difficulty

'We can be known only by the unfolding of our own unique stories within the context of everyday events', writes Gussin-Paley (1990), and certainly the conversations which I held with teachers in my doctoral pilot study provided that 'narrative Knowing' (Elbaz, 1993), which was essential in deepening my understanding of the nature of difficulty experienced by teachers. Without doubt, the particular qualities which a life history approach (Carter, 1993; Clandinin & Connelley, 1990, 1996; Goodson, 2013; Goodson & Numan, 2002; Goodson & Sikes, 2001) brings to the research encounter have helped me to get closer to the difficult lived experience of teachers. Life history as method and methodology has enabled me to uncover difficulty which, otherwise, I think I may have missed. It has done so in a number of important ways which I will now lay out.

First, life history situates an individual's life story in that 'ambiguous intersecting location between the personal and the professional' (Goodson & Sikes, 2001, p. 59), and I would suggest that this intersection is often the loci of difficulty – that point of tension where the personal and the professional collide and conflict. In one of my research conversations in the pilot study, for example, the teacher recalled his feelings of inferiority when he compared himself to other colleagues in his professional context. He wanted to be able to 'be like them', to emulate their confidence and self-belief, their unquestioning faith in the curriculum they were mandated to deliver. At the same time, beneath the radar, he railed against this curriculum and those who espoused it, believing it inappropriate for his pupils. He was confused, frustrated, angry and sad. On one occasion he tells of how subverted what in his eyes was a pedagogical straight jacket, by taking his English literature lesson outside of the classroom and in this 'small act of authorship' (Sannino, 2010, p. 289), he found some agency. He rejoiced in the engagement of his pupils, gathered around him on a small patch of playing field, listening to the words of George Elliot, read to them in the open air, in their new grassy classroom.

Using a life history method with its dual lens on the private and the public and its power to reveal what lies hidden in plain sight, I was able to provide a space for this teacher to tell the story in his own words; in doing so opening a window onto his difficulty. The life history lens gave me the eyes to see the teacher's turmoil: namely the conflict between a desire to conform and to please (Moore, 2006) and the equally powerful drive to rebel-to be true to his authentic teacher-self (Palmer, 1997).

Secondly, as I hope the above example shows, what story and life history methodology makes *visible*; it lifts the mask. The revelatory nature of story feels especially significant when we think of the challenges, of uncovering difficulty – the feelings of awkwardness, vulnerability and even of shame which are often associated with acknowledging difficulty (Eaude, 2012; Kelchtermanns, 2005). Stories, writes Bell (2002, p. 415), have 'a sense of being full' and with this fullness which captures the whole person, the whole teacher, I believe that we also access more of their truth. For, in the telling of the story, we go beyond the teacher as a one-dimensional 'matchstick figure', all too often the product of quantitative studies (Carter, 1993, p. 8). Instead, at ease, telling their own tale, on their own terms, the teacher/participant too takes off the 'suit of armour' (Gibbs, 2017, p. 719) which they may feel duty bound to wear in their professional work. And, with this shift, we can start to glimpse the interiority of the teacher, to learn about their emotionally patterned lived experience and to understand the fundamentals of their difficulty.

And, thirdly, and so importantly, I value story as my central research method as I am convinced of its capacity to *carry emotion* – emotion which we need to hear if we are to get to grips with difficulty, as Goodson (2013, p. 35) writes, 'the life history [told through stories] forces a confrontation with people's subjective perceptions'. There is no attempt to sidestep this messy, inconvenient and contradictory subjectivity – for all its difficulty, we embrace it, and, I would argue, in doing so we also embrace and value our participants; we see them more clearly, rather than reducing them to 'bloodless universals' (Goodson, 2013). To ignore this emotion, however difficult it may be to understand, is to miss out on a whole dimension of teacher experience. Palmer (1997, p. 71) writes that 'teaching tugs at the heart, opens the heart, even breaks the heart – and the more one loves teaching, the more heart breaking it can be' and, therefore, it is not surprising that with this emotional investment there is much at stake in the teacher's work (Kelchtermanns, 2005). It is a reasonable supposition then that the difficult conversations that thread through stories which teachers tell of their work will be riven with emotions, and by being alerted to feeling(s) in my participants' stories, I am likely to better understand another person's difficulty. Kazuo Ishiguro (2017) further posits that 'in the end, stories are about one person saying to another, this is the way it feels to me. Can you understand what I am saying?' If, then as researchers working with stories, we can understand this other person in their difficulty, I believe we accomplish so much in our enquiry.

I will now move on to share how I used an approach to data analysis (the Voice Centred Relational Method coined by Mauthner and Doucet (2003)), which, with its emphasis on listening 'beneath and beyond' (Tolman & Head, 2021, p. 155) to the words of the storyteller, helped me to listen *affectively*, and note the emotion so integral to teacher experience and to difficulty.

Pause for reflection

Bruner (1991) argues that meaning without mind is impossible. Above, the suggestion is made that meaning without emotion is equally impossible. Do you agree that this is the case and that by understanding emotion, we can access difficulty? Should we be have to be wary of the 'intelligence of the emotions' (Sayer, 2011, p. 37), or embrace it?

Part 2 'Listening beneath and beyond' (Tolman & Hood, 2021, p. 155): Analysis to get to the heart of the difficult conversation

I believe the best way to share the intricacies of the analysis and to capture how I listened and what I heard as researcher is to exemplify the process with extracts from analysis transcripts, but before I do so, I offer a little context on Voice

Centred Relational Method and the Listening Guide (Gilligan, 2015; Mauthner & Doucet, 2003; Tolman & Head 2021) – interpretative approaches which, I believe, were indispensable in helping me really *hear* my participants.

While I was grappling with the challenge of finding a method of data analysis which would preserve the richness, complexity and subjectivity of the teachers' stories, I was delighted when I came across an article about a form of data analysis which was completely new to me – the 'Listening Guide' approach, which draws on psychological paradigms (Tolman & Head, 2021). In making their case for this approach, they write, 'There is a difference between what is spoken and what can be discerned beneath and beyond' (p. 155). The Listening Guide methodology (Gilligan, 2015) gives the researcher the means to trace the polyvocality of participants' voices, that is to say the different voices within one voice, and in the process, to truly listen beyond – to look behind the mask. I went on to discover that two researchers (Mauthner & Doucet, 2003, 2008) had created an adapted version of the 'Listening Guide' called the 'Voice Centred Relational Method'. In my own analysis I worked with a fusion of these two approaches. The appeal of these innovative approaches to data analysis in relation to understanding the nature of difficulty is that they engage with difficulty by giving the researcher a tool to trace it in its many guises and contexts. The method involves a series of four discrete 'listenings' or 'tracings' (Mauthner & Doucet, 2003), which asks that the researcher attunes themselves to the many different layers of voice: listening for how the participant speaks of themselves, for how they speak of others, for how they speak of the wider structures around them, and (quite unusually for a data analysis approach) a further reflexive layer of listening which tunes into the researcher's own responses to the stories told. This polyphonic approach was invaluable in my quest to understand difficulty in that helped me to crystalise the nature of difficulty experienced by the participant and at the same time to turn the mirror on myself and to examine my researcher difficulty.

Now, with an example from one transcript, I would like to take you through some of the 'strands of difficulty' which weave through my interview/conversation with 'Billy', a young teacher in his fifth year in the classroom. I found it fascinating to attend to/listen to how Billy speaks of himself in this excerpt, the 'voice of the I' (**BLUE**) and equally how he speaks of other people. Noticing this polyvocality, I felt so much more attuned to the interplay of difficulty within his story:

Sally: Ah, right. Yeah … is that [the results] the bottom line, do you think?
Billy: **No, not for me. In the grand scheme of things** … that from the

perspective of the people who are in charge, they wouldn't know how those results were obtained anyway ... they just see it as it's our curriculum [that is why] we're making this progress.

Sally: [affirmative] Mmm!

Billy: And I'm not bothered about what that looks like on the outside, it's more about the reward you get on a day-to-day basis, being in the classroom. And that reward is completely intrinsic; it's not anything that has to be cemented by a tangible object ... something they have learned ... and just walking away with knowledge that they don't have before .... [extended pause] **not even knowledge, just something they can think about. I think** any interaction with a young person, **regardless of what it is about, should be treasured** by both people in the conversation ... 'cos I do think that you can learn more about a child and what they are fighting for, or what they are living for, **when you just have a natural conversation with them.**

My reading of difficulty in this excerpt is that contrary to what we might hear about the challenges of teaching in a secondary school, Billy does not experience difficulty in his interaction with the young adults he teaches. On the contrary, this is a source of personal fulfilment, something to be 'treasured'. He draws 'intrinsic' reward from these relationships, deriving great fulfilment from the 'natural conversations' which he has with children in his class. It is through these relationships that he learns about them as individuals. At the same time, there is a suggestion that these personal interactions happen beneath the radar; in another space that is not where the 'delivery' of the curriculum takes place. Billy speaks of how things appear 'on the outside', suggesting to me that there is another space, 'on the inside' where more meaningful educational interactions take place. However, as I went on to trace how Billy spoke of others in his professional world, 'the people who are in charge', difficulty, it seems, resides in the relationships with authority. Billy does not seem to trust their leadership, suggests they have no real knowledge or interest in the children whom he would seem to know so well, and he has little faith in the knowledge-based curriculum which they impose. By listening 'beneath and beyond" (Tolman & Head, 2021) I became aware of the intensity, rawness and vulnerability of this moment in the conversation. And by tuning-in into the different layers of Billy's voice I was able to locate the locus of difficulty in Billy's story: namely the acute tension between Billy's own vision for the best education of his pupils and that of an education system with very different goals and expectations.

Following the VCR and LC approaches, I reflected on my own 'reader response' (Mauthner & Doucet, 2003, p. 17) to Billy's deeply personal account of belief and tension. In the transcript my only utterance is an affirming 'Mmm!'; however, the reflexive lens of the analysis uncovered so much more of my hidden researcher self in that encounter.

Researcher's response: more resonance for me in this excerpt. While listening to Billy, I was aware of almost another 'film playing': of me in my classroom; and that tension between how and what I wanted to teach to support foreign language learning and the nagging, at times fearful, thought that if this method didn't 'pay off' on GCCE results day (by meeting the 'Aspirational Targets'), my capability as a teacher would be called into question. In other words, my affirmative 'Mmm' speaks volumes of my own experience as a teacher which resonated with that of Billy's. Listening again to Billy's long, third utterance, nearly a year on, I am just as warmed by his words. That is because, I think, they echo my philosophy of education: that teaching is profoundly relational – that teachers and their pupils too are bound up as selves and others.

In my experience, it is invaluable how this approach to analysis and interpretation allowed me to shine a light on the ghosts of my own difficult teacher past, the ' nagging and fearful thoughts' which were part of my daily teacher life. Difficulty was unspoken, but nevertheless utterly present for me in that research encounter, and thanks to this approach, it was uncovered. In uncovering it, putting it into words, I felt that, to some extent, I laid those difficult times to rest, that I understood myself somewhat better. This reflection resonated with Boler's work on educational research and emotion, and our need to be alert to 'emotion's absent presence' (Boler, 1999, p. xv). And I would argue that a self-understanding of what drives us to research is something very precious and necessary in our role. It makes us better, kinder and more effective in our search for new knowledge.

Pause for reflection

What does the concept of 'listening beneath and beyond' mean to you as a researcher? What does it involve, and how might it help us to pick up on the sources of difficulty/ tension in teachers' work, do you think?

Part 3: Harnessing storytelling: Professional learning for teachers to imagine their 'possible selves' (Markus & Nurius, 1996, p. 954)

Reflections on the value of story in the understanding of difficulty

In the preceding two sections, my intention has been to show how the threads of two experiences, that of researcher and the researched, are intertwined in the difficult conversation. I have argued that both the storyteller (the teacher) and the recipient (researcher) are bound together by the difficult content of the conversations through which the story is told and that there are challenges for both in this encounter. Storytelling in the context of research, I have come to realise, is something other than entertainment, a series of anecdotes, a chronology; it is more complicated, more *difficult*. It is difficult in that in the telling of their life story, participants ('Billy, whose story I have shared) unearth and interrogate their past and question their present. In this respect, there is something about storytelling in research which has the power to confront and disrupt (Goodson, 2013; Yoder-Wise & Kowalski, 2003) which makes us 'turn the mirror on ourselves' (Nias, 1989, p. 71) and both the participant and the researcher, are forced to look at their own reflection. Therefore, most certainly, storytelling may make us feel vulnerable and temporarily disorientated; it shocks us by what we discover about ourselves in removing the mask, but at the same time that very exposure to difficulty, to ourselves can be transformative. I say this not based on wishful thinking but drawing on the reflections of participants in my pilot study. After the interview had concluded and the recording had stopped, both 'Billy' and 'Molly' spoke of the new understandings which they had made in the telling of their life stories. Billy referred to the 'indulgence' of having the space to talk about the regrets, fears, hopes and joys associated with their work as a teacher. Both commented on how incredible and how unusual it was to have this space to reflect on themselves, as Molly put it, 'to make connections which I didn't know were there'. So, while in the telling of their individual stories both teachers shared profoundly difficult moments from their pasts, and it has to be acknowledged these memories must have been unsettling to revisit, neither regretted this 'encounter with themselves' which the retelling produced. On the contrary, it seemed to help them to view their professional past differently, less harshly, and with this awareness there was even some sort of closure – in Molly's words, 'it [her past] feels better for the re-telling'.

As a researcher of these two teachers' experience, I take no credit for any new insights gained by my participants – you only need to look at the excerpts from the transcript to see that I was very much positioned as listener rather than interrogator. Yet, perhaps the very fact of careful, compassionate listening, of being bound up, as selves-in-relation (Mauthner & Doucet, 2003) of sharing the space between us, was necessary to uncover difficulty, to make sense of it, and move to a new place. Consequently, as a researcher, moving slowly forward on my doctoral journey, I will never undervalue the art of 'listening beyond' (Tolman & Head, 2021, p. 155) of tuning in and attending to what is being spoken beneath (Gilligan, 2015), of trying to hear the many voices within one voice (Byrne et al., 2003; Gilligan & Eddy, 2017), therefore, of hearing the whole person and, possibly, their whole difficulty.

Concluding thoughts: A space for story in teachers' professional learning?

Researchers must, of course, never lose sight of the 'So what?' of their research, must be able to articulate their contribution to knowledge, to find 'gaps' in that knowledge and to fill them. The process of writing this chapter has crystalised for me that as much as creating a 'contribution to knowledge' what I really want to do (and should try to do) is to make a contribution to *people* – a contribution which would help teachers to thrive and to flourish. Turning my attention away from myself as researcher to teacher, I now want to imagine how this difficult yet rich interaction between teacher and researcher which I have tried to capture in this chapter can be taken out of the research context and transposed into ongoing teacher learning.

There are certainly many examples to build on which have been discussed in the literature around collaborative, conversational Teacher Learning (Feldman, 1999; Hargreaves & O'Connor, 2018; Netolicky, 2020) all of which are foregrounded by a belief that the richest and most transformative teacher learning is collaborative and dialogic in nature (Sachs, 2011). My imagined space in which teachers can share their difficulties is, I think, a kind of community of inquiry within a school (Osborn & Canfor-Dumas, 2018). Here, in this safe space, teachers working as selves-in-relation would be able to make sense of the daily difficulties they all encounter. It would be at once a sanctuary and a place to learn. Priestly et al. (2015, p. 38) ask the important question 'What do teachers do with their beliefs and aspirations?' In answering this question, I suggest that the professional learning could be re-imagined as a much-needed community of philosophical inquiry where teachers would feel free to articulate their thinking, to share what matters to them, and to hold rich conversations about the personal and professional dimensions of their everyday working lives and relationships. Although this would not be a space of certainty where we 'pin down' what 'effective' teaching entail, this space would embrace the dilemma and uncertainty. Solnit (2016, p. xii) writes, hopeful, aspirational thinking is generated in those places and spaces in our lives which are open, without boundaries, or prescription, and '[this] spaciousness of uncertainty is room to act'. Thus, in my imagined teacher space, teachers would not necessarily expect to leave with a quick fix, for they would continue to grapple with difficulty, inherent as it is in their work, but, crucially, they would not do so alone. And, through their shared conversations, embracing difficulty and openness, they would find themselves on the threshold of uncovering the solutions they seek, in a position to imagine their 'possible selves' (Markus & Nurius, 1986, p. 954), to better understand their emotional response to difficulty (Bibby, 2011) and to experience future-orientated agency (Priestly et al., 2015) – a glimpse of possible transformation. Of course, for now this vision resides in my imagination. Would it work, will it happen, I do not know, but what I do know is that my former teacher self, that isolated professional who I have spoken of earlier, would have welcomed such a space with open arms – would you or the teachers in your life?

References

Bell, J. S. (2002). Narrative inquiry: More than just telling stories. *TESOL Quarterly*, *36*(2), pp. 207–13. doi:10.2307/3588331.
Bibby, T. (2011). *Education – an 'impossible profession?': Psychoanalytic explorations of learning and classrooms*. Routledge.
Boler, M. (1999). *Feeling power: Emotions and education*. Routledge.
Byrne, A., Canavan, J., & Millar, M. (2009). Participatory research and the voice-centred relational method of data analysis: Is it worth it? International *Journal of Social Research Methodology*, *12*(1), pp. 67–77. doi:10.1080/13645570701606044.
Byrne, S., Trower, P., Birchwood, M., Meaden, A., & Nelson, A. (2003). Command hallucinations: Cognitive theory, therapy, and research. *Journal of Cognitive Psychotherapy*, *17*(1), pp. 67–84.
Carter, K. (1993). The place of story in the study of teaching and teacher education. *Educational Researcher*, *22*(1), pp. 5–18. doi:10.2307/1177300.

Clandinin, D. J., & Connelly, F. M. (1996). Teachers' professional knowledge landscapes: Teacher Stories – Stories of Teachers – School Stories – Stories of Schools1. *Educational Researcher, 25*(3), pp. 24–30. doi:10.3102/0013189X025003024.

Claxton, G. (1989). *Being a Teacher: a positive approach to change and stress.* Cassell.

Clough, P. (2002). *Narratives and fictions in educational research.* Open University Press.

Connelly, F. M., & Clandinin, D. J. (1990). Stories of experience and narrative inquiry. *Educational Researcher, 19*(5), pp. 2–14. doi:10.3102/0013189X019005002.

Dean, J. (2017). *Doing reflexivity: An introduction.* Policy Press.

Denzin, N. K., & Lincoln, Y. S. (2018). *The SAGE handbook of qualitative research.* SAGE.

Doucet, A. (2007). 'From her side of the gossamer wall(s)': Reflexivity and relational knowing. *Qualitative Sociology, 31*(1), pp. 73–87. doi:10.1007/s11133-007-9090-9.

Doucet, A., & Mauthner, N. S. (2008). What can be known and how? Narrated subjects and the listening guide. *Qualitative Research: QR, 8*(3), pp. 399–409. doi:10.1177/1468794106093636.

Eaude, T. (2012). *How do expert primary class teachers really work? A critical guide for teachers, headteachers and teacher educators.* Critical Publishing.

Elbaz, F. (1993). Responsive teaching: A response from a teacher's perspective.

Elbaz-Luwisch, F. (1997). Narrative research: Political issues and implications. *Teaching and Teacher Education, 13*(1), pp. 75–83. doi:10.1016/S0742-051X(96)00042-X.

Ellis, C. (2007). Telling secrets, revealing lives: Relational ethics in research with intimate others. *Qualitative Inquiry, 13*(1), pp. 3–29. doi:10.1177/1077800406294947.

Feldman, A. (1999). The role of conversation in collaborative action research. *Educational Action Research, 7*(1), pp. 125–47.

Gibbs, S. (2017). *Immoral Education. The Assault on Teachers' Identities, Autonomy and Efficacy.* Routledge.

Gilligan, C. (2015). The listening guide method of psychological inquiry. *Qualitative Psychology, 2*(1), pp. 69–77. doi:http://dx.doi.org/10.1037/qup0000023.

Gilligan, C., & Eddy, J. (2017). Listening as a path to psychological discovery: An introduction to the listening guide. *Perspectives on Medical Education, 6*(2), pp. 76–81. doi:10.1007/s40037-017-0335-3.

Goldin, D. (2019). Narrative as a mode of knowing. *Psychoanalytic Inquiry, 39*(7), pp. 512–24.

Goodson, I. (2013*). Developing narrative theory: Life histories and personal representation.* Routledge.

Goodson, I., & Sikes, P. J. (2001). *Life history research in educational settings: Learning from lives.* Open University Press.

Goodson, I. F., & Numan, U. (2002). Teacher's life worlds, agency, and policy contexts. *Teachers and Teaching, Theory and Practice, 8*(3), pp. 269–77. doi:10.1080/135406002100000422.

Greene, M. (1995). *Releasing the Imagination: Essays on Education, the Arts, and Social Change.* Jossey-Bass.

Gussin-Paley, V. (1990). *The boy Who Would be a helicopter: Uses of storytelling in the classroom*. Harvard University Press.

Hammersley-Fletcher, L. (2015). Value(s)-driven decision-making: The ethics work of English headteachers within discourses of constraint. *Educational Management, Administration & Leadership, 43*(2), pp. 198–213. doi:10.1177/1741143213494887.

Hargreaves, A. (1998). The emotional practice of teaching. *Teaching and Teacher Education, 14*(8), pp. 835–54. doi:10.1016/S0742-051X(98)00025-0.

Hargreaves, A., & O'Connor, T. (2018). Solidarity with Solidity: The case for effective professionalism. *Kappan* (20).

Ishiguro, K. (2017) Nobel prize Acceptance Speech https://www.nobelprize.org/prizes/literature/2017/ishiguro/lecture/.

Josselson, R. (1996). *Ethics and process in the narrative study of lives*. SAGE.

Kelchtermans, G. (1993). Getting the story, understanding the lives: From career stories to teachers' professional development. *Teaching and Teacher Education, 9*(5), pp. 443–56. doi:10.1016/0742-051X(93)90029-G.

Kelchtermans, G. (2005). Teachers' emotions in educational reforms: Self-understanding, vulnerable commitment and micropolitical literacy. *Teaching and Teacher Education, 21*(8), pp. 995–1006. doi:10.1016/j.tate.2005.06.009.

Markus, H., & Nurius, P. (1986). Possible Selves. *American Psychologist, 41*(9), pp. 954–69.

Mauthner, N. S., & Doucet, A. (2003). Reflexive accounts and accounts of reflexivity in qualitative data analysis. *Sociology* (Oxford), *37*(3), pp. 413–31. doi:10.1177/00380385030373002.

Moore, A. (2006). Recognising desire: A psychosocial approach to understanding education policy implementation and effect. *Oxford Review of Education, 32*(4), pp. 487–503. doi:10.1080/03054980600884201.

Netolicky, D. M. (2019) *Transformational professional learning: Making a difference in schools*. Routledge.

Netolicky, D. M. (2020). Transformational professional learning: What, why and how? *Independent Education, 50*(1), pp. 32–3.

Nias, J. (1989). *Primary teachers talking: A study of teaching as work*. Routledge.

Osborn, P., & Canfor-Dumas, E. (2018). *The Talking Revolution. How Creative Conversation Can Change The World*. Port Meadow Press.

Palmer, P. J. (1997). The heart of a teacher identity and integrity in teaching. *Change* (New Rochelle, N.Y.), *29*(6), pp. 14–21. doi:10.1080/00091389709602343.

Priestley, M., Biesta, G., & Robinson, S. (2015). Teacher agency: What is it and why does it matter? In *Flip the System* (pp. 134–48). Routledge.

Sachs, J. (2011) in N. Mockler, & J. Sachs (Eds.). *Rethinking Educational Practice Through Reflective Enquiry*. Springer.

Sannino, A. (2010). Teachers' talk of experiencing: Conflict, resistance and agency. *Teaching and Teacher Education, 26*(4), pp. 838–44. doi:10.1016/j.tate.2009.10.021.

Sayer, R. A. (2011). *Why things matter to people: Social science, values, and ethical life.* Cambridge University Press.

Sirois, F., & Rowse, G. (2016). The Role of Self-Compassion in Chronic Illness Care. Clinical Review *JCOM, 23*(11), pp. 521–7.

Solnit, R. (2016). *Hope in the Dark. Untold Histories. Wild Possibilities.* Canongate Books.

Thomassen, B. (2009) The Uses and Meaning of Liminality. *International Political Anthropology, 2*(1), pp. 5–28.

Tolman, D. L., & Head, J. C. (2021). Opening the black box: A primer for the listening guide method of narrative inquiry. *Qualitative Psychology* (Washington, DC), *8*(2), pp. 152–70. doi:10.1037/qup0000202.

Yoder-Wise, P., & Kowalski, K. (2003). The power of storytelling. *Nursing Outlook 51*(1), pp. 37–42. doi:10.1067/mno.2003.2.

11

Enabling Difficult Conversations about Childhood Trauma with Care Experienced Children and Young People in the Home: A Conversation between a Researcher and an Adoptive Mother

Debbie Watson and Alison Crowther

Introduction

In this chapter we focus on children's need for 'difficult conversations' with caregivers at home as a precursor to being able to engage in these at school with friends and teachers. We focus on a relatively small group of children[1] who have, at some stage, experienced being in care and/or have been adopted. Children and young people who experience the care system often have disrupted knowledge of their personal histories. Social workers address this disruption through life story work which aims to reconstruct the past. This takes the form of a life story book (mandated for children placed for adoption and seen as good practice for those that remain in care) and 'later life letters' which are written for young people once they are better able to understand the circumstances of their removal. Life story books attempt to create a timeline of the child's early, pre-care experiences and relationships into a chronology. But these are inherently challenging to prepare, and adopters and adopted children have reported feeling a lack of control and agency over the narratives conveyed which often leave the child with more questions than answers (Watson, Latter, & Bellew, 2015a, 2015b). Life story work mostly focuses on the 'big story' of why the child could not remain in their birth family but fails to address the everyday 'small' stories that make up children's memories of past family and placements. Moreover, both the big and the small stories are often avoided in the home through fear of inciting additional trauma and as such these become 'difficult conversations' – topics not to stray into for fear of the consequences in family life with adults often stuck in the dilemma of how honest or benevolent they should be (Levine, Roberts, & Cohen, 2020). Despite this, children and young people have emphasised their need to have these conversations with knowledgeable, confident adults they trust. This chapter draws on a ESRC-funded impact project, 'Difficult Conversations' in 2020/2021, in which children and adults in adoption and fostering spheres co-created training resources to support the adults in care experienced children's lives to have better life story conversations (Watson, Staples, & Riches, 2020).

We initially met at the launch of a previous Arts and Humanities Research Council (AHRC)-funded project called *trove*,[2] which Debbie led. *trove* involved co-designing a bag with care experienced children that could simultaneously hold important objects and serve as a memory prompt for children who have been physically parted from their past. The bag design incorporates an android phone and a bespoke multi-media storying app that enables children to attach stories onto precious toys and objects using Near Field Communication (NFC) tags and the reader in the phone, which can be accessed over time, providing the opportunity to hear themselves when they were younger, saying how they felt about the objects and what they know about their origins (Gray, Hahn, Cater, Watson, Williams, Metcalfe, & Meineck, 2020). In this way *trove* provides a space for children to creatively reflect and engage in memory work (Watson, Meineck, & Lancaster, 2018). Through the experience of the project, we also recognised children's need for information and conversations about their past and their concerns over how to ask for this information as well as parents who were oblivious to that need or just didn't know how to have these 'difficult conversations'.

This chapter is in the form of a conversation. Alison's specialism is facilitating difficult conversations – having worked in conflict resolution for twenty-five years and being the mother of a seven-year-old adopted boy, and Debbie's research and networks enriched the training provision for adopters, foster carers and social workers. We posed questions to each other about the experience of working on the project and the ensuing responses have been grouped under thematic headings. The data that we have presented as part of this received full ethical approval from the University of Bristol, Social Sciences and Law Research Ethics committee, and all participants have consented to their data being used in research outputs and have been anonymised.

Through this conversation, we also aim to address core concepts of the book including the importance of liminal spaces, how to nurture difficult conversations and the care required to do so. We argue that being supported to have these conversations has the potential for transformation in family life and children's identity outcomes.

The need for Difficult Conversations in adoption and fostering

Ali: I know you have heard some harrowing stories, talking one to one with parents and children. What did these tell you about the level of need for difficult conversations?

Debbie: Everything!! Across consecutive projects, I got to know some adoptive and foster care family stories from the child and parent's perspective, and I kept hearing dissonance between these stories. I was aware that parents had information about the child's birth family that they didn't know how to convey to their child, even when the child was a teenager. Some of this information was potentially catastrophic for the child who will at some time learn this history. I heard accounts of adopters hiding books, or parts of books from their child as they did not want to open 'Pandora's box' and did not feel supported to do so (Watson et al., 2015a, 2015b). Through work on *trove* (Gray et al., 2020; Watson et al., 2018) I also had glimpses into toy-mediated questions that children were raising (and had not previously raised with parents), and this made me question the extent of skill and knowledge of adults to deal with these questions. *trove* is potentially an important child-mediated tool, but it requires confidence on the part of adults in the child's life to be able to respond to the questions that might come up – the so-called 'difficult conversations'. Not answering these (and sometimes adults don't know the answer) can stock up potentially devastating future problems which could lead to placement breakdown, mental health difficulties, and difficulties engaging in school. I also strongly support the claims that we can overestimate the potential harm precipitated by 'difficult conversations' and adults tend to over-focus on short-term concerns rather than potential long-term benefits (Levine et al., 2020).

Bojesen (2019) defines conversation as a developmental and unpredictable act and for me, this is part of what makes these conversations difficult for children and parents/carers, as anxieties about where the conversation may go inhibit both child and adult from engaging. In conversing with another, Bojesen (2019) claims that there is an identity shift as the autonomy of each conversant is destabilised. This is inherently risky for children who already struggle with identity questions – to converse and engage in difficult questions about one's past demands a secure identity base from which to begin. This requires a level of trust in the adult concerned to care for them and there is a need for an ethics of care in this encounter where the child feels listened to and their questions are answered and valued (Noddings, 1992) and this is not possible in a context where adults fear the consequences of these conversations.

Debbie: Can you go back to the time when you discovered *trove* and how this discovery inspired our work together?

Ali: I had been worried that nobody seemed able to tell me exactly how I should be talking to my son about his past. Even social workers used phrases like '*your parents loved you very much but couldn't look after you*', which felt more like diminishing or side-stepping the conversation. I had worked in conflict resolution for years, and I knew that if we encounter an important issue which shapes our feeling and thinking, we need to bring it into the light so that we can jointly understand it and find a way forward. Transparency is crucial not only because it breaks or builds trust but because hiding information and feelings takes a lot of energy – including if you are hiding something from yourself. As I asked around other adoptive parents, I realised that they didn't know how to approach these conversations either, which exacerbated my worries. There is a duty on adoptive parents to tell the child about their history which is mandated in the Adoption and Children Act (Department for Education, 2002) and the advice we receive is to do it immediately and constantly – even to be talking about the child's history when they are very tiny babies so that the words are never a shock. However, it doesn't happen enough – precisely through the lack of adults' skill that you have already alluded to, Debbie. A friend I had spoken to about my worries sent me the flyer for your event [*trove* showcase], so I came along. I had wondered whether you had cracked the nut already and that *trove* was indeed the project which would give me the answers I was looking for. As it turned out, you shared that you had created *trove* for the material objects children possessed when they moved out of the birth family – often forcibly so this was no nicely curated set – normally what had been grabbed by a social worker. *trove* tracks how children feel about those items over time and how they add to them through various foster homes and eventually to adoption, if and when that happens. Children's physical objects often get lost, and subsequent carers sometimes do not understand the value to the child of significant items, and I know this has been a concern of yours in your work (Watson, Hahn, & Staines, 2019). You shared some stories from when you were trialling *trove* with children (Watson et al., 2018) and one specific story really got my attention.

You were interviewing an adoptive mum while her 4-year-old daughter was playing with *trove*. Mum was adamant that her daughter, having been placed for adoption at birth, would not understand the point of *trove* and did not have any questions about her past. What was fascinating was that within a few minutes of engaging with *trove* the girl was asking questions about her birth mum that had never been raised before (such as '*why was mummy too young to keep me?*') and how her adopted mum suddenly seemed anxious about how to address these with such a young child. A plethora of similar stories suggested that not only was *trove* helpful but that it had exposed a huge gap in knowledge and skills in adults about how to deal with difficult questions which would need to be addressed – and would be transformative when they were.

> ## Pause for reflection
>
> - In your area of work, what difficult conversations are going unaddressed? What might ease and be transformed if they were addressed?

Debbie: What had you heard from other adopters about difficult conversations they were encountering?

Ali: Rather than conversations they were encountering, it was what wasn't being said that concerned me. These conversations just weren't happening which I suspected would damage the child's identity and relationships later. Care-experienced author Lemn Sissay puts this very eloquently:

> *Memories in care are slippery because there is no-one to recall them with you as the years pass. In a few months I'd be in a different home with a different set of people who had no idea of this moment. […] This is how to quietly deplete the sense of self-worth deep inside a child's psyche. […] Family is just one set of memories, disputed, resolved or recalled between one group of people over a lifetime, isn't it? And if there is no-one to dispute, resolve or recall the memory, did it happen?* (2019, p. 88)

Other parents I came across said they mention past life, but get out the life story book very rarely, or they don't like to mention it because it prompts 'bad' behaviour in the children. Often the low quality of the life story books as you have found in your research (Watson et al., 2015a, 2015b), or worries about the story being too 'bad' and age inappropriate, plus not wanting to dysregulate that child are settled upon as reasons for not having conversations or leaving it until later. Looking after a traumatised child is incredibly emotional, and often physically hard, and there is little time for self-care, so increasing our child's anxiety, especially where there is not good advice on how to deal with that anxiety is a lot to ask.

Ali: You have worked with many social workers over the years, and with adoptive parents and carers. What has struck you about their perspectives on difficult conversations?

Debbie: If I start with adoptive parents and carers, as you just mentioned, the immediate challenge of getting through the day/week without upset is paramount. Most are aware of the need to have open conversations about the traumatic and the everyday pre-care experiences of their child – something Brodzinsky refers to as *'communicative openness'* (2006), whereby

> *The ability of children to express their feelings about being adopted, and the empathic sensitivity of parents to those feelings, is viewed as a critical process in healthy adoption.* (p. 5)

Most adoptive parents, however, feel they don't have the skills and often the actual knowledge to do this well. There is also an overwhelming feeling that more support is needed and not just in the immediate aftermath of adoption (when the child may still be very young) but also at milestones during the child's development (changing schools, becoming a teenager, accessing social media, getting access to their social work file, etc.). Most parents I have encountered feel the burden of the other family(ies) and genuinely want to be able to hold these previous relationships for their child, but this is emotionally complex work for them as they also navigate their own feelings about what has happened to the child who is now theirs. The adopted child is in a state of liminality, an in-betweenness which is always in flux and cutting across multiple temporalities. Such children exist and experience parenting outside of normative expectations of family where multiplicity and complexity is common:

> *Liminality could also be the condition of being suspended or even trapped between two different sets of role expectations, a condition often leading to impassivity, or even to a social impasse.* (Neumann, 2012, p. 474)

This in-betweenness felt by children is explored in papers related to the study where we document children and young people's views (Watson et al, 2020) and perspectives from adults in their lives (adopters, foster carers, social workers) (Staples, Watson, & Riches, forthcoming). In this latter paper, we draw on feminist new materialist theories of temporalities to understand where temporal states are *'bleeding through one another'* (Barad, 2017, p. 220) and argue that the child displaced from birth family is both in liminal space and existing in multiple temporalities, and this further exacerbates the difficulty of having conversations about their pre-care experiences:

> *a given entity can be in (a state of) superposition of different times. This means that a given particle can be in a state of coexisting at multiple times – for example, yesterday, today, tomorrow. However, temporality is not merely multiple, rather, temporalities are specifically entangled and threaded through one another such that there is no determinate answer to the question 'What is time'? There is no determinate time, only a specific temporal indeterminacy.* (Barad, 2017, pp. 219–20)

For me, this state of temporal indeterminacy of identity poses a specific challenge for carers and adoptive families of care experienced children and points to something else 'difficult' about these conversations. The responsibilities towards all the relational entanglements (Murris, 2020) in a child's life are multiple and pivotal. Child and adult together live their present and imagine their future, but also confront the histories that co-constitute them. Adopters are balancing their own love and protectiveness for their child with ambivalence or hatred of the perpetrators of abuse against their child. Many describe feeling they are left picking up the pieces of other people's abuse/ neglect and poor parenting and that feels unfair. Some carers have described a feeling of the child being stuck in their past and not being able to move forward:

> *He presents and perceives himself as a victim and thinks he will always be a victim and he can't move on from that. We want to help him move on from that by having these conversations.* (Des, Foster Carer)

While for social workers the priority is to keep children safe, and they want to enable new family formulations to be successful, most social workers I have encountered have expressed concern over how to contain the emotions that surface in having difficult conversations and in engaging in life story work where a child and their new family must come to terms with the absent family(ies) in their child's life, for example:

> *Just accepting that the adopted person is always a mixture of the whole lot, and it's not a choice.* (Jeanine, Adoption Social Worker)

Most social workers are desperately aware of the inadequacies in the system, which mean they have less time for direct work with children and families (and often less training and skill). They don't want to leave families in distraught situations where they are unable to continue to support them.

How did we do the research?

Ali: We used a 'sandboxing' method to collect data – what do you think this brought to the training that methods like interviews would not have done?

Debbie: Sandboxing as a method was developed from child psychologist Margaret Lowenfeld's psychotherapeutic 'World Technique' (1979). The approach foregrounds the child's view of the world allowing children to reflect in a non-verbal way, accessing aspects of their 'interior' that they might not have otherwise been able to (Lowenfeld, 1979). Our use of Sandboxing was based on previous research with children in care (Mannay, Staples, & Edwards, 2017).

All participants (children and adults alike) were invited to create a scene representing hopes and fears about 'difficult conversations' in a sandbox using a selection of figures and the sand. We then interviewed them individually about what they had created and explored aspects of having difficult conversations such as barriers, enablers, time, space and relationships. The sandbox below was created by one of our care leavers who talked explicitly about not fitting into her new foster care home and the challenges of being in 'No Man's Land' (Watson et al., 2020), an experience of liminality (Neumann, 2012) where she identified herself as a leech in the middle of the castle moat she had constructed:

> *That's no man's land, that's where I am. This side is my family life, it's very hectic, it's a war zone, there's crumbling – no stability in the buildings, [...] and the grass is always greener on the other side, this was my foster placement with, you know, big house, full of love all the time but I still don't feel like I fit in anywhere. You know, all the bad side, there's nowhere for me, I just sit on my own little island in the middle [...] I came from poor upbringing with you know, abusive environment [...] and it was always very hectic and I went into a placement with this massive house with very tight family connections, you know, dinner round the table [...] and it wasn't really spoke about – about the fact that going from somewhere where you have nothing and being shown all these things that you technically could have had, it's kind of like, well, you know – [...] it's hard – I feel like it's something not really spoke about.* (Sarah, 20)

Figure 11.1 Sarah's sandbox (20-year-old care leaver).

Ali: In what ways was this a powerful method?

Debbie: We found participants spent time crafting their sand scenes and in the interviews the scenes gave them something to focus attention on, rather than retaining eye contact in a traditional interview (Banks, 2001) as we asked them to explain what they had constructed. For some participants this enabled them to put into words things that they found difficult, such as adoptive parents' fears of starting a conversation that might go off in unpredictable ways (Bojesen, 2019). The metaphor of the sand scene enabled people to focus on the elements of this rather than to have to name their fears, in this case in the sense of a journey and separate territories:

> *You might be able to see a path over there but if there are dangers and that area is defended then you could get hurt trying to move across to there. Why would you want to try and move from one space to the other?* (Esme, Adoptive Parent)

Figure 11.2 Esme's sandbox.

Small stories and everyday conversations

Debbie: From your training in conflict resolution what did you feel were the most important elements of how we might help address these difficult conversations?

Ali: The first element is to enable the conversation to happen at all and reduce the fears that adults have about the consequences of things 'getting out of control'. Successful and sustainable 'conversations' in a family context are different to how we might think about conversation in, for example, an educational context because 'conversation' becomes so much more intimate – it is about connection and care and could be grounded in little acts such as a glance, a tickle, a comment, a word or a laugh – as one of the social workers in Difficult Conversations noted, children need access to the everyday memories of their lives, things we mostly take for granted:

> *What was I doing?' 'Who was loving me?' 'What did I enjoy doing?' and all that sort of thing, and I think if nothing else children should have that.* (Finn, Adoption Social Worker)

It's also about confidence; people need to feel secure that I, as a facilitator, know my craft and have 'been here' before. I manage expectations by doing what I say I will do. It's the same with conversations with children. In the training I have written for parents and carers, the first two modules focus entirely on the skills and strengths of the parent – building them up to be courageous and curious, finding out and exploiting their strengths authentically. You are always there to talk to, you are eager/curious, and, in fact, you are so confident with it that you can offer to go to a restaurant to try some food from their heritage because it's exciting. You seek out museums about the cultural history of the child so they can start to build an identity that is their own. To access this thinking in the training, we talk about how the parent can 'reframe' their mind and their child's mind by looking further back in history. The child is a result of millions of years of evolution, adaptation and success. There must have been a great many successful mothers and fathers in their heritage for them to exist today. If we reframe history and culture over a longer time, not just the last one or two generations, there can be more positivity and things to explore that also enables the child to have a deeper sense of connection with their heritage. It is far less scary for the adult too, and from those small steps, opportunities for deeper conversations begin to build. Remember, in all these conversations, you do not need to have the answers; you go on a quest together to find them. Like many children, my son loves me to regale our friends, in his presence, with stories of when he was little, how he used to love to eat grated cheese bit by bit in his fingers or how he managed to call the police with my phone five days into placement! Mums and dads of his friends, our extended family, my old friends and their families, his nursery teachers, play workers, therapists and teachers, our neighbours and even local shopkeepers are all guardians of his story. A keen sense of self and community gives the child and the family unit enough ballast to explore darker areas of their history with less fear of getting lost in it.

> **Pause for reflection**
>
> - Whose story do you hold? Is there anyone in your life who might like to hear reminiscences and update you on how they feel now?

Being vulnerable and showing our own emotions as the professional/caregiver is another element. Vulnerability, well managed, builds trust – and thus confidence in whatever process we are going through. To resolve conflict, participants need to share what is going on beneath the surface – the fears and hopes which lay behind our public 'positions' – to feel understood, so we can find a solution that meets everyone's needs. Facilitators of the Difficult Conversations training will develop participants' ability to talk about hopes, fears, and expectations and often the intense grief that we feel that our child may not travel an easy path into adulthood. Experiencing others displaying their vulnerability can show both adults and children that this feeling is common to everyone – adopted or not.

A final issue to highlight is repair. A facilitator must always address unsettled feelings in a room immediately because tense situations get worse. Often, we name it – 'I'm noticing that … ' – we acknowledge and wonder aloud what to do next, seeking help. The same is true with children. If a child has dysregulated around a difficult conversation, we can wait until they are in a state to hear us, and quietly, calmly acknowledge our part in making them feel big feelings. A favourite phrase is: 'I wonder if … (you are feeling sad because you thought about your birth mother today/you are angry because its near your birthday and you wonder what other people in your birth family are doing)'. We say sorry, hear more and wonder together how we may manage it better next time.

> **Pause for reflection**
>
> - If you have messed up a difficult conversation, how might you repair?

Ali: Why were the small everyday conversations important to the children and young people in the Difficult Conversations project?

Debbie: We explore this in the first film on *Metaphor and Identity*, where one young woman (Beth) told us that her social worker always had 'her' own agenda and didn't take much notice of Beth as an individual. She shared a story of going into a meeting with beautifully painted purple nails and her social worker not noticing these. The little things matter, and all build up into bigger memories and relationships which in turn enable better conversations:

> *A good conversation kind of looks like where you feel like you're listened to, where you feel like supported, you feel like they kind of actually care about the small things you want to say and not just major things they think they need to get through.* (Beth, 19)

As Lily (care leaver) reminds us below, life stories are not just rooted in the past, they are also about the present and future (Bamberg, 2011) and often these temporalities are co-existing (Barad, 2017):

> *It's not just a conversation about the negative, it's a conversation about life in general, it's not, 'hey tell me about your bad experiences.' It is, 'hey tell me what makes you, what made you, how, what process of growing up turned you into the person you are now'.* (Lily, 20)

Developing the training materials in the Difficult Conversations project

Debbie: If I asked you to distil down the essential features of what we have produced in the training materials, what might they be?

Ali: We have five Cs that frame the training. Our five Cs are centred around the first C, which is *Child*. The next four Cs are:

Courage – to have the conversation in the first place – I can't overestimate how difficult that might be for some families, especially those with the most tragic of circumstances. Planning, self-care and support are very much needed here.

Curiosity – about children's past life and extended family, history and culture. Sometimes we have so little to go on – we only know vague cultural backgrounds. That is enough to start some amazing conversations, helped by food, clothing, beliefs, architecture and even visiting countries or areas. For example, my son traces his culture back to several countries, one, he (slightly inaccurately) calls 'Roman', which fits beautifully with learning in school, museums, archaeology and story books like Mr Benn. When he was very small, he told someone, *'I'm part Roman, and I'm also descended from … amoeba!'*

Creativity – is needed by the parent/carer to think up some small actions that will land in the child's world but not dysregulate them too much. Our children often start deep conversations at the most inopportune of times and we need to be ready.

Community – encircles all these other 'Cs' because as humans we are communal creatures, built on relationships, and community is what keeps us safe.

> ## Pause for reflection
> - How can you help build a strong, helpful and sustainable community around any vulnerable children in your care?

Ali: Of all the tools we used in the research and training development, which one(s) struck you as being transformative?

Debbie: Using the transcripts of interviews with all our participants and transforming them into verbatim script for the films was something I always thought would be powerful, but I feel completely humbled by people's words and stories every time I watch them. I think these will be tools that social workers will draw on again and again. The films and the training materials we have developed are all available on our website and can be accessed to do training: http://difficultconversations.info. Some of these are available as samples and professionals can register online to access all of them for free.

Ali: I agree – and previously you spoke of liminal spaces. We hear from many adopted adults that they carry the weight of responsibility for bringing chaos onto their adoptive families, whom they love and don't want to upset by having difficult conversations. They represent the liminal space between birth family (perceived often as damaged and chaotic – otherwise why would the child have been taken away?) and the adoptive family. Sometimes the child blames themselves for being so bad they had to be taken away. If this training helps to gently bring some of this hidden shame into the open so that we can take that weight off adoptees, then we are transforming many lives and families.

Debbie: Can you give the readers an example of one of the training resources you developed and why you particularly think this will be useful?

Ali: Feedback so far suggests that people like the graphics about how important it is to effectively keep the mental 'wound' of not knowing about identity open. The picture (see Figure 11.3) shows how we need to allow it to granulate up from the bottom, just as we need to in our physical body sometimes, to prevent a wound closing too quickly and getting infected. This is a difficult task, but we do this by throwing in tiny bits of information, '*x and y met when they were studying A levels at school*' or '*your grandma would have loved to look after you, but she was a bit old*'. We don't need a long conversation – this is just a granule that the child can let percolate for as long as they want and ask questions about when they want to.

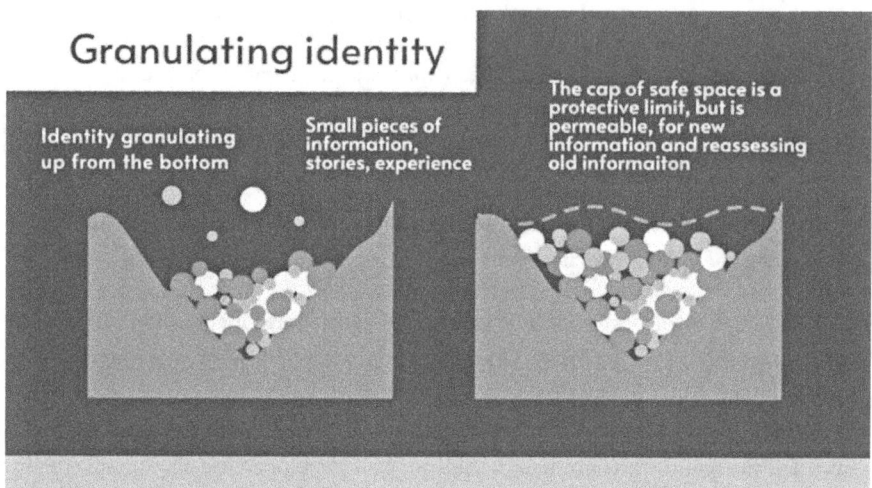

Figure 11.3 Granulating identity.

Pause for reflection

- What role is there for schools and teachers in conversations with care experienced children and what challenges do they face in doing this work?

Debbie: Can you give me an example of how you have used any of the ideas in the training in conversations with your son?

Ali: While I was writing the materials, my son was also having sessions with a specialist occupational therapist to see what sensory needs he had and whether we could help some of his behaviour in that way. This experience emphasised how useful metaphors are to describe what is going on in his head, and then we linked that to how he can use these metaphors in real life. We have developed a range of metaphors to discuss my son's condition and its implications for his actions. For example, we tend to say his brain is slightly different and it has some quickness and distractions built in that other people don't have. I say that to concentrate on his schoolwork, his brain is concurrently dealing with trauma, so he effectively must learn to drive a big red lorry at the same time. Some children are only walking or riding bikes at the same time as trying to learn, but he has a more complex task. Using the metaphor of the big red lorry and setting his learning as 'skills', make his efforts seem manageable and improvable – people learn to drive every day!

Conclusions

This chapter has explored 'difficult conversations' related to care experiences and trauma within the context of key theories in the book. We have noted the importance of liminality and temporalities whereby children are constantly managing relationships with more than one family/carer and the inherent narratives of their lives which are intimately bound up in these connections. The world presents many avenues for conversations that are 'difficult', and this chapter has considered this in everyday, intimate ways for children and parents/carers. Much of what we address here has resonance with conversations that could happen with any child and is not restricted to those who have been care experienced. We hope that the materials we have produced could be adapted to many contexts for parents/carers and other professionals, including those in educational contexts.

Difficult conversations are at the heart of good relationships and as adults we have a responsibility to nurture these in the children we care for and have the skills to support them to explore difficult topics in their lives – be this climate anxieties or questions about who was caring for them when they were younger. This demands more than a simple transaction of information – there needs to be an appreciation of the child's capacities to understand, to hear, and to process certain information and a willingness on the part of the adult to be challenged about their assumptions and prejudices and to foreground the child's emotional needs. This is potentially high risk and could result in adults and children alike feeling out of their depth with uncomfortable and distressing content to process. But with support, we strongly believe that engaging in these conversations could have transformative benefits for the child and family concerned. As poorly understood narratives are explored in safe incremental ways, there could be a shift from an unidirectional idea of adults as the 'care giver' to '*include a relational ethics in the shift to a "becoming together" with responsibility to and for each other*' (Caine, Chung, Steeves, & Clandinin, 2020, p. 272). We provide insights into this level of empathy and care on the part of children in this chapter. Such work has implications for the stability of adoption and care placements as well as for long-term mental health and educational outcomes for children.

Acknowledgements

While this is a conversation between two of us in the project, we also want to acknowledge and thank the wider team who have been involved. Massive thanks to Eleanor Staples and Katie Riches, who were the university-based researchers, Emma Callander and Nina Ross, who produced the films for the training, and to Stuart Gray and Calum Murray, who developed the Difficult Conversations website www.difficultconversations.info. But this project would not have been possible without our partners CCS Adoption, Gloucester Local Authority and Coram Children's Charity – thank you so much to Lindy Wootton, Emma Pask, and John Simmonds for your passion and wisdom and a huge thanks to the children, young people, parents/carers and professionals who participated and shared their experiences of difficult conversations with honesty and courage.

Notes

1. In 2021, 80,850 children were in state care, of which 2,870 were adopted: Children looked after in England including adoptions, Reporting Year 2021 – Explore education statistics – GOV.UK (explore-education-statistics.service.gov.uk).
2. *trove* (small 't'). See here for a film and information about how this was developed: https://stuartiaingray.com/trove/.

References

Bamberg, M. (2011). Who am I? Narration and its contribution to self and identity. *Theory & Psychology*, *21*(1), pp. 3–24.
Banks, M. (2001). *Visual Methods in Social Research*. SAGE.
Barad, K. (2017). Troubling time/s and ecologies of nothingness: Re-turning, re-membering, and facing the incalculable. *New Formations*, *92*(92), pp. 56–86.

Bojesen, E. (2019). Conversation as educational research. *Educational Philosophy and Theory, 51*(6), pp. 650–9.

Brodzinsky, D. (2006). Family structural openness and communication openness as predictors in the adjustment of adopted children. *Adoption Quarterly, 9*(4), pp. 1–18.

Caine, V., Chung, S., Steeves, P., & Clandinin, D. J. (2020). The necessity of a relational ethics alongside Noddings' ethics of care in narrative inquiry. *Qualitative Research, 20*(3), pp. 265–76.

Department for Education (2002). *Adoption and Children Act.* In DfE (Ed.). The Stationery Office. https://www.legislation.gov.uk/ukpga/2002/38/contents.

Gray, S., Hahn, R., Cater, K., Watson, D. L., Williams, K., Metcalfe, T., & Meineck, C. (2020). Towards A Design for Life: Redesigning for Reminiscence with Looked After Children. *CHI (Human-Computer Interaction)*, 25–30 April 2020, Honolulu, Hawaii, pp. 1–14. DOI: https://doi.org/10.1145/3313831.3376824.

Levine, E. E., Roberts, A. R., & Cohen, T. R. (2020). Difficult conversations: Navigating the tension between honesty and benevolence. *Current Opinion in Psychology, 31*, pp. 38–43.

Lowenfeld, M. (1979). *The World Technique.* Allen and Unwin Press.

Mannay, D., Staples, E., & Edwards, V. (2017). Visual methodologies, sand and psychoanalysis: employing creative participatory techniques to explore the educational experiences of mature students and children in care. *Visual Studies, 32*(4), pp. 345–58.

Murris, K. (2020). Posthuman child: De(con)structing western notions of child agency. In W. Omar, & B. Weber (Eds.). *Thinking, Childhood, and Time: Contemporary Perspectives on the Politics of Education* (pp. 161–78). Lexington Books.

Neumann, I. B. (2012). Introduction to the forum on liminality. *Review of International Studies, 38*(2), pp. 473–9.

Noddings, N. (1992). *The Challenge to Care in Schools: An Alternative Approach to Education* (Advances in contemporary education thought series, v. 8). Teachers College Press.

Sissay, L. (2019). *My name is why.* Canongate Books.

Van der Kolk, B. (2014). *The body keeps the score: Mind, brain and body in the transformation of trauma.* Penguin.

Watson, D. L., Hahn, R., & Staines, J. (2019). Storying special objects: material culture, narrative identity and life story work for children in care. *Qualitative Social Work, 19*(4), pp. 701–18. DOI: 10.1177/1473325019850616.

Watson, D. L., Latter, S., & Bellew, R. (2015a). Adopted children and young people's views on their life storybooks: The role of narrative in the formation of identities. *Children and Youth Services Review, 58*, pp. 90–8. doi:10.1016/j.childyouth.2015.09.010.

Watson, D. L., Latter, S., & Bellew, R. (2015b). Adopter's views on their children's life story books. *Adoption and Fostering, 39*(2), pp. 119–34. DOI:10.1177/0308575915588723.

Watson, D. L., Meineck, C., & Lancaster, B. (2018). Adopted children's co-production and use of 'trove' (a digitally enhanced memory box) to better understand their care histories through precious objects. *Clinical Child Psychology and Psychiatry, 23*(4), pp. 614–28. doi:10.1177/1359104518776359.

Watson, D. L., Staples, E., & Riches, K. (2020). 'We need to understand what's going on because it's our life': Using sandboxing to understand children and young people's everyday conversations about care. *Children and Society, 00*, pp. 1–17. https://doi.org/10.1111/chso.12432.

12

Ethical Complexities of Having Difficult Research Conversations: A Reflective Account and a Cautionary Tale on Speaking for 'Others'

Antonios Ktenidis

Introduction

This chapter explores the ethical complexities of engaging in difficult conversations with oneself as a researcher, especially when these conversations refer to 'privileged' researchers and 'marginalised' participants. A reflexive account is developed, looking into how 'I', as a white, cis-male, non-disabled, doctoral researcher, carried out research with young people with dwarfism[1] regarding their secondary schooling experiences in the UK. This chapter is partly inspired by another article, 'Using Others in the Nicest Way Possible: On Colonial and Academic Practice(s), and an Ethic of Humility', written by Henderson and Esposito (2019). Henderson and Esposito (2019) reflect critically on their involvement in past research projects, providing insights into ethical and methodological decisions they had to make at the time. Their reflections are frank, in terms of revealing the complexity of doing research and interrogating decisions which appeared to be right at the time they were made. In contrast to neat, often brief, methodological accounts of published research, the authors engage in difficult conversations with themselves and each other, shedding light on the messiness of (qualitative) research and acknowledging how their intersectional identities affected every single aspect of their research, such as the recruitment of and interaction with participants.

Taking a similar approach to Henderson and Esposito (2019), I engage in difficult conversations between my 'past self' (when I carried out my doctorate) and my 'current self' (three years after completing my doctorate and currently working as a lecturer), providing an insight into the complexities of doing qualitative, social justice research. These conversations focus specifically on different methodological and ethical aspects of my research, including the rationale for this research, the recruitment of participants, navigating the fieldwork and its embodied encounters, and the analysis of the data and representation of participants. These conversations take the form of vignettes, written in *italics*.

The theoretical framework that shapes and structures these conversations is Linda Alcoff's (1991) text 'Speaking for Others'. In this text, Alcoff elaborates on the dangers of speaking for others and proposes four 'interrogatory practices', which researchers should engage with when choosing to speak for others. In this chapter, I use these practices to interrogate my methodological and ethical decisions as a non-disabled researcher doing research with disabled young people.

Something worth clarifying early on is that this chapter is not aiming at my 'catharsis' (as a researcher), meaning that I am not writing this chapter to resolve any internal conflicts I had or still have regarding my doctorate. Henderson and Esposito (2019) point out how academics often publish papers where they disclose the conflict they experience due to publishing findings which could upset their participants, to which participants have no access nonetheless. Instead, this chapter aims to illuminate the complexity of doing social justice research as a 'privileged' researcher with 'marginalised' participants, and propose a feminist, ethical framework, which all researchers (from novice ones to more experienced) should draw on when they engage in such research. I argue that an engagement with Alcoff's interrogatory practices (outlined later) should be considered a researcher's ethical duty, as they constitute a means of engaging in a reflexivity of discomfort (Pillow, 2003), which fosters difficult conversations with oneself and can be transformative in relation to how one comes to understand their research and the decisions they make as part of it. I also see this chapter as a 'cautionary tale' for other researchers, who might find themselves in similar positions, and I highlight the value of shedding light on those difficult conversations we need to have with ourselves instead of treating them as the proverbial elephant in the room. As Ellingson (2017, p. 31) argues, 'We neaten up our stories of "what happened" to sound credible and get published. The rejection of the messy details of research is a legacy of positivism.'

Before moving to the main body of this chapter, I consider it essential to provide a brief account of the research I carried out as part of my doctorate. As previously stated, my research focused on the secondary schooling experiences of young people (between the ages of 11 and 30 years old) with dwarfism in the UK. I adopted a qualitative approach, which invited participants to share with me their stories from their schooling experiences. Participants could choose how they preferred to share their stories, with options including oral stories (participating in a semi-structured narrative interview), visual stories (participants could draw their stories), written stories (for instance, stories communicated via email), poetry, and digital storytelling (stories shared in a private weblog I had created). These stories were then analysed through thematic analysis (Braun & Clarke, 2012) and a range of themes and sub-themes were generated, such as stories of bullying, interactions with teachers and teaching assistants, etc., embodied experiences of school spaces (Ktenidis, 2020). Nevertheless, what this account fails to capture is the range of challenges I encountered during this research and the ongoing difficult conversations I had with myself while doing this research.

The structure of this chapter is as follows: each section first introduces an interrogatory practice proposed by Alcoff (1991). I then provide vignettes of the difficult conversations I had with myself, which I analyse and make sense through reference to the literature. Each section also involves pauses for reflections for the reader, during which the reader can consider how these discussions might relate to their own experiences as researchers or readers of research.

Why do you want to speak for others?

Alcoff's (1991) first interrogatory practice proposes a critical interrogation of one's impetus to speak for others, especially for academics. She points out that due to certain privileged identities – white privilege, cis-male privilege, class privilege – some people are convinced that they should always be the speakers, as they know 'better' than others, even when they speak for those others. Alcoff (1991, p. 24) refers to this impetus as 'a desire for mastery domination' and argues that it should be interrogated and resisted.

In a research context, this can be manifested when 'privileged' researchers claim to 'give voice' to marginalised groups, perpetuating the discourse that these groups do not have a 'voice' in the first place (Ajjawi, 2022). Moreover, it is rarely the case that a marginalised community has approached a privileged researcher to 'give them voice'; instead, it is researchers that decide to research this specific community (Henderson & Esposito, 2019).

On the other hand, Alcoff (1991) acknowledges how problematic the opposite position – the position of retreating or, differently said, to speak only for oneself – is. The option to retreat is a manifestation of privilege itself, Alcoff argues. Bridges (2001, p. 381) refers to this as 'social solipsism', proposing that

'There is a real danger that if we become persuaded that we cannot understand the experience of others and that "we have no right to speak for anyone but ourselves", then we will all too easily find ourselves epistemologically and morally isolated, furnished with a comfortable legitimation for ignoring the condition of anyone but ourselves.'

> ### Pause for reflection
>
> - How do you make sense of the above quote and how does it make you feel?
> - Are you an academic? Do you consider yourself a privileged speaker?
> - Have you ever considered and reflected on your impetus to speak for others? What are its origins?

This topic – who speaks for whom – is highly pertinent within disability studies, which has triggered difficult discussions of who should do disability research (and who should not). Both in the United States (Charlton, 1998) and in the UK (Branfield, 1998), it has been suggested that disability research should be conducted by disabled people, who have a direct experience of it. Richards and Clark (2018, p. 200) discuss how the researcher's own status of dis/ability – which must be 'confessed' – is related to their 'expertise' and the authenticity of the knowledge they produce 'about and for the disability community'. Charlton (1998, p. 128), for instance, refers to the 'innate inability of able-bodied people, regardless of fancy credentials and awards, to understand the disability experience'. Moreover, Kitchin (2000, p. 33) considered how some disabled people who had participated in research 'felt they had been exploited – their knowledge and experiences "mined" by the researcher(s), who they then never heard of again'.

Throughout my PhD journey I was more than often questioned about why I chose this topic. I had to respond to questions like the ones outlined below:

- *Why am I doing this research or what is the rationale for my research?*
- *Am I 'eligible' to do this research?*
- *Why people with dwarfism?*
- *Why young people between the ages of 11 and 30 years old?*
- *Why secondary education?*
- *Why UK (and not Greece, which is where I am originally from)?*

And I would often include reflections on my thinking in my research journal, e.g.:

I always feel very grateful towards the people asking me these questions, it feels like they are genuinely interested in what I am doing, and they make me reflect further on my research. However, these questions also make me feel quite nervous, as I feel I need to justify 'myself' for doing this 'research'. Many Disability Studies books I have read often start with a disclosure of the author's disability, which sometimes is used to claim a better understanding of the topic under investigation. However, this is not the case with me, I do not have a diagnosis of dwarfism. Therefore, I feel under more pressure to justify my rationale for my research. Why people with dwarfism?

It is true that in my own research with people with dwarfism; it was not a charity or an association or a member of the dwarfism community that asked me to carry out any sort of research. As Henderson and Esposito (2019) argue, it is rarely the case that privileged researchers have been invited to do research on behalf of a marginalised community. My initial interest was around the role of height/ism in (secondary) schools due to being a person of short stature myself. However, after reading a paper by Shakespeare et al. (2010) ('No laughing matter: medical and social experiences of restricted growth'), and due to my introduction to disability studies during my undergraduate studies, dwarfism was an impairment which would enable me to consider the intersectional role of disability/disablism and height/heightism in education. After immersing myself in the relevant literature, I came across what I coined as the m/educational narrative; that is how medical discourses, which pathologise dwarfism (and shortness), permeate education, with young people with dwarfism being interpellated into certain deficit subjectivities, e.g. less smart, less capable (Ktenidis, 2020).

This was one of the impetus to conduct this research, the idea of listening to young people's first-hand accounts of their schooling experiences, which had been marginalised so far, as it was often other stakeholders describing those experiences, e.g. teachers, parents (Holmes et al., 1982), as well as to explore the disruptive potential of their stories or how these stories could act as counter-narratives (McLaughlin & Coleman-Fountain, 2019), which could speak back to 'master narratives', such as the m/educational one. Unlike the m/educational narrative, that positions the 'problem' on the individual bodies which are constructed and understood in fixed ways through the medical and psychological lens, I wanted to utilise a sociological lens to make sense of the first-hand accounts of young people with dwarfism as it shifts the attention away from the individual body to the disabling structures and attitudes (Goodley, 2016).

> **Pause for reflection**
> - What were the drivers for your research?
> - What did you aspire to achieve with your research?
> - How did you feel about speaking for 'others'?

Rather than retreating into a position of silence, I decided to pursue this research, without necessarily being fully prepared for the challenges that I would face. I was conscious that I was putting myself in a position of speaking for others, who had often been spoken for before. This was one of the first difficult conversations I had to have with myself, acknowledging the existent power relations of the non-disabled researcher doing research with disabled participants (Tregaskis & Goodley, 2005). Having these conversations with myself early on was crucial in order to mitigate instead of reinforcing those power relations and thinking of ways I could achieve this (Tregaskis, 2004).

Where are you speaking from?

Alcoff's second interrogatory practice emphasises the need to interrogate where one's speech is 'coming from', that is, one's positionality. However, she warns against the autobiographical narratives, e.g. disclosing one's identities, that are often used as disclaimers, especially when they are meant to justify one's ignorance. Pillow (2003) problematises the use of reflexivity as a tool for confession (where the researcher discloses their identities to their readers) or catharsis (where researchers feel that such a disclosure is sufficient in explaining the prejudices they bring in their research as part of their positionality and, as a result, they do not have to address them anymore). Instead, Pillow calls for a 'reflexivity of discomfort' (pp. 187–8), which draws on difficult conversations with oneself to reflect critically on uncomfortable matters (Hamdan, 2009). Uncomfortable reflexivity, Pillow (2003, p. 187) argues, should 'go beyond being a methodological exercise ... it is rendering the knowing of the self or the research subjects as uncomfortable and uncontainable'.

> *I have received my ethics approval from my institution, which means I can officially start my fieldwork, including identifying, reaching out and recruiting participants etc. I have heard from other doctoral researchers and supervisors that this is the*

most exciting part of the PhD! However, I am having mixed feelings. On the one hand, I am excited to talk to people about their schooling experiences, listen to their stories. On the other hand, I am really anxious! Will people (choose to) talk to me? Will they respond to my invitation to take part in the research? How will I negotiate access to participants with gatekeepers? How long should I give them until I hear back? How many times can I message them? What is the best channel/platform to advertise my research? But the main question that was occupying my mind was: 'Will they trust me, considering I am a person without dwarfism?'

The discursive practice I focus on in this section in relation to my positionality as a non-disabled researcher is recruitment and online gatekeeping. However, I consider it crucial to explain first what it means to understand gatekeeping as a discursive practice. Reviewing the existent literature on gatekeepers, Crowhurst (2013) argues that there is a gap in reflexive accounts on the ever-evolving gatekeeper-researcher relationship, particularly on issues around trust and power. Crowhurst 2013 (p. 464) attributes this gap to a 'mechanistic model that reduces the gatekeeper to an instrument in the field and the "passing through the gate" as a matter of course'. Such a model is frequently found in mainstream social research textbooks, reducing gatekeepers to a disembodied, neutral and objective figure whose role and functions are confided to a specific, discrete stage of the research process (Crowhurst, 2013, p. 473), and concealing the 'complex dynamics in which gatekeeping is operationalised in the field, and the multiple ways in which gatekeepers impact upon the research' (Crowhurst & Kennedy-Macfoy, 2013, p. 457). In contrast to this mechanistic model, Crowhurst (2013, p. 471) proposes a poststructuralist approach to gatekeeping, where, '"the gate" itself ceases to be viewed as a purely mechanistic instrument, guarded by a neutral figure, but rather can be seen as a discursive construction, giving meaning and making sense of the research encounters between socially embedded actors in the field.'

Gatekeeping, Crowhust and Kennedy-Macfoy (2013, p. 458) suggest, is 'a historically situated, social and cultural process that embodies the power relations of the contexts in which it takes place'. Within this approach, gatekeepers are viewed 'as social actors embedded, participating in and influencing relations of power' (Crowhurst, 2013, p. 464). Gatekeepers cease to be understood as static figures, but they are seen 'as a cluster of institutional practices, truths, funding regimes, disciplinary conventions, power relations and discourses' (Eldridge, 2013, p. 483). Rather than demonising (or celebrating) gatekeepers as individuals who hinder (or facilitate) access to potential participants, this approach seeks to understand gatekeepers (and the researchers themselves) as discursive subjects who draw on the contextual power relations that produce and inform their encounters with the researcher (Crowhurst, 2013; Eldridge, 2013). Crowhust (2013, p. 472) emphasises the 'need for a reflexive approach on the part of the researcher to consider the social relationships, identities and discourses which inform the encounters with gatekeepers in the field and the effects these have on the research process'.

Among the six associations of people with dwarfism that functioned as gatekeepers, I was eligible for membership only in two of them. Except for these two associations, the rule was that membership was granted only to those with a dwarfism diagnosis or those with a family member with dwarfism. Nevertheless, the process of gaining access is not static but dynamic, 'shaped by transformative encounters between researchers, gatekeepers and participants' (Crowhurst & Kennedy-Macfoy, 2013, p. 364). Despite these membership criteria, some of the associations that I could not be member of still allowed me to advertise my research on their Facebook pages, giving me online access to potential participants. This was not a straightforward process of course, as there had been many messages in between with me explaining the purposes, the rationale and the importance of my research and distancing myself from the depiction of the researcher as a mere 'collector of stories', who, after the completion of the fieldwork, is nowhere to be seen (Kitchin, 2000). In my online interactions with gatekeepers, I also came across the issues that Crowhurst and Kennedy-Macfoy (2013) raise, such as issues of authenticity and trust.

I keep checking how many people have seen and/or liked the short video I recorded and uploaded on the social media groups, in which I introduce my research and myself. I then go straight to the messages, but there are none. I have not heard from anyone yet. My recruitment method has proved ineffective. Although I did manage to get access to the groups through the gatekeepers/administrators, I have still not managed to recruit any participants. I am reminded of Crowhurst's (2013, p. 472) words:

> The fact that gatekeepers grant access should not necessarily unleash the researcher to un-problematically carry out her/his research – ultimately, it is the potential respondent who should be able to decide whether he/she wants to take part in the research, and the researcher has the responsibility of understanding and ensuring that this is the case.

I need to reconsider my methods of recruitment. I need to explore new options, as what I am doing is not working.

Only a small number of participants reached out to me on social media. This could be explained by the fact that I was not a member of the associations, which meant no access to the in-person events where trust could be developed, and I was also seen as an 'outsider' researcher.

The difficult conversations I had with myself shed light on the affective dimensions of doing disability research fieldwork, which are rarely acknowledged (Valente, 2017), such as the stress and anxieties that a researcher experiences in the recruitment process. Moreover, these difficult discussions made me reflect further on the limitations of the recruitment method I had chosen and the possibilities of other methods, which I utilised later.

> ### Pause for reflection
> - How did you feel when you were about to start your fieldwork?
> - To what extent did such feelings link with your positionality?
> - How were you perceived by participants?

To whom are we accountable for our research?

In her third interrogatory practice, Alcoff proposes that speaking comes with accountability, or, put differently, one should be held accountable for what they say. Furthermore, they should remain open to criticism. In particular, Alcoff (1991, p. 25–6) calls for an interrogation of the impulse to turn down criticism immediately and she proposes instead that one should 'attempt actively, attentively, and sensitively to 'hear (understand) the criticism'.

Regarding the issue of accountability, a range of responses have been given to whom a researcher is accountable, including the institution within which the research is taking place, the funding body, the participants of the research (Levinson, 2010), the various gatekeepers and the community (Levinson, 2010). However, different levels of power are accredited to each of the aforementioned stakeholders in terms of how they can hold the researcher accountable.

Alcoff links accountability with an openness to criticism, so here I would like to show how I dealt with criticism with reference to two critical incidents: one during the fieldwork, and another during a conference.

I am just about to walk in the hotel where the event is being hosted. The main purpose of me attending this event is to identify and recruit participants. I am feeling so nervous. Will I able to speak to potential participants and see if they are interested in taking part? How should I introduce myself? How should I approach participants? This is not a space/time designated for research activities, so I do feel as a 'space intruder'.

Pause for reflection

- How did you feel when you appeared somewhere that you were not meant to be per se?
- How did you prepare for such fieldwork encounters?

This was an example of a difficult conversation I had with myself in terms of feeling that I was occupying a space that was not meant for me; however, this would constitute one of the most effective approaches to recruiting participants. Was it right for me to be in that space and use it for purposes that it was not designated for (despite having been granted permission to do so by the organisers)?

Once I entered this space (in the hotel), where a presentation would take place, there were only two people inside. I felt that my presence (or my right to be there) was immediately interrogated. 'What are you doing here?' I was asked by the one person in the room. I introduced myself and explained that I was a member of the association, and I was also attending the event to talk with people for my project. The other person rushed to explain: 'He's not one of them; he's not here for the weekend and then we will never hear back from him again.' My earlier thoughts had come true.

A recruitment strategy I adopted in my research was venue-based sampling (Rockliffe et al., 2018), which took place through attending two events that were held by one association. After becoming an affiliate member of certain associations, I was permitted to attend their annual conventions. These events constitute a 'safe' space (Hogde & Runswick-Cole, 2013), a getaway from ableism's omnipresence materialised in the hostile attitudes and disabling structures that people with dwarfism encounter in their everyday lives (Pritchard, 2020).

During these events I felt at certain occasions that my body (short, but not with dwarfism) was interrogated and the disclosure of my identity as a researcher brought about even more scepticism about my presence in the events and about my intentions. In the incident described above, both people had dwarfism and were members of the associations. I had already met one of them in a past event, so he was aware of both, my membership and my project. It was the first time I encountered the other person. The levels of mistrust towards research and researchers (with and without dwarfism) who become members of the association could suggest that the members might feel as though their experiences and stories had been appropriated and misrepresented (Kitchin, 2000). This was particularly palpable with the second person referring to researchers as 'one of them', indicating that mistrust, which was absolutely justified.

In order to mitigate such feelings, during my face to-face interactions with potential participants I claimed what Mulling (1999, p. 340) refers to as 'positional space' – areas where the situated knowledges of both parties in the interview encounter engender a level of trust and cooperation. These positional spaces, however, are often transitory and cannot be reduced to the familiar boundaries of insider/outsider privilege based on visible attributes such as race, gender, ethnicity or class. For instance, when I was asked by potential participants about the rationale of the research, I was open and honest about my personal drives, including my own experiences of heightism during schooling – a form of discrimination that we both shared experiences of, without this implying that such experiences were identical. Moreover, by taking part in the different activities that the associations had planned, such as dinners and disco events, I got to know potential participants better in informal settings – and so did they – and develop a relationship of trust. Both I and the potential participants had the opportunity to come to know each other not only as 'the researcher' and 'the participant' but as members of the same association who spend time together. At these moments our embodied differences ceased to matter, as we both focused on what brings us together rather than what differentiates us from each other. This was the big difference that the face-to-face encounters made compared to the online encounters. Being able to claim such positional space was crucial in mitigating feelings of mistrust towards my embodied identities and my identity as a researcher and in recruiting participants who felt safe to share their stories with me.

Returning to the difficult conversation about whether I should be there or not, what I was reminded of and learnt during the fieldwork was that my identity as a researcher and the identities of the participants were just one of the identities we held, meaning that we could connect on more levels than just the subjectivity of 'researcher' and 'participant'.

The second incident took place at a conference, during which an academic interrogated my 'right' to speak for people with dwarfism as a 'short' (but without dwarfism) person. Although the paper I presented at this particular conference was a discussion of how shortness has been medicalised and my own experiences of heightism, this scholar felt that I was equating shortness with dwarfism.

> *Why am I being 'interrogated' like this? Do other academics get interrogated in similar terms? For instance, have middle-class academics researching working class families been questioned in similar ways? I felt that the criticism was unfair and I was trying to find ways to dismiss it.*

Initially, I was caught off guard and wondered where such questioning was coming from. Although I did attempt to respond to the question, pointing out some of the issues I have mentioned so far, such as how the retreating position is equally problematic, I could see that the colleague was not convinced by my response. Being 'questioned' like that in front of an audience was quite discomforting to say the least. However, in hindsight, I was able to speculate and reflect on the origins of such a question(ing). For instance, in their published work, this scholar identifies as an insider researcher, with such a positionality giving them a more accurate insight into experiences that people with dwarfism have. Therefore, there is an epistemological difference in our understanding of positionality and 'who' has the 'right' to do 'research' with particular groups. Moreover, although I do not claim that shortness and dwarfism are the same thing, I remain conscious of the dangers created by the perpetuation of a hierarchy of shortness, similar to the reproduction of a hierarchy of impairments (Deal, 2003).

The difficult conversations I had with myself made me more aware of my defence mechanisms towards criticism, such as being quick to dismiss it. Partly, such mechanisms might have to do with my own privileged identities (e.g. white, or cis-male) which may often afford me the credibility of arguments that may, as a result, be rarely questioned. However, although this questioning from the colleague felt quite personal, as it had linked to my positionality, it was at the same time really helpful in developing my understanding of the epistemological differences I might have with colleagues who work in similar fields further.

Pause for reflection

- Have you considered to whom you are accountable for your research?
- How do you react to criticism?

Where does the speech go and what does it do?

The fourth interrogatory practice Alcoff proposes is to pay attention to the effects one's words can have on the discursive and material world. As Alcoff (1991, p. 26) proposes, 'one must look at where the speech goes and what it does there'. To illustrate this point, Alcoff refers to a 'First-World person' who is speaking for an individual or a group in the 'Third World'. At a discursive level, the researcher is constructed as the authoritative, knowledge subject, while the individual/group is reduced to the object of research, which needs to be empowered. The discursive effects then perpetuate racist, imperialist research relations (Alcoff, 1991; for a further critique see Spivak, 1988).

Writing from a postcolonial perspective, hooks (1990, pp. 151–2) also considers how the speaker might act as the coloniser:

> *Often this speech about the 'Other' annihilates, erases: 'no need to hear your voice when I can talk about you better than you can speak about yourself. No need to hear your voice. Only tell me about your pain. I want to know your story. And then I will tell it back to you in a new way. Tell it back to you in such a way that it has become mine, my own. Re-writing you, I write myself anew. I am still author, authority. I am still the coloniser, the speaking subject, and you are now at the centre of my talk.'*

> *To what extent did I act as the colonizer of the participants' stories? What 'editing'[2] rights do I have over the participants' stories? How am I re-presenting the participants? Will participants find their representations and the way I made sense of and interpreted their stories fair?*

These were the questions that I kept asking myself over the course of the analysis process and the writing up of the thesis. These are also the questions that I still ask myself. As the author of the research, I had the 'third dimensional power' (Hoffmann, 2007, p. 321), which has to do with the authorial/authoritative power of the researcher to re-tell the participants' stories, including the researcher's theoretical frameworks (the lenses through which the stories are discussed) and analytical choices (which stories and/or which parts of the selected stories are listened to and which ones are silenced). The issue of authorial power was highly pertinent to my research, considering my positionality as a researcher without dwarfism.

> *I have listened to those stories of school violence again and again. I am honoured participants shared them with me. Nevertheless, I am really struggling to write them into my thesis. To start with, I am scared if my interpretation of them, the*

way I make sense of them, the theoretical frameworks I draw on, do justice to what the participants meant in the first place. Moreover, I am equally worried that, if I let those stories to 'stand alone', that is, without offering an/my interpretation, they might be read as another tragic story of disability, provoking feelings of pity towards the participants. How should I re-write those stories?

While I was writing my thesis, there was a case of a child with dwarfism that was getting bullied at school that made it to the news.[3] The child, recorded by his mother, was visibly upset (in tears) and was threatening that he would take his own life. The video went viral and triggered a range of reactions, such as targeting and critiquing the mother for recording her child in this condition, questioning the child's age, proposing that he is an adult and others claiming that this was yet another story that made it to the news, but not affecting any change. One of the responses was also a crowdfunding to get the child to go to Disneyland, as if such a trip would cease bullying from happening. Part of the problem with the above case, in my view, was the representation of the child with dwarfism as the 'poor victim' of bullying due to his disability, and the solution to the problem of bullying was sending the child to Disneyland.

This was one example that made me even more conscious of and concerned about the discursive and material effects that such stories can have. To an extent, such an interpretation of this case perpetuated a disablist narrative, in which disability was the reason the child was getting bullied (Ktenidis, 2022). Goodley and Runswick-Cole (2012) have called for further reflection on the readings one draws on to make sense of disabled children's experiences, especially readings that can perpetuate disablist, pathological narratives, such as the one above. In particular, they raise their concerns about how such experiences can become the object of voyeurism and be sensationalised by the media, feeding into the 'tragedy' of disability (Goodley & Runswick-Cole, 2013). Moreover, Hyden (2013, p. 225) discusses 'the potential harm the circulation of narratives on sensitive topics may cause the involved, since they might be reinterpreted beyond the narrator's control' and 'by passing them on to new audiences, we pave the way for possible new meanings – and as they are passed on, they make entrance into new power relations' (p. 231). I had similar concerns when I was re-telling stories of disablist school violence (Ktenidis, 2022).

What am I supposed to do with these stories? Should I leave them out? Should I silence them, as if I had never heard them? If I did so though, wouldn't it be an 'abuse' of my authorial power? On the other hand, how can I 'protect' those stories from being sensationalised, especially when I do not have full control over how they might be read? What should I do?

Ultimately, rather than silencing these stories due to these risks, what I chose to do was to let these stories out with my interpretation of them, which was shaped by a range of critical theoretical frameworks, such as critical disability studies (Ktenidis, 2022). Following hooks (1989), I did not merely name these experiences but I situated these experiences within theoretical contexts, which shed light on what brought such experiences into existence in the first place. Listening to Alcoff and Gray (1993, p. 269), I positioned these stories 'in violent confrontation' with the dominant discourses, which makes possible subversive speaking's aim to have a disruptive effect on such discourses and not giving the space to be appropriated by them (Ktenidis, 2022).

However, even while I am writing this chapter, I am still contemplating the ethics of 're-writing the "other"'. These difficult conversations led me to engage in further reading around those matters (Eakin, 2004; Hardesty & Gunn, 2019) as well as explore other methods of analysis, which can be more reflective, e.g. reflexive thematic analysis (Braun & Clarke, 2019). They also made me more conscious about the multifaceted nature of analysis and its implications, in terms of not being just a technical task during which codes, themes and subthemes are constructed but how every single part of analysis involves ethical decisions.

Pause for reflection

- Have you ever considered the discursive and the material effects when you speak for others?
- If you are a researcher, have you had a discussion of such effects with your participants?
- Did you encounter any struggles in trying to 're-present' your participants and their experiences fairly?

Concluding thoughts

In this chapter, I engaged with Alcoff's interrogatory practices as a means of fostering difficult conversations with myself as a researcher, reflecting on specific methodological and ethical decisions I made at the time when I carried out my doctoral research. These interrogatory practices enabled me to reflect on my impetus to speak for others, especially as a privileged researcher doing research with a marginalised group, my positionality, my accountability and openness to criticism, and the effects of my research. These reflections took the form of difficult conversations, which held great value for me, as they enabled me to become a more reflexive researcher, an invaluable quality, especially in qualitative research. These difficult conversations further shaped the direction of my research by considering the ethical complexities of different aspects of it, such as the rationale of the research and the 'problem' of speaking for others, the ethics of gatekeeping, the ethics of accountability, and the ethics of analysis and representation. Rather than providing neat methodological accounts of our research, I argue that there is need for the messy details of our research to get out there, in order to 'humanise' our research.

Moreover, this chapter showed one way of how a researcher could engage with Alcoff's interrogatory practices and difficult conversations with themselves as researchers. Far from proposing that my reflections are generalisable, I argue that engaging in those practices/conversations should be an ethical duty for every researcher (novice or more experienced), as they and their research would benefit greatly from such an engagement. They will acquire a deeper insight into the reasons that led to certain methodological and ethical decisions and will be more aware of the power dynamics of their research. These difficult conversations with oneself hold a transformative potential for researchers in terms of making them acknowledge the privileged identities and values they enter their research with and how these shape their course of action. However, as proposed earlier in relation to reflexivity, such difficult conversations should not be used as an (other) tick-box exercise through which researchers could be excused for their wrongdoings or to be absolved from taking responsibility for those, but difficult conversations should result in some form of transformation in how one understands and does research.

Finally, although these difficult conversations might trigger some discomfort, because they make us confront our privileged identities and their impact on our research, for instance, such a feeling should not be a reason to avoid them. On the contrary, the 'difficulty' of these conversations, and the 'discomfort' that comes with them, is where their transformative potential lies.

Notes

1 Dwarfism refers to a medical condition resulting in a height of 4 feet and 8 inches or below.
2 See for example Hardesty and Gunn (2019).
3 I want to maintain the anonymity of the case, hence the lack of reference.

References

Ajjawi, R. (2022). Problematising voice in qualitative health professional education research. *Focus on Health Professional Education: A Multi-disciplinary Journal, 23*(2), pp. 69–78.

Alcoff, L. (1991). The problem of speaking for others. *Cultural Critique, 20*(20), pp. 5–32. https://doi.org/10.2307/1354221.

Alcoff, L., & Gray, L. (1993). Survivor discourse: Transgression or recuperation? *Signs: Journal of Women in Culture and Society, 18*(2), pp. 260–90.

Branfield, F. (1998). What are you doing here? 'Non-disabled' people and the disability movement: A response to Robert F. Drake.

Braun, V., & Clarke, V. (2012). *Thematic analysis*. American Psychological Association.

Braun, V., & Clarke, V. (2019). Reflecting on reflexive thematic analysis. *Qualitative Research in Sport, Exercise and Health, 11*(4), pp. 589–97.

Bridges, D. (2001). The ethics of outsider research. *Journal of Philosophy of Education, 35*(3), pp. 371–86.

Charlton, J. I. (1998). *Nothing about us without us: Disability oppression and empowerment*. University of California Press.

Crowhurst, I. (2013). The fallacy of the instrumental gate? Contextualising the process of gaining access through gatekeepers. *International Journal of Social Research Methodology, 16*(6), pp. 463–75.

Crowhurst, I., & Kennedy-Macfoy, M. (2013). Troubling gatekeepers: methodological considerations for social research. *International Journal of Social Research Methodology, 16*(6), pp. 457–62.

Deal, M. (2003). Disabled people's attitudes toward other impairment groups: A hierarchy of impairments. *Disability & Society, 18*(7), pp. 897–910.

Eakin, P. J. (Ed.) (2004). *The ethics of life writing*. Cornell University Press.

Eldridge, A. (2013). Gatekeeping and drinking cultures: how do we talk about drinking? *International Journal of Social Research Methodology, 16*(6), pp. 477–89.

Ellingson, L. L. (2017). *Embodiment in qualitative research*. Routledge.

Goodley, D. (2016). Disability studies: An interdisciplinary introduction. *Disability Studies*, 1–296.

Goodley, D., & Runswick-Cole, K. (2012). Reading Rosie: The postmodern disabled child. *Educational and Child Psychology, 29*(2), p. 53.

Goodley, D., & Runswick-Cole, K. (2013). The body as disability and possability: theorizing the 'leaking, lacking and excessive' bodies of disabled children. *Scandinavian Journal of Disability Research, 15*(1), pp. 1–19.

Hamdan, A. K. (2009). Reflexivity of discomfort in insider-outsider educational research. *McGill Journal of Education, 44*(3), pp. 377–404.

Hardesty, M., & Gunn, A. J. (2019). Survival sex and trafficked women: The politics of re-presenting and speaking about others in anti-oppressive qualitative research. *Qualitative Social Work, 18*(3), pp. 493–513.

Hodge, N., & Runswick-Cole, K. (2013). 'They never pass me the ball': exposing ableism through the leisure experiences of disabled children, young people and their families. *Children's Geographies, 11*(3), pp. 311–25.

Hoffmann, E. A. (2007). Open-ended interviews, power, and emotional labor. *Journal of Contemporary Ethnography, 36*(3), pp. 318–46.

Holmes, C. S., Hayford, J. T., & Thompson, R. G. (1982). Parents' and teachers' differing views of short children's behaviour. *Child: Care, Health and Development, 8*(6), pp. 327–36.

Hooks, B. (1989). *Talking back: Thinking feminist, thinking black* (Vol. 10). South End Press.

Hooks, B. (1990). Postmodern blackness. *Postmodern Culture, 1*(1).

Hyden, M. (2013). Narrating Sensitive topics. In M. Andrews, C. Squire, & M. Tamboukou (Eds.). *Doing Narrative Research* (pp. 223–39). Sage.

Kitchin, R. (2000). The researched opinions on research: Disabled people and disability research. *Disability & Society, 15*(1), pp. 25–47.

Ktenidis, A. (2020). *Short'Stories of Young People with Restricted Growth of Their Schooling Experiences (Secondary Education) in the United Kingdom* (Doctoral dissertation, University of Sheffield).

Ktenidis, A. (2022). En/counters with disablist school violence: experiences of young people with dwarfism in the United Kingdom. *British Journal of Sociology of Education, 43*(8), pp. 1196–215.

Levinson, M. P. (2010). Accountability to research participants: Unresolved dilemmas and unravelling ethics. *Ethnography and Education, 5*(2), pp. 193–207.

Limes-Taylor Henderson, K., & Esposito, J. (2019). Using others in the nicest way possible: On colonial and academic practice(s), and an ethic of humility. *Qualitative Inquiry, 25*(9–10), pp. 876–89.

McLaughlin, J., & Coleman-Fountain, E. (2019). Visual methods and voice in disabled childhoods research: Troubling narrative authenticity. *Qualitative Research, 19*(4), pp. 363–81.

Mullings, B. (1999). Insider or outsider, both or neither: some dilemmas of interviewing in a cross-cultural setting. *Geoforum, 30*(4), pp. 337–50.

Pillow, W. (2003). Confession, catharsis, or cure? Rethinking the uses of reflexivity as methodological power in qualitative research. *International Journal of Qualitative Studies in Education, 16*(2), pp. 175–96.

Pritchard, E. (2020). *Dwarfism, spatiality and disabling experiences*. Routledge.

Richards, S., & Clark, J. (2018). Research with disabled children: Tracing the past, present and future. *Dis/abled Childhoods? A Transdisciplinary Approach*, pp. 187–209.

Rockliffe, L., Chorley, A. J., Marlow, L. A., & Forster, A. S. (2018). It's hard to reach the 'hard-to-reach': the challenges of recruiting people who do not access preventative healthcare services into interview studies. *International Journal of Qualitative Studies on Health and Well-Being, 13*(1), p. 1479582.

Shakespeare, T., Thompson, S., & Wright, M. (2010). No laughing matter: medical and social experiences of restricted growth. *Scandinavian Journal of Disability Research, 12*(1), pp. 19–31.

Spivak, G. C. (1994). Can the subaltern Speak?[1988]. *Colonial Discourse and Post-Colonial Theory: A Reader*, pp. 66–111.

Tregaskis, C. (2004). *Constructions of disability: Researching the interface between disabled and non-disabled people*. Psychology Press.

Tregaskis, C., & Goodley, D. (2005). Disability research by disabled and non-disabled people: Towards a relational methodology of research production. *International Journal of Social Research Methodology, 8*(5), pp. 363–74.

Valente, J. M. (2017). Anxiety as a tool for critical disability studies fieldwork. *Review of Disability Studies: An International Journal, 13*(2).

13

Fairness, Fruitfulness, Fact: An Argument for the Belonging of People with Profound Intellectual and Multiple Disabilities within Research

Joanna Grace

Introduction

The limits of language for difficult conversations

Moments of profound meaning are often unreachable with language. We know through the living of our lives that there is meaning outside of language, beyond it, as well as behind it. Those of us who are users of mouth words[1] tend to get tangled in the meaning they hold; we fall out of contact with other meanings: embodied, felt, lived meanings. We only encounter these other meanings when we find ourselves living through experiences that render our lexicon of words puny. However, if we seek out people who do not use mouth words, and learn to listen to them, we can reconnect with day-to-day 'other meanings' as well as the more profound ones that life throws our way.

People with profound intellectual and multiple disabilities live authentically in the meaning they experience. In not having access to standardised forms of communication, due to the profound nature of their intellectual disability, they rarely fall victim to the mistake of considering words as meaning, rather than as tools for expressing meaning. They are exceptional communicators who use limited resources to express themselves (Raphael & Clarke, 2011). However, conversations with people with profound intellectual and multiple disabilities are frequently viewed as difficult, if not impossible. The difficulty of these conversations, or their apparent impossibility, is only heightened when we seek to conduct them in a research environment. Ethics committee shy away from work which involves people who cannot give informed consent, and the creative methods needed in order that people with profound intellectual and multiple disabilities are afforded their rightful belonging within research are not well established or even conceived of yet. To examine this affordance, this chapter aims to explore the roots of the exclusion of people with profound intellectual and multiple disabilities from research, before going on to explore the concept of 'being with' as a way of realising the belonging of people with profound intellectual and multiple disabilities within our philosophical considerations as well as within research. Advice is given for those seeking to attempt to be with people with profound intellectual and multiple disabilities, and readers are offered a glimpse of the meaning it is possible to apprehend through being with people with profound intellectual and multiple disabilities.

Excluded from inclusive research and advocacy

The added value of inclusive research (Walmsley et al., 2018) has been well rehearsed by those who have led the way in developing the field (Bigby et al., 2014; de Haas et al., 2022; Milner & Frawley, 2019; Nind, 2017; Walmsley, 2001). Inclusive research is research in which people with disabilities are 'not studied by academics as an object' but are instead 'involved as active participants' (Woelders et al., 2015, p. 529). 'Inclusive research adds value when there is a distinctive contribution which only co-researchers with intellectual disabilities can make' (Walmsley et al., 2018, p. 751). Walmsley et al. (2018) go on to highlight that this added value comes about through the reaching of knowledge that authors could not otherwise reach, and by reflecting upon insider cultural knowledge. People with profound intellectual and multiple learning disabilities experience life in very different ways, and lead very different lives from the majority of the population, so there is no doubt that they have a unique experience of knowledge and that they represent a population with distinctive cultural experience. Inclusive research involves 'standing with' those whose issues are being explored or investigated (Walmsley et al., 2018, p. 758) – something I do in my work through 'being with' people with profound intellectual and multiple disabilities, as discussed below.

As the inclusive research movement has developed, there has been a drive, motivated by the need to fulfil the requirements of funding offered specifically for inclusive research, to firm up definitions of what constitutes inclusive research. Pioneers of the movement have both offered up definitions of what counts as inclusive research and argued for the field to remain fluid (Bigby et al.,

2014; de Haas et al., 2022; Nind, 2017; Nind & Vinha, 2014; Walmsley et al., 2018). The development of inclusive research happened in answer to the call of the disability rights movement that advocates for research celebrating the motto of 'Nothing about us without us' (Charlton, 1998). It is important to acknowledge that 'self-advocacy is not readily available for all'. However, this same call underpins the 'People First' movement, which seeks to champion self-advocacy for people with learning disabilities through the setting up of groups that aim to empower their members (Goodwin et al., 2023). Great strides forwards have been made, but people with profound intellectual and multiple disabilities have been left behind, excluded by criteria that demand capacity they do not possess (Seale et al., 2015), and unheard as a result of rules which say that only the voice who can speak for them is their own (Atkinson & Walmsley, 2010; Davy, 2019; Palmer & Walmsley, 2020).

In a world more embracing of diversity it is well recognised that people from minority populations carry unique and valuable insight into their own lives and communitas, the experience of social connection with other marginalised people (Turner, 1969). It is clear that if we want to learn about the lives of people with profound intellectual and multiple disabilities, then there are no better people to learn from than people with profound intellectual and multiple disabilities themselves; this much is undisputed. I wish to go further and to argue that people with profound intellectual and multiple disabilities carry insight not only of value to their own lives but also of value to the lives of others.

However far you take the argument as to the value of including people with profound intellectual and multiple disabilities within research, you very quickly realise that it has not happened. People with profound intellectual disabilities are the 'lost voices' of research (Atkinson & Walmsley, 1999, p. 204); they are 'ignored' (Klotz, 2004, p. 93; Simmons & Watson, 2015, p. 51) and excluded (Hart et al., 2020; Jones et al., 2020; Kellett & Nind, 2001); they are the 'most silenced' 'most marginal group of disabled people both in society and in research' (Mietola et al., 2017, p. 264) and, I argue, it is important we understand why.

Why are people with profound intellectual and multiple disabilities excluded from research?

Too difficult and of no use

People with profound intellectual and multiple disabilities are disregarded as suitable participants in research by those who view them as having nothing to offer (Hart et al., 2020), and who consider them not to be knowers even within their own lives (Parsons et al., 2022), or to be 'worthless' (PMLD Network, 2003, p. 20). Beyond such blinkered notions people with profound intellectual and multiple disabilities are left out of research because it is considered too difficult to include them (Ashman et al., 2010; de Haas et al., 2022; Kellett & Nind, 2001; Maes et al., 2021; Ware, 2004). Including them would involve having difficult conversations. First, there is the difficulty of negotiating access to them, through ethics committees and gate keepers and then there is the difficulty of communicating across an intellectual divide.

Barriers to inclusion: Recruitment and consent

Researchers note recruitment and consent as two of the biggest barriers when it comes to trying to include people with profound intellectual disability within research (Carey & Griffiths, 2017; Swaine et al., 2011; Tilley, 2016). There is a need for ethical procedures that understand the vulnerability of people with profound disabilities, and offer protection but not through exclusion (Hart et al., 2020; Kellett & Nind, 2001; Mietola et al., 2017; Tuffrey-Wijne et al., 2008). Some have found the barriers to be so substantial that they felt it necessary to exclude people with profound intellectual and multiple disabilities from their work (Hill et al., 2016). Happily, others see the barriers and recognise the need to dismantle them, believing that people with profound intellectual and multiple disabilities both *can* (Grace & Bell, 2022; Seale et al., 2015; Simmons & Watson, 2015; Walmsley et al., 2018a) and *should* (Holt et al., 2019; Krisson et al., 2022; Scott et al., 2006) be included in research.

It is important that inclusion within research is not predicated upon intellectual capacity, and that intellectual capacity or the lack thereof is fully recognised, not glossed over, denied or stigmatised. Emma Murphy, who is a parent to Hugh, a young man with profound intellectual and multiple disabilities, articulates this clearly in Goodwin et al. (2022, p. 23):

> and it's that presuming competence and a level of cognition and then that's so offensive in some ways because actually you're saying that that's the only important way of understanding – and it's not, it's not the only way of connecting … so presuming competence then really undermines his experiences of the world, which are just as valid, but different.

A sentiment echoed by Vorhaus (2014, p. 616), who states that 'a profoundly disabled person may be unable to speak or contribute to a process of rational argument, but even when these capacities are absent, she remains a conscious agent, whose acts reveal human intentions and purposes'. If people with profound intellectual and multiple disabilities *can* and *should* be included in research, and if the barriers of recruitment and consent are surmountable, what further blocks them from assuming a place of belonging and what do we need to do to remove these blockades?

Barriers to inclusion: The researcher themselves

Once a researcher has navigated around the barriers mentioned above, of gate keepers and ethical procedures, as well as those not mentioned (time, money, technology, healthcare and various other logistics), they face a more human barrier: themselves.

Being with people with profound intellectual and multiple disabilities can be challenging, confronting, uncomfortable (Goodwin & Griffiths, 2022), and attempting to hear their point of view can feel 'taxing' (Atkinson & Walmsley, 2010, p. 275). People may experience attempts to converse with people with profound intellectual and multiple disabilities as less enjoyable than conversation with other partners (Ware, 2012); people can feel anxious (Shevlin, 2003) and even threatened (Blascovich et al., 2001) by the differences they perceive. Goodwin (2019, 2022) writes with searing honesty about the self-doubt she experienced as she attempted to be with children whose cognitive and physical impairments led to them appearing almost entirely passive. The discomfort of entering the world where the norms of 'being with' differ from our own established ways of interaction or communication can be destabilising (Bhabha, 2004). However, this 'disturbance' is argued to be necessary if one is to truly engage with the other whose lived experience is significantly distant from one's own (Bhabha, 2004). Moreover, this engagement can provide a window into our developing understanding of what it means to be with difference – a difference that may or may not resemble some of our own divergent ways of being. Without this disturbance, our worlds are limited to the part of humanity that exists within the periphery of our own capacities to be – worlds that can be considered exclusionary, and somewhat mono-perspectival.

It is at this point that it becomes relevant to position myself as an autistic researcher. For while I recognise the nature of the concerns above, and have certainly wondered whether I am making a fool of myself in front of others, or inadvertently patronising the person I am conversing with, my experience of communication as someone with a social communication difference does, at times I think, gives me an edge when seeking to communicate with people with profound intellectual and multiple disabilities. In my day-to-day life, I operate in a world in which social communication follows rules and traditions that suit a neurotype other than my own. I work hard to consciously follow these rules with varying degrees of success (Grace, 2021a, 2021b), and it is at times exhausting. However, I know when I meet a person with profound intellectual and multiple disabilities, they will not have these expectations of social conformity of me. In them I meet a communication partner that offers me total freedom. Within the communitas that we occupy together, we share the commonality of us both belonging to groups who find their preferred communication style to be marginalised, and although their experience of this communitas is far deeper than mine, it is through this shared experience that I am able to attune myself to be with them. I know that *we* will, between us, decide on how *we* communicate, and that what we decide will be based on our own unique needs and abilities, and not on conventions dictated by others. This is a beautiful freedom and one I would invite all who are daunted by the barriers to having these conversations to consider.

Being with in order to research with

In my own work as a doctoral researcher studying identity and belonging for people with profound intellectual and multiple learning disabilities, I recognise the value of 'being with' people with profound intellectual and multiple disabilities. 'Being with' is not an activity; it is not a form of doing. It is, as we described in Haas et al. (2022, p. 7), a 'mode of being'. It allows you to attune yourself to your communication partner (Forster, 2011; Forster & Iacono, 2014) and share meaning in a way that is bespoke to you. The importance of 'being with' is highlighted by many researchers who seek to share in the insight held by people with profound intellectual and multiple disabilities (Goodwin, 2013; Forster, 2020; Morris, 2003).

My aim within my work is to do research *with* people with profound intellectual and multiple learning disabilities. As I write, this work is in its infancy so it is premature to report on its progress, but I hope that readers reading these words upon publication will be able to look up how the work has unfolded. I hope to demonstrate that people with profound intellectual and multiple disabilities belong within the third wave of inclusive research (Milner & Frawley, 2019), no longer a population upon whom research is done but a population that plays an active role in the doing of research. I am developing my methodological approach for this work *with* people with profound intellectual and multiple disabilities through a process of spending time 'being with' (Parsons et al., 2022).

My desire to ensure that I work *with* people with profound intellectual and multiple disabilities comes neither from a sense of fairness nor of fruitfulness, but rather it is a forcible recognition of ontological fact: to quote (Trilling, 1972, p. 91), commenting on Wordsworth: these people exist as 'forcibly human'. Our work should include them because they are a part of what our work is about. It is fair to include them, it is fruitful to include them, and our work will be incomplete without them. For if we are seeking to account for the human experience, then as phenomenologists interested in the experience of living, we cannot do this without them. Their presence as a part of our society, a part of humanity, a part of our collective wisdom is undeniable, and if we want our theories, our methods, our models to account for lived experience, then they must stretch to encompass the experience of all people.

Advice for being with

In my work at The Sensory Projects (www.TheSensoryProjects.co.uk), conducted prior to taking up my doctoral studies, I regularly deployed 'being with' as a part of the facilitation of projects such as the Structured Sensory Art Project, the Sensational Sensory Selection Salon Project and The Sensory-being Project. In the Sensory-being Project a team of consultants, who were all described as having profound and multiple learning disabilities, and a team of designers, who were all in their second year of a sustainable design degree, work together to conceive and create objects intended to inspire sensory wonderment. The project has seen multiple iterations, and my practice within it has developed, supported by the opportunity to reflect with Simon Andrews (Andrews & Grace, 2019), course leader for the sustainable product design degree that the design team are enrolled upon.

Initially, I supported the design team by providing them with training in regard to sensory engagement (Grace, 2018), but through reflecting with Simon, I came to realise the value in offering the design team guidance around how to be with people with profound intellectual and multiple disabilities. We found this enabled them to better work with and understand the consultants. In 2019 the project won Creative Learning Guild's award for visual art and design in recognition of its meaningful co-design process – a process underpinned by the ability of all involved to be with each other and to listen in different ways.

I claim no expertise with regard to being with, only practice-based knowledge. I share here the advice I give to the design team on the understanding that those new to the idea of being with may find insight within it of value to them.

I tell the design team that when they meet the consultant team they will meet a group of people who are wholly unfacaded, people who are authentically themselves in every moment. I challenge the designers to bring their authentic selves to those meetings. I remind them that the consultants will not care what their hair looks like, will not be interested in their body weight or their fashion sense and care not for their skin colour or their religion – all the consultants are interested in is their presence in that moment. Being able to exist in your skin, as your authentic self, is a challenge to people of any age and location, but perhaps a particular challenge to the design team who are all in their late teens and early twenties and living through a time in life when appearance is particularly significant.

I advise them when greeting the consultants to think about how they do this across sensory modalities. If you are greeting someone who does not understand language you can still say hello and announce your name, but you must recognise as you do so that this may not register as a greeting in the way that it might with someone who uses words. You may want to extend the intention of your greeting to a sensory presence, moving your body so that it is in a position equal to theirs; this could mean bending, crouching or sitting – after all, the typical nose-to-navel meeting caused by the disparity in height between wheelchair users and people standing up is not ideal for anyone. You can further extend this with a touch if it feels right; I often find a squeeze of a person's forearm to be a good way of announcing my presence. Once introduced, usually an intensive interaction (Nind, 1996) conversation will be struck up, in the way that saying 'hello' to a user of mouth words usually precedes a longer conversation. Intensive Interaction is an approach to communicating with people with profound intellectual and multiple disabilities and I encourage readers unfamiliar with it to explore the seminal text by Nind and Hewett (1994), *Access to Communication: Developing Basic Communication with People Who Have Severe Learning Difficulties*, or engage with a brief introduction to this topic in Chapter 3 of this collection. In essence within an intensive interaction conversation, you can expect to find communication partners engaged in being with one another and responding to one another's expressive communication through the use of sounds, movements, facial expressions and posture.

Once your introductions are complete and the person is aware of your presence, it is important to be, not do. Users of mouth words are often tempted to try and prompt conversation with words, or to place their own words in the mouths of others, uttering what we imagine they would say as if they were a puppet we were interacting with. The aim, when seeking to be with a person with profound intellectual and multiple disabilities, is nothing more complicated than simply being with them. In doing this we enter a liminoid period that brings us into a place where we can gain new insights through an experience of communitas in which we engage with the unknown or unfamiliar (Turner, 1969). However, simplicity is often one of the hardest things to achieve. How often in your waking life do you spend time being, and not doing? The way of being with is achieved through presence and time. It takes time to be with someone, and you need to be with them not just physically but mentally too. You attend to their being; you are being together: being with. Much of this is achieved by giving yourself permission to do it and letting go of concerns about what those around you might think of your perceived inaction. Once in the mode of being with, you will find that you naturally respond to the being of the person you are with. You will notice in your own body where their body is tensing or relaxing. If they extend a limb or make a loud noise, you will find in yourself an instinct to join them in that action. Feeling those instincts and following them keeps you with them. It is as if you were walking down the street with a friend and they broke into a run, it is likely that you would begin to run too, even if you did not know what motivated their running. You are with your friend, so you run. Likewise, when you seek to be with people with profound intellectual and multiple disabilities you will naturally find yourself responding to how they are, doing the things they do and enjoying an expressive conversation without words.

What is it to be with?

I return now to where I began this chapter, with a realisation that no matter how carefully crafted, words cannot express all things, cannot convey all meanings. What is it, the reader might rightly ask, to 'be with' a person with profound intellectual and multiple disabilities? How can she, they might go on to ask, seriously suggest she is developing methodology *with* people whose intellectual impairments mean that they cannot even understand what that word means (do you notice in the question that slip back to thinking that understanding words is being the pinnacle of apprehending meaning?)? Of course these are questions I cannot answer in words, and questions that can only be fully answered by personal experience. To offer you what I can here, I present a series of pictures that, I hope, will enable you to make meaning of the 'unspoken conversation' I experienced with one of the participants.

In these pictures you see a conversation unfolding. No words were spoken. But the meaning, I believe, is evident even in this poor one-dimensional rendering of the experience:

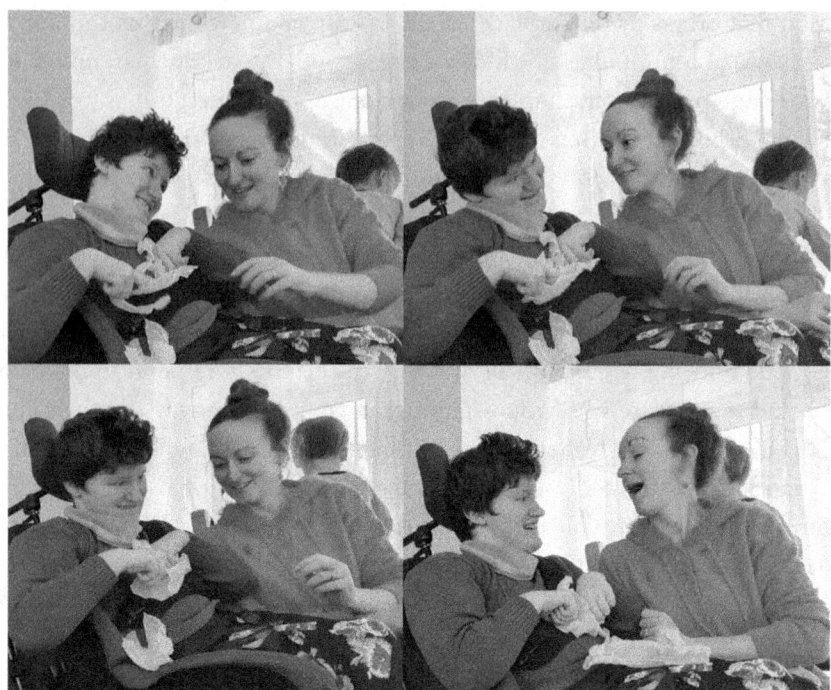

Figure 13.1 Jo and Chlöe chat.

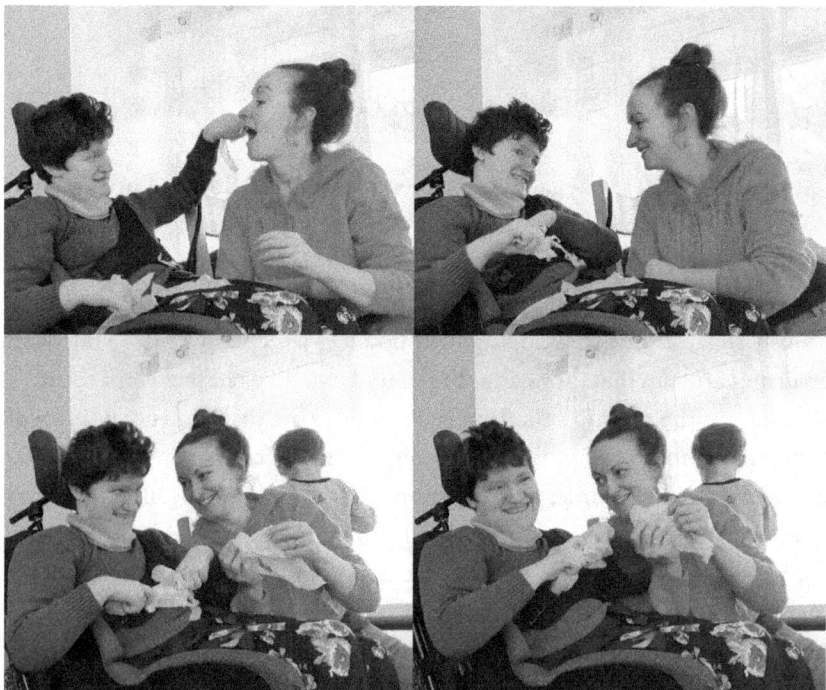

Figure 13.2 Jo and Chlöe with the tissue paper.

Figure 13.3 Jo and Chlöe embrace.

Concluding thoughts

Reason alone does not account for what it means to be human, and language cannot capture the whole experience of life. As research seeks to better understand the lives we lead, it needs to do so with a recognition that new creative methodologies are necessary. We can, and we should, include people with profound intellectual and multiple disabilities within research and philosophy, not solely to address the unfairness of their exclusion, nor purely to benefit from the fruitfulness that their inclusion brings but in order to maintain our own integrity as researchers seeking to understand life as lived recognising the fact of their presence as people living lives. The act of including people with profound intellectual and multiple disabilities can at first glance appear impossible; sharing meaning across an intellectual divide appears to require difficult conversations, but as the photos included here convey far more eloquently than my words ever could: these are not difficult conversations. These conversations can be joyous – rich with connection and meaning. As we enter into these 'difficult' conversations we come to realise that the act of including is not a one way thing, we also need including. To include people with profound intellectual and multiple disabilities in research and philosophy involves joining them in a shared communitas within which our understandings and our practice change. We do not bring research to them to look at them, nor tack them on as an afterthought to our philosophical models; we change research, and we change philosophy so that their human belonging in these spaces is realised.

Note

1. The online autistic community favour reference to the use, or otherwise, of mouth words over phrases such as non-verbal when describing people's communication. They suggest that we do not know when we encounter someone who does not speak words what command they have over language, and contend that alternate phrasings suggest totality in their description of ability or impairment. A definition of mouth words can be found at. https://aucademy.co.uk/books/.

References

Andrews, S., & Grace, J. (2019). Sensory Products for Sensory Beings. In *Design Research for Change* (pp. 100–1). Falmouth University.

Ashman, B., Ockenden, J., Beadle-Brown, J., & Mansell, J. (2010). Person-centred active support and people with complex needs. In J. Mansell, J. Beadle-Brown, B. Ashman, & J. Ockenden (Eds.). *Person-Centred Active Support: A Handbook* (pp. 161–77). Pavilion.

Atkinson, D., & Walmsley, J. (1999). Using autobiographical approaches with people with learning difficulties. *Disability & Society*, 14(2), pp. 203–16. https://doi.org/10.1080/09687599926271.

Atkinson, D., & Walmsley, J. (2010). History from the inside: towards an inclusive history of intellectual disability. *Scandinavian Journal of Disability Research*, 12(4), pp. 273–86. https://doi.org/10.1080/15017410903581205.

Bhabha, H. K. (2004). *The location of culture*. Routledge.

Bigby, C., Frawley, P., & Ramcharan, P. (2014). Conceptualizing inclusive research with people with intellectual disability. *Journal of Applied Research in Intellectual Disabilities*, 27(1), pp. 3–12. https://doi.org/10.1111/jar.12083.

Blascovich, J., Mendes, W. B., Hunter, S. B., Lickel, B., & Kowai-Bell, N. (2001). Perceiver threat in social interactions with stigmatized others. *Journal of Personality and Social Psychology*, 80(2), pp. 253–67. https://doi.org/10.1037/0022-3514.80.2.253.

Carey, E., & Griffiths, C. (2017). Recruitment and consent of adults with intellectual disabilities in a classic grounded theory research study: Ethical and methodological considerations. *Disability & Society, 32*(2), pp. 193–212. https://doi.org/10.1080/09687599.2017.1281793.

Charlton, J. I. (1998). *Nothing about us without us.* University of California Press. https://doi.org/10.1525/9780520925441.

Davy, L. (2019). Between an ethic of care and an ethic of autonomy: Negotiating relational autonomy, disability, and dependency. *Angelaki – Journal of the Theoretical Humanities, 24*(3), pp. 101–14. https://doi.org/10.1080/0969725X.2019.1620461.

de Haas, C., Grace, J., Hope, J., & Nind, M. (2022). Doing research inclusively: understanding what it means to do research with and alongside people with profound intellectual disabilities. *Social Sciences, 11*(4), p. 159. https://doi.org/10.3390/socsci11040159.

Forster, S. (2011). *Affect attunement in communicative interactions between adults with profound intellectual and multiple disabilities and support workers.* Thesis. Monash University. https://doi.org/10.4225/03/58901eba376a2.

Forster, S. (2020). Approaching a person with profound intellectual and multiple disabilities: What do you think, what do you do? In M. Nind, & I. Strnadová (Eds.). *Belonging for People with Profound Intellectual and Multiple Disabilities* (pp. 133–58). Routledge.

Forster, S., & Iacono, T. (2014). The nature of affect attunement used by disability support workers interacting with adults with profound intellectual and multiple disabilities. *Journal of Intellectual Disability Research, 58*(12), pp. 1105–20. https://doi.org/10.1111/jir.12103.

Goodwin, J. (2019). *Sharing an Aesthetic Space of Refuge Within a School for Pupils with Profound and Multiple Learning Disabilities: Golden Tent* [PhD Thesis, University of Winchester]. https://winchester.elsevierpure.com/en/studentTheses/sharing-an-aesthetic-space-of-refuge-within-a-school-for-pupils-w.

Goodwin, J., & Griffiths, E. (2022). *'Being With' in Sensory Theatre.* https://oilycart.org.uk/resources/being-with-in-sensory-theatre/

Goodwin, J., Nind, M., Dunne, L., Howe, Z., Martin, K., Mellor, C., & Ward, A. (2023, forthcoming). Exploring Belonging Through Arts-based Practice. *PMLD Link, 35*(2) Issue 105.

Goodwin, M. (2013). Listening and Responding to Children with PMLD – Towards a Framework and Possibilities. *The SLD Experience, 65*(1), pp. 21–7. https://www.ingentaconnect.com/contentone/bild/sld/2013/00000065/00000001/art00005.

Grace, J. (2018). *Sensory-being Sensory Beings.* Routledge.

Grace, J. (2021a). Neurodiversity and maternity 1. Hidden barriers to healthcare access. *Practising Midwife, 24*(2). https://doi.org/10.55975/SRAP4956.

Grace, J. (2021b). *The Subtle spectrum.* Routledge.

Grace, J., & Bell, S. (2022). Listening to 'voiceless' subjects: gathering feedback to a sensory story from participants with profound intellectual and multiple disabilities. *Good Autism Practice, 23*(2), pp. 5–12.

Hart, S. M., Pascucci, M., Sood, S., & Barrett, E. M. (2020). Value, vulnerability and voice: An integrative review on research assent. *British Journal of Learning Disabilities, 48*(2), pp. 154–61. https://doi.org/10.1111/bld.12309.

Hill, V., Croydon, A., Greathead, S., Kenny, L., Yates, R., & Pellicano, E. (2016). Research methods for children with multiple needs: Developing techniques to facilitate all children and young people to have 'a voice'. *Educational and Child Psychology, 33*(3), pp. 26–43. https://www.scopus.com/record/display.uri?eid=2-s2.0-84994593528&origin=inward&txGid=7f8841a7358c2d25699b17b0529fa4ce.

Holt, L., Jeffries, J., Hall, E., & Power, A. (2019). Geographies of co-production: Learning from inclusive research approaches at the margins. *Area, 51*(3), pp. 390–5. https://doi.org/10.1111/area.12532.

Jones, K. E., Ben-David, S., & Hole, R. (2020). Are individuals with intellectual and developmental disabilities included in research? A review of the literature. *Research and Practice in Intellectual and Developmental Disabilities, 7*(2), pp. 99–119. https://doi.org/10.1080/23297018.2019.1627571.

Kellett, M., & Nind, M. (2001). Ethics in quasi-experimental research on people with severe learning disabilities: dilemmas and compromises. *British Journal of Learning Disabilities, 29*(2), pp. 51–5. https://doi.org/10.1046/j.1468-3156.2001.00096.x.

Klotz, J. (2004). Sociocultural study of intellectual disability: moving beyond labelling and social constructionist perspectives. *British Journal of Learning Disabilities, 32*(2), pp. 93–104. https://doi.org/10.1111/j.1468-3156.2004.00285.x.

Krisson, E., Qureshi, M., & Head, A. (2022). Adapting photovoice to explore identity expression amongst people with intellectual disabilities who have limited or no verbal communication. *British Journal of Learning Disabilities, 50*(1), pp. 41–51. https://doi.org/10.1111/bld.12373.

Maes, B., Nijs, S., Vandesande, S., Van keer, I., Arthur-Kelly, M., Dind, J., Goldbart, J., Petitpierre, G., & Van der Putten, A. (2021). Looking back, looking forward: Methodological challenges and future directions in research on persons with profound intellectual and multiple disabilities. *Journal of Applied Research in Intellectual Disabilities, 34*(1), pp. 250–62. https://doi.org/10.1111/jar.12803.

Mietola, R., Miettinen, S., & Vehmas, S. (2017). Voiceless Subjects? Research Ethics and Persons with Profound Intellectual Disabilities. *International Journal of Social Research Methodology, 20*(3), pp. 263–74. https://doi.org/10.1080/13645579.2017.1287872.

Milner, P., & Frawley, P. (2019). From 'on' to 'with' to 'by': people with a learning disability creating a space for the third wave of Inclusive Research. *Qualitative Research, 19*(4), pp. 382–98. https://doi.org/10.1177/1468794118781385.

Morris, J. (2003). Including all children: finding out about the experiences of children with communication and/or cognitive impairments. *Children & Society, 17*(5), pp. 337–48. https://doi.org/10.1002/chi.754.

Nind, M. (1996). Efficacy of Intensive Interaction: developing sociability and communication in people with severe and complex learning difficulties using an approach based on caregiver-infant interaction. *European Journal of Special Needs Education, 11*(1), pp. 48–66. https://doi.org/10.1080/0885625960110104.

Nind, M. (2017). The practical wisdom of inclusive research. *Qualitative Research, 17*(3), pp. 278–88. https://doi.org/10.1177/1468794117708123.

Nind, M., & Hewett, D. (1994). *Access to communication: Developing basic communication with people who have severe learning difficulties* (Second Edition). David Fulton.

Nind, M., & Vinha, H. (2014). Doing research inclusively: bridges to multiple possibilities in inclusive research. *British Journal of Learning Disabilities, 42*(2), pp. 102–9. https://doi.org/10.1111/bld.12013.

Palmer, C., & Walmsley, J. (2020). Are people with profound and multiple learning disabilities welcome in the wider learning disability community? In M. Nind, & I. Strnadova (Eds.). *Belonging for People with Profound Intellectual and Multiple Disabilities: Pushing the Boundaries of Inclusion* (pp. 129–32). Routledge.

Parsons, S., Kovshoff, H., & Ivil, K. (2022). Digital stories for transition: Co-constructing an evidence base in the early years with autistic children, families and practitioners. *Educational Review, 74*(6), pp. 1063–81. https://doi.org/10.1080/00131911.2020.1816909.

PMLD Network. (2003). *Valuing People with Profound and Multiple Learning Disabilities.* https://www.scie-socialcareonline.org.uk/valuing-people-with-profound-and-multiple-learning-difficulties-pmld/r/a11G00000017uHDIAY.

Raphael, C., & Clarke, M. (2011). Christian. *PMLD Link, 23*(68), pp. 18–20.

Scott, J. K., Wishart, J. G., & Bowyer, D. J. (2006). Do current consent and confidentiality requirements impede or enhance research with children with learning disabilities? *Disability & Society, 21*(3), pp. 273–87. https://doi.org/10.1080/09687590600617550.

Seale, J., Nind, M., Tilley, L., & Chapman, R. (2015). Negotiating a third space for participatory research with people with learning disabilities: An examination of boundaries and spatial practices. *Innovation: The European Journal of Social Science Research, 28*(4), pp. 483–97. https://doi.org/10.1080/13511610.2015.1081558.

Shevlin, M. (2003). Preparing for contact between mainstream pupils and their counterparts who have severe and profound and multiple learning disabilities. *British Journal of Special Education, 30*(2), pp. 93–9. https://doi.org/10.1111/1467-8527.00290.

Simmons, B., & Watson, D. (2015). From individualism to co-construction and back again: Rethinking research methodology for children with profound and multiple learning disabilities. *Child Care in Practice, 21*(1), pp. 50–66. https://doi.org/10.1080/13575279.2014.976179.

Swaine, J., Parish, S. L., Luken, K., & Atkins, L. (2011). Recruitment and consent of women with intellectual disabilities in a randomised control trial of a health promotion intervention. *Journal of Intellectual Disability Research, 55*(5), pp. 474–83. https://doi.org/10.1111/j.1365-2788.2011.01399.x.

Tilley, S. (2016). *Doing respectful research*. Fernwood Publishing.
Trilling, L. (1972). *Sincerity and authenticity*. Harvard University Press. https://www.hup.harvard.edu/catalog.php?isbn=9780674808614.
Tuffrey-Wijne, I., Bernal, J., & Hollins, S. (2008). Doing research on people with learning disabilities, cancer and dying: ethics, possibilities and pitfalls. *British Journal of Learning Disabilities*, 36(3), pp. 185–90. https://doi.org/10.1111/j.1468-3156.2008.00519.x.
Turner, V. (1969). Liminality and communitas. *The Ritual Process: Structure and Anti-structure*, 94(113), pp. 125–30.
Vorhaus, J. S. (2014). Philosophy and profound disability: Learning from experience. *Disability and Society*, 29(4), pp. 611–23. https://doi.org/10.1080/09687599.2013.831749.
Walmsley, J. (2001). Normalisation, emancipatory research and inclusive research in learning disability. *Disability & Society*, 16(2), pp. 187–205.
Walmsley, J., Strnadová, I., & Johnson, K. (2018). The added value of inclusive research. *Journal of Applied Research in Intellectual Disabilities*, 31(5), pp. 751–9. https://doi.org/10.1111/jar.12431.
Ware, J. (2004). Ascertaining the views of people with profound and multiple learning disabilities. *British Journal of Learning Disabilities*, 32(4), pp. 175–9. https://doi.org/10.1111/j.1468-3156.2004.00316.x.
Ware, J. (2012). *Creating a responsive environment for people with profound and multiple learning difficulties*. Routledge. https://doi.org/10.4324/9780203065266.
Woelders, S., Abma, T., Visser, T., & Schipper, K. (2015). The power of difference in inclusive research. *Disability & Society*, 30(4), pp. 528–42. https://doi.org/10.1080/09687599.2015.1031880.

Afterword

This book was inspired by the possibilities we experienced in the Community of Philosophical Inquiry (CoPI) pedagogy (Lipman, 2003), an approach that we have embedded in our roles as educators and in our research. We were also inspired by Osborn & Canfor-Dumas's thought-provoking book, *The Talking Revolution: On the Power of Conversations to Change the World* (2018). With its focus on conversation as a strategy to confront and address societal ills, their book ignited and invigorated our hopes for dialogue to transform individuals and contribute to societal change on societal issues such as racism, disability rights and neurodivergence.

'Difficult conversations' are the central theme in this book and address conversations about ideas and concepts that challenge our taken-for-granted assumptions about how the world works or should work. Drawing on philosophical and sociological literature (Freire, Lipman, Bhabha), we adopted the concepts of liminality, dialogue, transformation and ethics of care to act as the framework for articulating the authors' take on the place and relevance of difficult conversations in their respective fields (Chapter 1).

The authors approached the task from professional, research, pedagogical and personal perspectives and interrogated their practice and experiences in relation to the value and place of 'difficult conversations' within the realm of education and beyond. Specifically, their stories are threaded together through the following concepts: the 'difficult conversations' with others and the self, 'third spaces' to enable 'difficult conversations' and celebrating difference through 'difficult conversations'.

Directing our attention to consider the normative and entrenched educational practice that dominate education in the context of autism, Chapter 2 asserts the necessity for educational practitioners to engage in 'difficult conversations' by reflecting deeply on their own values and practice. The theme of 'difficult conversation with the self' is also prominent in Chapter 9, which provides a compelling discussion on the climate change emergency as a topic that is a vital and current aspect of educational debate. Likewise, Chapter 12 gives an insightful perspective on 'difficult conversation' as a dialogue with oneself to exemplify how researchers can critically appraise their positionality and consider the position of the 'researched'. One of the methodological approaches to interrogating one's belief systems is the life history methodology captured in Chapter 10, where the author positions 'difficult conversation' about teachers' professional lives as the focus of the discussions.

To address the role of 'third spaces' in co-created curricula in HE, the authors of Chapter 7 offered an honest and captivating discussion on the role of 'difficult conversations' in shifting lecturer-student hierarchical differentials. Although universities are often perceived as 'spaces' for freedom of speech and academic freedom (two concepts that have recently been conflated in the context of HE), Chapter 8 presents an engrossing perspective of this conflation as a barrier for exploring 'difficult knowledge' or challenging the 'status quo'. Also situated in the HE context, Chapter 6 highlights the value of the CoPI approach as a liminal space for nurturing and sustaining anti-racist practices and cultures in universities.

In celebrating difference, Chapters 3 and 13 confront everyday assumptions and reservations about what counts as communication with individuals with complex needs and disabilities and offer fascinating insights into research and dialogue that doesn't rely on using *'mouth words'*. The teacher's agency, curiosity and willingness to ask the 'beyond' questions were particularly amplified in the exploration of the ethics in a 'difficult conversation' about death with a student with severe learning difficulties (Chapter 4). While the above chapters address educational practice in settings, Chapter 5 illustrated how co-production can enable 'difficult conversation' through a humanising dialogue between parents and carers and teaching practitioners to transform parent-practitioner partnership in and beyond institutional boundaries. Another example of practitioner-parent collaboration through 'difficult conversations' was illustrated in a profoundly moving personal-professional account about the value of using objects as stimuli for conversations about adoption in Chapter 11, offering the reader a window into the practice of having 'difficult conversations' for transformation.

Through this rich diversity of topics covered, the chapters highlight the necessity for educating professionals, universities, schools and ourselves as individuals to be open to 'difficult conversations', challenge the 'status quo' and ultimately transform individuals and society. Nonetheless, we also recognise that besides the willingness to engage in 'difficult conversations' the skills and dispositions needed for effective dialogue also need addressing. As trained dialogic facilitators, we have first-hand experience of the challenges of difficult but fruitful conversations (Bhabha, 2004; Freire, 1970; Lipman, 2003; Ahmed,

2018; Ferner and Chetty, 2019). Human beings are predisposed to be defensive, unreasonable and unquestioning, particularly when their dearly held values are questioned. This implies that in the context of this collection, incorporating the ethics of care and the willingness to be in the liminal state of uncertainty and unpredictability requires training in conversation practices, examples of which are outlined in Chapters 6, 7 and 8.

A further area of consideration relates to the range of topics included in this collection. We recognise that current topics such as gender, identity, migration and 'culture wars' are unrepresented. Despite this limitation, we are hopeful that the accounts in this collection can offer readers a useful way of thinking about and articulating the challenges and promise of 'difficult conversations' in any contested topic. Our reflections on the book's topics have nevertheless left us with some unanswered questions such as: *Can any topic become a focus for difficult conversations?*, *Who decides what is and is not a suitable topic?*, *What counts as a suitable or desirable topic?*, *Can everyone benefit from the transformation through 'difficult' conversations?* or *When is the disruption of 'difficult conversation' dis/empowering?*

Overall, the book was underpinned by a commitment to social justice and a desire to start a conversation about the transformative possibilities of 'difficult conversations'. By questioning some of the commonly held assumptions about research, language, race, pedagogy and inclusive teaching practices among others, the authors encourage readers to notice the different ways injustice can manifest in educational contexts. This collection provides important insights into how we might begin to understand and address some of the challenges in our professional practices. Moreover, we feel that the authors powerfully demonstrate how social justice can become more action-orientated, and how engaging in 'difficult conversations' can be a tool for personal and societal transformation. Thus, we would like to make a strong case for the value of engaging in 'difficult conversations' as a worthwhile response to the challenging and complex world in which we now live.

Index

academic freedom 4, 129–31, 133, 138–9, 240
    as conversational practice 134–7
    value of understanding academic freedom 136–7
accountability 35, 53, 95, 211, 217–18
activist professionalism 68–70
adaptive communication 52
adoption 96, 156, 185, 187–99, 200 n.1, 240. *See also* carers/caregivers, difficult conversations with
Adoption and Children Act (2002) 188
Advance HE Sustainability conference workshop 155
advocacy 51, 67–8, 95, 149, 224–5
age-appropriateness approach 64–6
Alcoff, L. 5
    criticism 211
    'First-World person' 215
    interrogatory practices of 204–18
    'Speaking for Others' 204
Alternative Provision (AP) Improvement Plan 74
ambiguity 11, 83, 118
Anthropocene 145
anti-racist/racism 94, 96, 103, 106, 240. *See also* race/racism
    anti-racist behaviour 98
    anti-racist educator 96–8
    and difficult conversations 97–8
    growth zone 103–4
Arts and Humanities Research Council (AHRC) 186
attunement 41–8, 53–4, 138, 153–4
    affect attunement 45, 48–50, 53
augmentative and alternative communication (AAC) 44, 66
authentic/authenticity 27, 48, 64, 66, 70, 100, 105, 133, 174, 206, 210, 230
autism
    autistic interaction 29
    deficit model of autism 28–9
    double empathy problem 29–35
    as neurodevelopmental disorder 27–8
    self-harm and suicide (autistic adults) 30, 36
autistic children, schooling experiences of 2, 23
    attainment data 23–4
    difficult conversations 25–6
    disruptive behaviour 24
    double empathy problem in mainstream primary schools 30–5
    bullying (social exclusion) 32–4
    emotional labour of being good 33–5
    undesirability of difference 31–2
    in mainstream schools 23–5, 28, 36
    mental distress 24
    in primary school 24, 31, 34
    unlawful exclusions 24
awareness, conversations 5, 7, 9–10, 15, 24, 44, 48, 50, 52, 60, 63, 74, 83, 86–7, 94, 101, 152, 158, 179

BAME (Black and Asian Minority Ethnic) 97, 100–1
banking model of education 4, 112–13, 115–16, 122
barriers, conversation 5, 60, 74, 77, 80, 83, 85, 93, 96, 105, 113, 119, 123, 149, 159, 192, 228, 240
    to difficult conversations on climate change 151–5
    human barriers (researchers themselves) 227–8
    institutional and structural 93
    recruitment and consent barriers 226–7
    to transformation through co-creation 121–2
behaviourist approach/behaviourism 69–70
'being with,' people with PMLD 49, 224, 227–31

Bendell, J., 'Navigating Climate Tragedy' paper 146, 150
BERA workshop 155
Bhabha, H. K. 11, 15, 42
Black Lives Matters (BLM) movement 3, 13, 95–6, 100
Bojesen, E. 134–6, 187
Buber, M. 8–9, 14, 62
   I-thou space 14
   types of dialogue 62–3
Butler, J. 138

Canfor-Dumas, E. 74, 82, 85, 87
   principles of creative conversation 70
   The Talking Revolution: On the Power of Conversations to Change the World 239
carers/caregivers, difficult conversations with 3, 14, 24, 51, 73–4, 77, 185–201, 240
   elements of addressing difficult conversation 193–6
   encounters of other adopters 189
   granulating identity 198
   importance of everyday conversation 195–6
   one to one with parents and children 187–8
   perspectives on difficult conversation of other adopters 189–91
   sandboxing method 191–4
   tools/training materials development 197
   training in conversations 199
   training resources 197–8
   trove 188–9
categorization 100–1, 104
Chapple, E. 35
charities 24, 156
Children and Families Act (2014) 75, 83–4
Client Earth, environmental law charity 156
climate and ecological emergency (CEE) 4, 145–8, 150, 152–4, 157, 239
climate change 4, 146–58. *See also* eco-anxiety
   adaptation conversation 156–7

   barriers to difficult conversations on 151–5
   beyond self 154
   defences to support climate communications 152
   eco-anxiety 152–3
   self-conversation 153–4
   self-support 152
   climate reality 146, 154–5, 157–9
   role of educators 148–51
Climate Psychology Alliance (CPA) 152, 158
co-creation 3, 5, 111–13, 115–20, 123–4
   barriers to transformation through 121–2
   transformative nature of 119–20
collaborative knowledge 113
collective resistance 16–17, 28
collective responsibility 102–4, 138
communication 1–3, 5, 8–9, 41–2, 44, 47, 49–55, 59, 74–5, 77–80, 85, 87, 120, 150, 158, 223, 227, 230
   adaptation/adaptive communication 52, 156–7
   climate communication 152–4
   communication book 59, 69
   communicative openness 190
   diversity in classroom 2, 52–4
   social communication 29, 50, 227–8
communitas 12, 225, 228, 231, 233
Community of Philosophical Inquiry (CoPI) approach 3–4, 9, 93–4, 99, 106, 118, 123, 239–40
   difficult conversations on racism 100–3
   reflections of 104–5
conversation(s) 86–7, 134
   academic freedom as conversational practice 134–7
   value of understanding 136–7
   barriers (*see* barriers, conversation)
   Bojesen on 134–6
   on climate change (*see* climate change)
   conversation of mankind 134
   creative conversations 75, 79, 85
   defined 134–6
   difficult (*see* difficult conversations)

meaning-making 6, 8, 13–14, 46, 51, 54, 69–70, 85, 94, 97, 105–6, 114, 134–6, 156, 177, 209, 223, 228, 231–3
non-verbal (*see* non-verbal conversations)
pedagogies of conversation 134
person-appropriate conversation 65
practices during 86
on race 97–8
research (*see* research conversations)
uncomfortable conversations 1, 4, 10–13, 15, 26, 33, 42, 46, 111, 115, 123, 135, 148
verbal conversations 8, 32, 42–3, 48
co-production 3, 82, 84–5, 87–8, 240
defined 77–8
and difficult conversations between parents and SENCOs 73–85, 87
power imbalance 83–5
courage 8, 42, 53, 82, 104, 171, 196
courageous conversations 17
Covid-19 pandemic 7, 13, 23, 116, 146, 155
craft knowledge 69
creative conversations 75
principles of 79, 85
creativity 44, 53, 79, 88, 197
critical dialogue 93, 150
criticality 1, 4, 8, 10, 28
critical pedagogy 4, 7–8, 131
critical reflection 1, 12, 41
critical thinking 28, 122
curiosity 13, 16, 138, 196, 240
curricula/curriculum 3, 14, 24, 59, 63, 66, 93, 111, 121–2, 124, 148, 174

Deep Adaptation process 157
democratic education system 16, 112, 114, 120–1, 124
Dewey, J., on dialogue 8
dialogic pedagogy 14
dialogue(s) 2–5, 8–9, 14, 16, 35, 49, 69–70, 74, 86–7, 99, 101, 103–4, 121, 239
critical dialogue 93, 150
genuine reciprocal dialogue 63
monologue-disguised-as-dialogue 62–4, 66
rational dialogue 9
research dialogue 168, 172

student-teacher relationships 112–14, 119–21, 123–4, 138
technical dialogue 63
transformative dialogue 9
different learners 61
difficult conversations 59–62, 66, 68, 70, 73–5, 77, 80–4, 86–8, 94, 100, 105–6, 116, 119, 122–4, 129–31, 136, 139, 145, 167, 203, 211, 233, 239–41
about death 60
agency 3–5, 8, 11, 16, 42, 50, 82, 102, 116, 174, 181, 185, 240
analysis 175–8
for anti-racist thinking and action 97–8
with caregivers (*see* carers/caregivers, difficult conversations with)
challenges 4–6, 8, 12–14, 16, 26, 28–9, 34–6, 74–5, 78, 80, 83, 87, 94, 111–12, 114, 134, 136, 168, 172, 205, 208, 240–1
on climate change (*see* climate change)
and co-production 78–80
criticism/critical incidents 211–12, 214, 218
difficulty in 8–11, 131, 168–70
fear 4, 9–10, 15, 33, 46, 80, 94, 103–5, 114–17, 123, 149–50, 153–4, 179, 185–6, 192–4
in higher education (*see* higher education (HE))
identity, impacts on 5, 10–15, 26, 35, 45–6, 49, 64–5, 96, 100, 106, 113, 115–16, 131, 152, 168, 187, 189, 191, 194, 198, 212–13, 228, 241
interview with a teacher 176–7
language limitations for 223–4
between parents and SENCOs 78, 81–5, 87
practical activities for 139–41
on racism (case study of CoPI) 100–3
reader/researcher's response 178
reflections of research participants 179–80
'Difficult Conversations,' ESRC-funded impact project (2020/2021) 5, 186
difficult knowledge 137, 152, 240
dilemma of difference 61, 71

dilemma of possibility 61–4, 70–1
Dimmock v The Secretary of State for Education and Skills case 149
disability(ies) 1, 7, 23, 25, 50–1, 53, 131, 157, 206, 216, 223, 239
    inclusive research and advocacy 224–5
    PMLD (*see* Profound Intellectual and Multiple Learning Disabilities (PMLD)
Disability Rights movements 13, 225, 239
disability studies 206–7
discomfort 2, 12–13, 16–17, 26, 33, 45, 112, 150, 158, 218, 226
    emotional 94
    pedagogies of 137
    reflexivity of discomfort 204, 208
discrimination 8, 53, 74, 79, 100, 132, 213
diverse/diversity 2, 7, 13, 15, 26, 28, 42–5, 47, 50–5, 59, 65, 69, 80–2, 86, 95–6, 112, 118, 130, 149, 225, 240
Donelan, M. 130, 137
Doucet, A. 169
Downs Syndrome 59, 65
dwarfism 5, 203–8, 210–16, 218 n.1

eco-actions 155
eco-anxiety 4, 148, 152–3. *See also* climate change
Education, Health and Care Plans (EHCPs) 23, 73–7, 79, 81–4
    timescales and development 76
'Education in Climate Emergency,' University of Worcester 155
education system 25–6, 35–6, 130–2, 146–7, 177
emotions/feelings 8–10, 13, 15, 30, 33–5, 43–4, 48–50, 76, 87, 150–1, 153–4, 157–8, 174–5, 178, 191
    emotional discomfort 94
    emotional education 158
empathy 13–14, 16, 49, 51, 60, 88, 99, 104, 120, 151, 172, 200
    double-empathy problem 29–35
empowerment 115–16
Engagement Model (Standards and Testing Agency) 66
Engagement Profile and Scale 66
England 201 n.1
    SEND reforms in 23, 75

English as an Additional Language (EAL) 52
environmental/climate education 146–50
Equality Act (2010) 94–5
equity 35, 93–4, 113
    race and equity in HE 95–6, 98–100, 104, 106
Esposito, J., 207
    'Using Others in the Nicest Way Possible: On Colonial and Academic Practice(s), and an Ethic of Humility' 203
ethics of care 2, 8–9, 14–17, 55, 63, 74, 83, 167, 170, 172, 187, 239, 241
ethnicity 28, 95, 131, 213
expressed needs of children 63, 66. *See also* inferred needs of children

feedback procedure 115–18, 121, 155, 197
Floyd, G., murder of 93
Foote, E. 151
'The Foundations of Educational Thinking' module 131
freedom of speech/free speech 4, 129–31, 137–9, 240
Freire, P. 9, 12, 35, 42, 112, 122, 148

gatekeepers/gatekeeping process 112, 209–11, 218, 226
gender 26, 53, 65, 131, 149, 213, 241
    gender pay gap 7
genuine reciprocal dialogue 63
Giroux, H. A. 7, 28
global warming 150, 158
Goodson, I. 13, 171, 174
Gore, Al, *An Inconvenient Truth* film 149
group pain 74
growth/growth zone 7, 10, 13, 16, 54–5, 97–8, 103–4
'Guide to Having Climate Conversations' 156

Hawking, S. 13–14
Hewett, D., *Access to Communication: Developing Basic Communication with People Who Have Severe Learning Difficulties* 230
Hickman, C. 158

hierarchies 4, 13, 35, 46, 74, 83, 111–12, 117, 119, 122, 124, 148, 214, 240
   academic hierarchy 115
   and power dynamics in HE 114–16
Higher Education: Free Speech and Academic Freedom report (2021) 129–30
higher education (HE) 1–4, 94, 117, 122–4, 130–1, 240
   power dynamics and hierarchies in 114–16
   race and equity in 95–6, 98–100, 104
   student-teacher relationships 112–14
   student voice in 111
hooks, B. 215, 217
humanity 8, 11, 50–1, 53–4, 145, 227, 229

inclusive education/classroom practices 1, 3, 23, 45, 47, 50, 59, 62, 66–9, 112–13
inclusive research 224–5, 228
inequalities, social 6–8, 46, 76, 83, 104, 118, 122, 130, 146
   structural inequalities 6, 122
inferred needs of children 63, 65–6. *See also* expressed needs of children
initial teacher education (ITE) 171
institutional racism 93, 96, 98. *See also* structural racism
Intensive Interaction (II) approach 45–51, 53–4, 230
   in education 50–1
   imitation in 46, 48–50, 53
   overview 47–9
   techniques 47–8
internal dialogue/conversations 2–3, 59, 61–4, 67, 70
The International Disability Alliance 157

language 41–4, 49, 52, 101, 135, 146, 150, 158, 162, 178, 230, 233
   limitations for difficult conversations 223–4
   non-verbal 42–5
   sense of infinite in 135
   spoken language 41, 43–4
leadership 96, 101, 177
learning community(ies) 2, 35, 52–4, 112, 118–19, 121–2, 124

diverse learning communities 52, 118
   partnerships in 117–19
learning disabilities 50–1, 225
legislation 23, 75, 83, 95
'Letters to the Earth' project 153
life history approach 5, 167–8, 171, 173–4, 240
life story book 185, 189
life story work 185, 191
Limes-Taylor Henderson, K. 207
   'Using Others in the Nicest Way Possible: On Colonial and Academic Practice(s), and an Ethic of Humility' 203
liminality 11–12, 15, 32, 46, 55, 105, 154, 190, 199, 239
liminal period 11–12
liminal spaces 2, 5, 8, 11–13, 15, 17, 26, 32, 35, 46, 49, 53, 64, 70, 151, 158, 168, 173, 186, 190, 197, 240
Lipman, M. 9, 44, 99, 151
listening 'beneath and beyond' 175
Listening Guide (LG) approach 176, 178
lived experiences 11–15, 41, 45, 51, 63, 102, 105, 112–13, 124, 151, 173–4, 226–7, 229
local authorities (LAs) 23, 36 n.1, 75, 81, 83–4

mainstream schools 23–6, 28, 43–4, 59, 67, 81
   double empathy problem in 30–5
Makaton sign language 52
managerial professionalism 68
marginalized groups 5–7, 13, 47, 67, 93, 97, 120, 122, 129, 131, 133, 137, 156, 203–5, 207, 217, 225, 228
mechanistic model 209
mental health 148, 155, 187, 200
metaphor 134, 169, 193, 198
Metaphor and Identity film 195
Milton, D. 29
mimicry 50
minoritization 100
minority group 28–9, 35, 61, 95–7, 100, 104, 225
monologue-disguised-as-dialogue 62–4, 66
   Buber's notion of 63

'mouth words' 2, 5, 41–3, 45–7, 49–51, 53–5, 223, 230, 234 n.1, 240
multimodal interactions 41–2

narrative life history approach 167
National Autistic Society 24
National Standards for SEND 77
Near Field Communication (NFC) tags 186
neurodivergent children/pupils 25–6, 33, 45, 52, 239
neurodiversity 2, 26–8
Nind, M., *Access to Communication: Developing Basic Communication with People Who Have Severe Learning Difficulties* 230
Nodding, N. 14, 55
   ethics of care 63
   inferred/expressed needs of children 63
non-verbal conversations 2, 8, 41–9, 52–3, 55, 234 n.1
   communicating through non-verbal language 42–5
   more knowledgeable 45–6

openness 5, 52–3, 70, 79, 82, 99, 113–14, 137–8, 181, 190, 211, 217
oppression/oppressive 8, 26, 67–8, 83, 116, 131, 137, 150
Osborn, P. 74, 82, 85, 87
   principles of creative conversation 70
   The Talking Revolution: On the Power of Conversations to Change the World 239

parents of special needs children 3, 11, 24–5, 194, 197, 199, 226, 240
   adoptive 189–91
   co-production between parents and SENCos 73–7, 81–5, 87
   difficult conversations between parents and SENCOs 78, 85–6
   and EHCP process 82, 84
   one to one with parents and children 187–8
   parent-infant interaction 47
partnerships in learning communities 117–19

The Path to Net Zero (2020) 154
pedagogies of conversation 134
pedagogies of discomfort 137
People First movement 225
people of colour 7, 95, 97
personal classroom experience 131–3
personal pain 74
personal responsibility 79
personal tragedy model 27
person-appropriate conversation 65
Philosophy of Children (P4C) pedagogy 99
Picture Exchange Communication System (PECS) 52
'Political Impartiality in Schools' guide 149
positional space 213
power relations/dynamics 29, 74, 83, 111–12, 114–16, 119, 208–10, 216, 218
practitioners, educational 1, 42, 44, 48, 50–1, 53, 63–6, 68–9, 80, 131, 139, 152, 239–40
The Prevent Duty 147, 149
problem-posing education 112–13, 122–3
professionals, education 1, 73–5, 77–9, 82, 84–5, 197, 199, 240
Profound Intellectual and Multiple Learning Disabilities (PMLD) 5, 47, 223–5, 233–4
   exclusion from research 225–9
   'being with' 49, 224, 227–31
   communication difficulties 225–6
   human barrier (researchers themselves) 227–8
   recruitment and consent barriers 226–7
   unspoken conversation 231–4
Project Drawdown 150
Pupil Referral Units 24, 36 n.2

Race Equality Charter 96
race/racism 1, 3, 53, 93–5, 97–8, 131, 157, 239. *See also* anti-racist/racism
   difficult conversations on (case study of CoPI) 100–3
   reflections of 104–5
   and equity in HE 94–6, 98–100, 104
   institutional 93, 96, 98
   structural 7, 106

Race Relations Act (Amendment) (2000) 94–5
rational dialogue 9
re-assimilation 11
recruitment method for participants 210–12
reflections 1–2, 15, 17, 26, 30–5, 41–3, 46, 48, 52, 54, 59, 63, 94, 103–4, 138–9, 170, 172, 179–80, 207, 218, 241
   on CoPI 104–5
   critical reflection 1, 12, 41
   embodied reflection 140
   self-reflection 9, 12, 14, 152, 155
reflexivity 152, 218
   reflexivity of discomfort 204, 208
relational pedagogy 14, 16, 178
religious education (RE) 59–60, 66–70
research conversations (teachers/researchers) 167–8, 172–3
   analysis of difficult conversations 175–8
   difficulty of difficult conversations 168–70
   professional learning of teachers 179–81
   reader/researcher's response 178
   reflections of research participants 179–80
   researcher's experience of difficulty 171–3
   teacher's experience of difficulty 173–5
research positionality 171, 208–9, 214–15, 217, 239
resistance 8, 15–17, 28, 122, 154
responsibility 16, 70, 81, 94, 100, 102–4, 191
   collective responsibility 102–4, 138
   ethical responsibility 16, 159
   individual responsibility 102–4
   institutional responsibility 104
   personal responsibility 79, 104
   societal responsibility 148

safe space 16, 44, 87, 105–6, 180, 212
   uncomfortable and or about climate conversations 150–1
sati (funeral pyre) in colonial India 68

The Saturday event (on World Environment Day) 155
self 2–3, 8, 10, 12, 49
   self-advocacy 225
   self-awareness 43, 86, 169
   self-belief 171, 174
   self-care 16, 86, 157–8, 172, 189
   self-compassion 17, 55
   self-concept 31, 34, 64
   self-doubt 10, 70
   self-examination 97, 104, 106
   self-exclusion 24
   self-knowledge 106
   self-preservation 16
   self-realization 9, 94
   self-reflection 9, 12, 14, 152, 155
   self-understanding 55, 178
Sensational Sensory Selection Salon Project 229
The Sensory-being Project 229
sensory engagement 198, 229–30
The Sensory Projects 229
separation 7, 11, 83, 116, 150
Severe Learning Difficulties (SLD) 59, 61–6, 68
sex education 64
sexism in education 131–2, 138
sexuality 7, 28, 53, 131
shared decision-making 82, 84
Sharing the World: Educational Responses to Extremism 139
Singer, J. 28
skills of expression 9, 82
social capital 85
social change 26, 28, 46, 123, 146, 149
social class 53, 101, 131
social inequalities. *See* inequalities, social
social interactions 29, 43–4, 47, 51, 154
social justice 13, 17, 28, 35, 52–4, 74, 79, 98, 101, 105, 120, 204, 241
social media 132, 190, 210–11
Social Role Valorisation Theory (SRVT) 65–6
social solipsism 205–6
social workers 8, 185–6, 188–91, 194, 196–7
societal pain 74
special educational needs 23–4, 27, 64

Special Educational Needs and Disabilities
    (SEND) 3, 36 n.1, 59, 61–2,
    65–6, 70, 73, 75, 79–80, 84–5, 87
  National Standards for 77
  SEND Code of Practice 27
Special Education Needs Coordinators
    (SENCos) 3, 81–2, 84, 87
  co-production between parents and
    73–7, 81–5, 87
Spivak, G. C. 9, 67
stakeholders 3, 5, 46, 50, 54, 73, 75, 77, 80,
    83, 121, 207, 211
status quo 8, 25, 28, 36, 93, 104–5, 112,
    116, 122, 124, 129, 131, 137, 240
STEM education 131
storytelling 158, 179, 205
structural inequalities 6, 122
structural racism 7, 106. *See also*
    institutional racism
Structured Sensory Art Project 229
students 1–4, 16, 42, 65, 69, 93–7, 100–2,
    118–23, 131–4, 137–8, 149, 240.
    See also teachers
  in higher education 112–15
  passive student identities 115–17
  student councils 111, 116
  student empowerment 115–16
  teacher-pupil relationships 43–4,
    112–14, 119–21, 123–4, 138
Sustainability and Climate Change (S&CC)
    strategy 146–7, 149, 155
Sustainable Development Goals (SDGs) 149

teachers 25, 31–2, 61–4, 68, 148–9, 155,
    167–8, 213, 228. *See also* students
  inclusive teacher 64, 70
  religious education 59–60, 63
  research conversations (*see* research
    conversations (teachers/
    researchers))
  teacher planning 68–9
  teacher-pupil relationships 43–4,
    112–14, 119–21, 123–4, 138
  values and beliefs of 5
Teach the Future 148
technical dialogue 63
temporal/temporalities 12, 155, 190–1,
    196, 199
third space 112–14, 123, 239–40
Thompson, E. 153

transformation 2, 8–10, 13–17, 36, 70, 74,
    82, 94, 98, 100, 106, 119, 133,
    150, 172, 181, 218, 239–41
  barriers to transformation through
    co-creation 121–2
  of educational practice 52–4
  communication in classroom for
    social justice 53–4
  communicative diversity in
    classroom 52–3
transformative dialogue 9, 14
transparency 3, 78, 124, 168, 188
trauma (experienced by children) 1, 36,
    44, 52, 54, 137, 186, 189, 199
trove, AHRC funded project 186–9
trust 3, 14, 78–80, 82, 117–19, 187,
    209–11, 213
  trusting partnership 117, 119
Turner, V. 11, 15, 31

UKRI, South Coast Doctoral Training
    Partnership 5
uncomfortable conversations 1, 4, 10–13,
    15, 26, 33, 42, 46, 111, 115, 123,
    135, 148
uncomfortable reflexivity 204, 208
unconscious bias training 93, 95
under-represented groups 95
UN Paris accord 157

values, conversations 97–8, 113, 118, 122,
    131, 134, 136–7, 171, 175, 179, 218,
    224–5, 228–9, 239–41
  in different time/situation 80–3
  values-based approach 74, 77, 79, 83,
    85, 87
verbal conversations 8, 32, 42–3,
    48
virtual learning environment 132
Voice Centred Relational (VCR) Method
    175–6, 178
vulnerability 8, 17, 46, 53, 113, 138, 174,
    177, 195, 226
Vygotsky, L. 69

Warnock Report 61
Williamson, G. 129
Wray, B. 158

Yeampierre, E. 157

www.ingramcontent.com/pod-product-compliance
Lightning Source LLC
Chambersburg PA
CBHW071815300426
44116CB00009B/1322